TREASURY

of

ENGLISH VERSE

NEW *and* OLD

by

A. S. COLLINS, Ph.D., M.A.

Lecturer in English at University College, Leicester
Editor of "Treasury of Modern Poetry," Palgrave: "Golden Treasury, Book III"
Macaulay: "Essay on Milton," Author of "English Literature of the
Twentieth Century"

LONDON
UNIVERSITY TUTORIAL PRESS LTD.
CLIFTON HOUSE, EUSTON ROAD, N.W. I

First Published 1931 5504
Reprinted 1934, 1941, 1943, 1946, 1948, 1954

PRINTED IN GREAT BRITAIN BY UNIVERSITY TUTORIAL PRESS LTD, FOXTON
NEAR CAMBRIDGE

PREFACE.

THIS Treasury is a collection of some of the best of English poetry from the early sixteenth century down to the present day: it is particularly suited for school and college use, but it also makes a definite appeal to the general reader interested in poetry for the pleasure and satisfaction which it gives.

No volume of a manageable size could contain all that may be regarded as " best," and so the present Editor has been compelled to omit much that is undeniably immortal poetry, as for example Coleridge's *Ancient Mariner*. He has, however, tried to make the best use of the space at his disposal: our greatest poets have been given their proper prominence, yet as many as possible of the outstanding poems of lesser poets have been given too; a poem like *The Ancient Mariner* has been passed by because its length would have prevented the more varied selection from Coleridge's poetry which its omission has made possible, and the same principle has been followed elsewhere.

No two readers shall easily be found to agree on what is absolutely the best selection in any given body of poetry, and considerations of space have moreover had to be taken into account here, but the Editor has included nothing in this Treasury which does not seem to him essentially good of its kind. He has had in mind those readers who have yet to make a full acquaintance with English poetry, and therefore he has on the whole chosen poems which, by general consent, are those which all who aspire to a knowledge of English poetry should know.

While aiming at giving some of the best of our poetry, this Treasury seeks also to give a collection both representative and varied: to be a true reflection of the English Muse through the centuries, and to show her in all her various moods from grave to gay. Most of the poetry chosen consists of lyrics, but to confine a collection of poetry to lyrics would be to lose much: therefore, many passages have been taken from long poems, and from dramatic poetry. Indeed, to include such passages was essential if the Treasury were to be truly representative and varied.

To help the reader to appreciate the continuous development of English poetry a brief introductory survey is prefixed to the Treasury, and the poems of each poet are prefaced by a short critical and bio-graphical note in order to show the reader how the poets stand in relation to their time and to one another, and, by making the poet more than a mere name, to inspire and aid the reader to explore his other beauties for himself.

The Glossary not only gives unusual dialect and archaic words, but also adds such explanatory notes as are often needed for an understanding of allusions, particularly the classical ones beloved of our older poets. Whereas a reader quite rightly feels that a dictionary is no true table-companion for a volume of poetry, it is hoped he will find this Glossary a helpful and acceptable substitute.

A. S. C.

UNIVERSITY COLLEGE,
     LEICESTER.

ACKNOWLEDGMENTS.

THE best thanks of the Editor for permission to insert copyright poems in the book are due to the authors, to the publishers mentioned below, and to the literary executors of Rupert Brooke, W. S. Blunt, J. E. Flecker, Thomas Hardy, George Meredith (through Mr. W. M. Meredith), and R. L. Stevenson.

Messrs. Ernest Benn, Ltd.

HUMBERT WOLFE.—*A Thrush in the Trenches* from "Requiem"; *A Botticelli Face* from "News of the Devil."

W. B. YEATS.—*The Man who Dreamed of Faery-land, The Lake Isle of Innisfree, When You are Old,* from "Poems by W. B. Yeats."

Jonathan Cape, Ltd.

W. H. DAVIES.—*Leisure, Oh, Sweet Content, The Moon, Sweet Stay-at-Home, Raptures,* from "Collected Poems of W. H. Davies."

Macmillan and Co., Ltd.

T. E. BROWN.—*My Garden* from "Collected Poems of T. E. Brown."

G. W. RUSSELL.—*Babylon* from "Collected Poems by A. E."

RALPH HODGSON.—*The Bells of Heaven*; *Time, You Old Gipsy Man.*

W. S. BLUNT.—*St. Valentine's Day.*

LAURENCE BINYON.—Extract from *The Sirens.*

THOMAS HARDY.—*The Darkling Thrush*; *Shelley's Skylark*; *Song from The Queen of Cornwall*; *The Oxen*; *In Time of "The Breaking of Nations"*; *"Men Who March Away."*

RUDYARD KIPLING.—*If—* from "Rewards and Fairies."

W. B. YEATS.—*The Song of the Wandering Aengus* from "Selected Poems by W. B. Yeats."

Constable and Co., Ltd., and Messrs. Charles Scribner's Sons, New York.

GEORGE MEREDITH.—*Love in the Valley* (Stanzas I., II. and VI.); *The Orchard and the Heath*; *Lucifer in Starlight*; *Juggling Jerry*.

The Poetry Bookshop.

HAROLD MONRO.—*Milk for the Cat.*

ROBERT GRAVES.—*A Boy in Church*; *In the Wilderness.*

CHARLOTTE MEW.—*The Changeling.*

William Heinemann, Ltd.

JOHN MASEFIELD.—*Sea Fever, Up on the Downs,* Extract from "*The Daffodil Fields,*" Extract from "*The Everlasting Mercy,*" *Beauty,* from "Collected Poems by John Masefield."

A. C. SWINBURNE.—*Chorus from "Atalanta in Calydon"*; *A Forsaken Garden.*

Martin Secker, Ltd.

J. E. FLECKER.—*The Old Ships, The Dying Patriot,* from "Collected Poems by J. E. Flecker."

M. BARING.—*In Memoriam, A. H.,* from "Poems 1914-1919 by M. Baring."

J. M. Dent and Sons, Ltd.

G. K. CHESTERTON.—*The Donkey.*

Messrs. Methuen and Co., Ltd.

RUDYARD KIPLING.—*Recessional, Sussex,* from "The Five Nations."

G. K. CHESTERTON.—*The Song of Quoodle* from "The Flying Inn."

Oxford University Press.

ROBERT BRIDGES.—*Spring Goeth all in White, A Passer-By, London Snow, On a Dead Child,* from "The Poetical Works of Robert Bridges."

Burns, Oates and Washbourne, Ltd.

ALICE MEYNELL.—*Chimes; Renouncement; To a Daisy; The Shepherdess.*

FRANCIS THOMPSON.—*The Kingdom of God; Nocturn; To a Snowflake; Daisy.*

G. K. CHESTERTON.—*A Cider Song.*

John Lane, The Bodley Head, Ltd.

J. DAVIDSON.—*In Romney Marsh; A Runnable Stag.*

Ingpen and Grant.

EDWARD THOMAS.—*Adlestrop; Out in the Dark; Lights Out,* from " Collected Poems by Edward Thomas."

R. Cobden-Sanderson, Ltd.

E. BLUNDEN.—*The Long Truce; Midnight.*

Gerald Duckworth.

EDITH SITWELL.—*The Little Ghost Who Died for Love,* from " Troy Park."

HILAIRE BELLOC.—*The South Country; Lines to a Don.*

Chatto and Windus.

R. L. STEVENSON.—*I will Make You Brooches; Christmas at Sea; To S. R. Crockett; Requiem.*

R. NICHOLS.—*The Tower.*

John Murray.

SIR HENRY NEWBOLT.—*He Fell Among Thieves, Vital Lampada, Drake's Drum,* from " Poems New and Old."

Sidgwick and Jackson, Ltd.

RUPERT BROOKE.—*The Soldier, The Old Vicarage, Grantchester,* from " Collected Poems by Rupert Brooke."

Sidgwick and Jackson, Ltd.—continued.

JOHN DRINKWATER.—*Olton Pools, The Midlands,* from " Collected Poems by John Drinkwater."

W. J. TURNER.—*Romance* from " The Hunter and Other Poems."

Thanks are also due to the Editor of *The Times* for permission to insert Laurence Binyon's *For the Fallen* and to Messrs. James B. Pinker and Sons, Literary Agents, for W. de la Mare's *Silver, The Children of Stare, Nod, The Sunken Garden,* and *The Linnet.*

CONTENTS.

Contents.

Contents. xiii

Contents.

Contents.

Contents.

Contents.

INTRODUCTION.

EARLIEST ENGLISH POETRY.—Our poetic heritage is a richer one than we sometimes realise. Chaucer is not, as, in the wake of Dryden, we used until quite recently to call him, the Father of English poetry; in fact he came five centuries and more later than the eldest of our inspired singers. Scholars of last century, zealously followed by those of our own day, have given us back the poems of our ancient bards, and recent years have seen the appearance of popular translations of them. The thickest mists of time have rolled away, and a strange world has been revealed, though, inevitably, there still lies over it the haze of antiquity. Yet it is a world neither so strange as to be alien nor so dim as to conceal many a resemblance, physical and spiritual, to our own England and the spirit of her people. Other countries of modern Europe have their early literature, but none so old is so rich as ours. Let us then doubly rejoice in our unique and honourable heritage.

In this Treasury, however, we must regretfully pass by the poetry of this far-off world. The ancient forms of our language must adorn the pages only of a scholar's treasury. This volume is to confine itself to those poems whose beauties require no interpreter. But where the translator is at hand to lead the way, it is to be hoped that the lover of English poetry will not be slack to follow, and here at least in this brief survey we should be churlish not to pay our tribute.

There are fragments of heathen poetry which Time the devourer has spared us, but the faith of Christ was in the land before the bulk of our ancient poetry took the shape in which it has descended to us. If there is any name which we can reverence as that of the Father of English poetry it is that of Caedmon. To him, simple unlearned cowherd of Whitby, an angel

appeared and bade him sing of divine things; then he
became a lay brother of the Abbey, and being taught
the Bible story is said to have translated his learning
into the sweetest English song. But Time has dealt
even more hardly with Caedmon's poems than with
the noble Abbey of Whitby where he wrote them He
probably founded a poetic school of whose work no
mean part survives, but of his own undoubted com-
posing there lives only a little hymn in praise of God
and His creation. His followers versified a good deal
of the early books of the Old Testament, and these
poets of the late seventh or early eighth century were
most inspired when their theme was war, as though
the leaven of Christ had not yet fully worked within
them.

But by about the year 720 some unknown poet had
wrought from old tales of Denmark and Southern
Sweden a fine poem, in which the pagan virtues of
strength and warlike prowess are, in the ideal
character of the monster-quelling hero Beowulf,
softened by the presence of the Christian graces.
Beowulf, saviour of peoples, is a chivalrous prince to
whom young nobles may look up for an example.
The setting in which his valiant deeds are done might
well be the Northern coast of England, and though
the story, compact of myth and imagination over-
laying a basis of historical fact, is not of England, it is
of peoples who only two centuries before had been
neighbours of the English in the Continental home
from which they descended upon Britain.

Later in the eighth century arose the poet Cynewulf. In *Christ* his spirit soared in an ecstasy of
adoration, and elsewhere he speaks as one whose soul
has been profoundly stirred by the vision of the
Cross. It is of the Christian faith and its saints
that he writes, and always with a keen sense of the
beauty of nature. It has been a temptation to ascribe
to him several poems which declare a like poetic gift,
but which it is safer to leave anonymous.

AFTER THE NORMAN CONQUEST.—Time is both kind and cruel: it takes away so much, and yet leaves us often such rich fragments. Many, doubtless, are the manuscripts of our pre-Conquest poets which fire and other merciless enemies have snatched from us, but in the Caedmonian poems, in *Beowulf*, in the work of Cynewulf, and in several other poems of high merit, there is enough to testify that in the three centuries before the Normans came England had borne poets who had advanced poetry very far indeed from the humble beginnings of their craft. It is probable that this literary movement had reached its peak, and that, being already in decline, the advent of the Normans did no more than hasten its passing.

From the end of the tenth century to the dawn of the thirteenth there was almost complete silence among our poets. Then about the year 1200 English poetry began afresh. Our first period of English poetry had nearly run its course before the poetry of France began, but, while England was silent, the poetic soul of France found expression, and in the new period of English poetry it was the poetry of France which was our inspiration. From France came, indirectly, the courtly love songs of the Provençal lyrists, and, directly, the romances of King Arthur and his Knights, of Charlemagne and his Peers, and of the old tale of Troy. Here was abundance of fresh matter, and the strain of courtly gallantry, though soon to become a fast convention, was a new manner. Over and above all this, France gave us a new poetic form. Our earlier poets had used a verse form whose ornament was not rhyme but alliteration, and whose rhythm was governed by stress and fell into no very regular pattern. The verse our poets now learnt from France was the short rhyming couplet of eight syllables where stress was replaced by the iambic rhythm based on a metrical foot consisting of one unaccented syllable followed by one accented syllable.

Poetic skill, so long disused, was not to be regained in a day. The thirteenth century passed away and very little poetry of any lasting merit had been produced when the fourteenth century dawned. Another fifty years went by and still there was no master such as Cynewulf had been. But the standard of achievement was rising steadily as romance succeeded romance, and the more serious writers put their muses to the service of religion and history. Notably high was the standard reached by anonymous lyrists of the early fourteenth century who sang of Spring's return, of love, of the Virgin Mary, and of other themes secular and religious.

CHAUCER.—At last, in the seventies of the fourteenth century, came Chaucer. His genius, fostered first by French poetry, strengthened then by Italian, and deepened through the years by experience, overtopped the talents of all his competitors in the house of Fame. To his contemporaries and to his successors of more than a century he was " the prince of poets all," and to us, even more than to them, he is the one great poet of that age. Judged upon *The Canterbury Tales* alone (and he has masterpieces outside those) his achievements in narrative and description and characterisation as well as in mastery of verse form and of metre are amazing. It is our greatest loss in this Treasury that his English is still just too old-fashioned for most of us to read him with ease.

Chaucer was of the new school which owed its inspiration primarily to France. There was in the second half of the fourteenth century another poetic school. The tradition of pre-Conquest poetry had not died; it lived on, we can safely infer, among popular bards who despised or were unacquainted with the new poetry of the French-speaking court. Soon after 1350 it reappeared, with the old alliterative verse form slightly modified, and with a vigour which suggests that its re-appearance was not so sudden as, in the absence of other poems probably lost, it now seems to have been. The spirit no less than the form had survived, a spirit in many ways different from that of the new school. The gay brilliant show of life did not attract these poets; not for them were the conventions of the Court of Love and the cheerful sunshine of a May morning. Imbued with the serious reflective spirit of poets like him who wrote *Beowulf* they looked on the dark problems of contemporary life. Chaucer was the artist with whom poetry stood first, Langland, the greatest of this other school, was the teacher for whom poetry was secondary. Chaucer and Langland thus express two sides of our national character, two undying strains which when found in harmony often yield our greatest song as in the work of Spenser and of Milton. Chaucer is our Cavalier, Langland our Puritan.

AFTER CHAUCER.—The death of Chaucer in the year 1400 was like the setting of the sun in the firmament of poetry. There followed a century of twilight in which poets stumbled as they tried to keep their feet upon the path lit now only by the reflected light from the vanished luminary. Chaucer was the acknowledged master of Lydgate and Occleve, but they had hardly a spark of their master's genius; moreover, the English language was rapidly losing its inflections and approaching in form the English of to-day—to the great metrical confusion of the poets. Between 1400 and about 1520 the best poetry was written by Scotsmen, and notably Dunbar, for the Scots, while they, too, took Chaucer as their master, had more of genius and greater originality; the English poet of most mark was Skelton, whose vigorous poetic eccentricity lifts him out of the rut. But the anonymous writers of popular ballads more than compensate for the absence of great poets; it was during the fifteenth century and the first half of the sixteenth that the ballads assumed the form in which we have them, and from their rich abundance we have begun the culling of this Treasury.

It was not only their inborn talents that made Dunbar and Skelton greater poets than their predecessors of the fifteenth century. Lydgate and Occleve remained men of the middle ages, weak survivors of a passing world. Dunbar and Skelton were men of the dawning modern world. Before they died there had been printing in England for some half a century, Greek was being taught at Oxford, America had been discovered, and the Reformation was well on its way; the mould of the medieval world had been shattered; everywhere the Renaissance was bringing a new world to birth.

WYATT AND SURREY.—Dunbar and Skelton stood between the medieval and the modern. It was not for them, but for younger men wholly of the new world, to open the door to the next great age of poetry. Sir Thomas Wyatt, followed by the Earl of Surrey, turned his eyes to the sonnets and songs of the Italians. Wyatt, who was the elder, introduced the sonnet into English poetry, translating and imitating the sonnets of Petrarch. Surrey, his disciple, wrote sonnets with more grace and ease, quite eclipsing in artistry the somewhat clumsy efforts of Wyatt in whose lines it is often hard to discern an iambic rhythm. Both poets used other lyrical forms, and to them in large part we owe the impulse behind the great lyrical profusion of the Elizabethans. Wyatt, too, wrote some of our first formal satires, and Surrey introduced blank verse into English in his translation of two books of Virgil's *Aeneid.* Once again, as had happened before in the thirteenth century, poetry had undergone a change of spirit and of form, and for this change we owe these two men our greatest debt. Their poems undeniably have their intrinsic merits, but yet hardly one has that degree of charm or beauty which is the hallmark of immortality.

ELIZABETHAN POETRY.—As Chaucer came only after long years of preparation, so many years of poetic experiment were to pass before the new promise born with Surrey and Wyatt reached its fulfilment in Spenser. It was not till 1557, ten years after the later of the two men had died, that their poems were for the first time published in Tottel's *Miscellany*. But their verses had been circulated in manuscript, and had stimulated the lyrical vein in others. After 1557 more and more lyrical pieces appeared in enlarged editions of Tottel and in other miscellanies with such delightful titles as *The Paradise of Dainty Devices* (1576). Many of these poems were weak effusions, poetic exercises and no more, but some showed real skill and talent. All, however, were insignificant in comparison with *The Shepherd's Calendar* of 1579, which at once proclaimed Spenser to be " the new poet " for whom England had been waiting. Its various metres declare that Spenser too is at this stage still experimenting, but these are the experiments of a master.

The great Elizabethan period of poetry was now begun. Notably in the lyric there is a rich abundance from which the anthologist who does not confine his Treasury to these years alone can carry away but a few of the beauties he would like to rifle. The sonnets published in the fifteen–nineties number some two thousand. The plays of the forerunners of Shakespeare—Greene and Peele and Lyly—and the plays of Shakespeare himself and of his successors, have their many charming gems of interspersed songs. Outside the plays and the volumes of sonnets, there are lyrics enough, too, by Sir Philip Sidney, Drayton, Daniel, Marlowe, Spenser, Sir Walter Raleigh, and others less famous. Fresh rich liquid beauty is everywhere—a spontaneous outpouring of poetry as from men so happy that they sing by nature.

Nor were lyrics, slight like Lyly's *Appelles' Song* or of sustained magnificence like Spenser's *Prothalamion,* even the major part of the poetic splendour of this age. Our day, too, has brought forth a profusion of good lyrics, mostly short, but it has not rivalled the Elizabethan age in producing as well anything like the number of fine long poems, of which the greatest of all in Elizabeth's day was Spenser's *Faerie Queene.* If, in this Treasury, we have taken comparatively little from these longer poems, it is that the lyrics, masterpieces complete in themselves, are more than plentiful enough to fill the space at our disposal; and, secondly, because, while the long poems maintain a high level of poetry, it is not easy to find passages which compel as high an admiration when detached as do the lyrics—in other words, the poets wrote their long poems, as they should do, as a whole, maintaining a poetic level rather than straining after " purple patches."

Again, with Shakespeare ever in our minds, it is hardly necessary to refer to the wealth of poetry in the drama of the Elizabethans. In his earlier plays Shakespeare was a greater poet than he was a dramatist, and to the end he was as great a poet as a playwright. Of Marlowe it has been said that his genius lay more truly in poetry than in drama, and of Peele it can be said without fear of contradiction. When the great Queen's death in 1603 saw the passing of " the spacious days " and in the drama the gradual decline set in which led at last to the closing of the theatres by Parliament in 1642, still the drama remained full of poetry in the hands of Beaumont and Fletcher, of Webster, and of others.

THE METAPHYSICAL POETS.—While Spenser was still writing his *Faerie Queene,* a young man by name John Donne, later Dean of St. Paul's, was beginning to write poetry, soon to initiate a quite new poetic movement in England. The poetic genius of Donne was strong, original, passionate, subtle, analytic, and intellectual. Beauty extending through many consecutive lines is not common in his poems, though his tantalising flashes of beauty convince us that he could have written more beautifully. He turned his back upon the clear, sensuous beauty of Spenser and his fellows, and set down, in verse which laid aside metrical smoothness for an irregular rhythm ruled by his passion of the moment, and in strange, unexpected imagery conceived by his subtle mind, his thoughts and feelings of love which were marked by a sincerity and self-analysis unknown to the simpler Elizabethans. Early in the seventeenth century his thoughts turned to religion, and he wrote his Divine Songs and Sonnets, and in these also displayed the same qualities of heart and mind, and the same perverse obscurities of expression and irregularities of metre, now in the analysis of his soul and not of his love-worn heart.

The perverseness of Donne—his search after strained similes, his delight in absurd comparisons, his tortuous pursuit of originality—became the model for many, and occasionally marred the work of poets so remote from Donne in spirit as Milton and Dryden. But there were some who not only followed Donne in style, but who also shared his intensity of religious emotion, to pierce even more deeply than he into the spiritual world. These men, of whom the chief are George Herbert, Crashaw, and Vaughan, are, together with Donne, generally called our metaphysical poets. Donne is perhaps too intellectual to be a true mystic, but these others are undeniably what we call mystics— men endowed with a particularly keen sense of the reality of the unseen world, into which in moments of spiritual exaltation they are granted brief visions, later to be expressed by such as are poets as clearly as symbolism will allow.

THE CAVALIER LYRISTS.—In spite of this movement of reaction from the Elizabethans, their tradition did not die for a long while. Ben Jonson, the greatest dramatist of the time next to Shakespeare, was an admirable lyrist, and, while some were taking Donne as their master, Herrick and others declared themselves " sons of Ben." Jonson, as his plays declare, was learned in the classics, and his lyrics are not uninfluenced by his classical leanings. Sometimes he would take the idea of a classical lyric and expand it into English, and in doing so, or in writing a lyric not thus suggested, he would write with a conscious desire to be lucid and restrained as the classical poets of Rome had taught him to be. Thus in the work of Ben and his " sons," though the Elizabethan spirit lived on, there was less spontaneity; their poems are easy, graceful, and generally natural, but they strike us as being wrought with more attention to polish and elegance. Further, especially in the songs of Herrick, Carew, and Suckling, there is a less serious note than in the Elizabethans, and now and again a flippancy and cynicism; these are the Cavalier lyrists, who, while England under Charles I. was passing into civil strife, kept their muses lightly undisturbed by all that was dark and portentous around them.

MILTON.—Between these two groups of metaphysical poets and Cavalier lyrists stood the figure of John Milton, towering high above them, a greater poet even than Spenser. Spenser, as the notes to his *Shepherd's Calendar* confessed, had owed much to Chaucer; and in addition to the medieval strain (including this influence of Chaucer) his poetry shows clearly the mingling of the forces of the humanism of the Renaissance, and of the Reformation. The poetry of Milton, who, in his turn, confessed a debt to Spenser, again shows the working of the two forces of the Renaissance and the Reformation, but he has largely passed beyond the spell of the middle ages, and in being free from that his poetry more perfectly represents the finest product of the new humanism, fed by the classics, disciplined by the Puritanism which had followed on the Reformation, and now inspired by the example of the Elizabethans.

But the poetic soul of Milton "was like a star, and dwelt apart." He leant to neither of the contemporary schools of poetry, except that he indulged in a stray metaphysical extravagance. So wide was his learning that he owed rich debts everywhere, to Italian, and to Hebrew, to Greek and to Roman, and to his own countrymen, but his debts are of the kind that can with difficulty be collected, for the gold that he took he remelted, and the pure fresh metal of his moulding bears only one imprint—that of John Milton. Yet, standing alone as he does, there is something Elizabethan about his work, from the happiness and luxuriant beauty of his early poems down to the spacious grandeur of *Paradise Lost* and its two severer successors, *Paradise Regained* and *Samson Agonistes*.

THE CLASSICAL SCHOOL.—For at least thirty years before Milton died in 1674, there had begun a new school of poetry, overlapping (in respect of time) the metaphysicals and the Cavalier lyrists, and destined to become supreme and to be the ruling school for well over a century. These new poets, the first of whom were Waller and Denham, sought by careful attention to poetic form to cure poetry of the ills from which it suffered at the wilful hands of the metaphysicals. They succeeded in imposing upon most of the poets of the times of Dryden, and Pope, and Johnson their " reform of our numbers " as it has been called, and were in fact regarded by such critics as Dryden and Johnson not only as the founders of the so-called classical school of poetry in England but almost as the first " correct " English poets, two of the chief elements of " correctness " being smoothness and ready intelligibility. Thus Dryden declared " the excellence and dignity of [rhyme] were never fully known till Mr. Waller taught it; he first made writing easily an art "; and Dr. Johnson called Denham " one of the fathers of English poetry." There is, of course, exaggeration in such statements, but the perspective of Johnson is true enough when he says of Waller: " He certainly very much excelled in smoothness most of the writers who were living when his poetry commenced. The poets of Elizabeth had attained an art of modulation, which was afterwards neglected or forgotten."

The unhappiest feature of extravagance in literature lies in the reaction that assuredly must follow. If poets go out of their way to write with irregularity, obscurity, and fantastic imagery, and if they succeed in making such poetry a strong fashion of their day, then there follows, as the night the day, a reaction to regularity, everyday clearness, and commonplace comparisons. So poetry, after its wild fling in the first half of the seventeenth century, was placed in a straight jacket to be taught how to behave itself more soberly.

So, from about 1640, the classical reaction set in, and the new school of poetry was characterised by a reversal of the values hitherto predominant in poetry. Because Form had been treated too laxly, Form was now exalted, and the closed couplet in particular became a tyrannous convention. Because Imagination had run riot, now Reason was the master, and Imagination was suspect. Because Passion had held the reins, now it was the turn of Restraint. Because poets had talked so much of themselves, that is subjectively, now they turned to man and society, to satirise them, and to teach them, writing objectively. Nature having had her day, the Town came into its day. The Metaphysicals and Cavaliers having preferred the lyric, the classicals now favoured the longer didactic or satirical poem—not that they quite neglected the lyric, but their lyric, whether it is a sonorous Ode by Dryden or some tripping verses by Prior, is one which has undergone a sea-change to something less rich and strange.

Great poetry was still written: Dryden and Pope were greater poets than any since Spenser, with the exception of the solitary Milton, and Pope was one of the most consummate poetic artists England has known. But it should be clear why comparatively little of their poetry comes into an Anthology such a this: when imagination and passion, the countryside, personal emotion, and the lyrical form are out of favour, the poetry which achieves immortality wins, nevertheless, a place which is rather at the back than in the front of the house of Fame. Pope has his ardent advocates, but those who love the poetry of Spenser or Shelley are more numerous.

THE ROMANTIC REACTION.—Man is always a medley. A man may have very little imagination or humour, but the man who has *none* is a mere figure of speech. So we must guard ourselves against thinking that, because the classical school of poets gave imagination and nature very subordinate places, therefore they were unimaginative and unmoved by nature. Pope, classical poetic dictator though he almost was, nevertheless declared: " the more I examine my own mind the more romantic I find myself." Even Wordsworth admitted that " a passage or two " in *Windsor Forest* contained new images of nature.

Yet it is undeniable that Pope and his school suppressed almost completely such romantic strains as they had. Other eighteenth-century poets, however, though in much they were in harmony with the poetic taste of their age, gave a freer rein to their romanticism. In 1726 Thomson began to publish his *Seasons*; he was clearly inspired to a great extent by Milton, and wrote in blank verse, and, above all, he wrote of Nature as one who had lovingly observed her. Yet he was still sufficiently of his own day to mingle with his descriptions of nature much of that kind of reflection and moralising which Pope has in his *Essay on Man*, and, though breaking away from the current poetic vein, he did not break away so far as to alienate readers: his work was very popular, and Pope, far from playing the part of a jealous dictator rejecting the new, wrote some lines which Thomson included. In his *Castle of Indolence* Thomson departed still farther from the school of Pope, and caught a good deal of Spenser's spirit.

Thomson was the greatest of those whose poetry showed that there was a strong romantic current flowing below the surface of early eighteenth-century classicism. There were several lesser poets. While the satirical and didactic poetry of Pope and the closed couplet still held sway, imitation of Milton and Spenser became increasingly common. Dyer's delightful picture of the countryside in *Grongar Hill* shows a mind most happily sensitive to the beauty of wood and stream and hill, and to the inspiring charm of Milton's *L'Allegro*.

By the middle of the century the revolt from the school of Pope was boldly declared. Collins and Gray revived the true lyric. Collins, certainly, was for a few years neglected, and Gray indulged often in stilted diction, but both were inspired singers and their work before long won its deserved appreciation. The love of the remote past, a prominent feature of the romantic spirit, was shown by both: by Collins in his *Ode on the Superstitions of the Highlands* and by Gray in his versions of Old Welsh and Norse poems. This love began to be felt by others, and inspired the "medieval" forgeries of Chatterton, and Percy's collection of old ballads in his *Reliques*. Dr. Johnson, with the powerful artillery of his criticism and conversation, still held the classical fort, and Goldsmith still wrote closed couplets, though with a softer music and a greater tenderness of spirit than the satirical users of that form, but before Johnson and Goldsmith were dead the day of classicism was over.

The eighties of the eighteenth century saw the arrival of the heralds of the fully romantic age of poetry soon to begin. In that decade Crabbe, Cowper,

Blake, and Burns all wrote much of their best poetry. Crabbe was the closest of them all to Pope's school; realistic satirist and user of the heroic couplet, he has been called "Pope in worsted stockings" and a "poetical Hogarth," but his interest in the poor, where Pope had almost ignored them, and his pictures of nature, though they do not pierce beyond the surface, proclaim the new spirit. Cowper's poetry is much more romantic: it reveals deep personal feeling, love of liberty, and a sense of the brotherhood of man, tenderness for animals, and an appreciation of nature that preludes Wordsworth's insight into her mysterious life. Blake, before he became the visionary prophet expressing himself in tortuous symbolism, wrote many fine lyrics which possess a simplicity and melody reminiscent of the Elizabethans: he has a passionate sympathy for oppressed children, and is a mystic who sees "heaven in a wild flower." Burns, with his ardent nature, brought back sincere personal feeling into the lyric in his songs of love; and Burns, like Cowper and Blake, loved nature and was tender towards animals, and preached in poetry the cause of freedom and the equality of men.

THE ROMANTIC REVIVAL.—By 1800 Cowper and Burns were dead, Blake had written his best, and Crabbe had for some years been silent as a poet, to resume later but in the same style and spirit. In 1798 a new age was inaugurated by the publication of *Lyrical Ballads* by Wordsworth and Coleridge. Wordsworth rejected the poetical diction of the school of Pope, and turned to simple themes and, above all, to nature: in his own words, his aim was "to open out the soul of little and familiar things," and he became, says Matthew Arnold, "a priest to us all of the wonder and bloom of the world." Coleridge, in *The Ancient Mariner*, which appeared in *Lyrical Ballads*, turned to the supernatural. Both wrote by the light of imagination, and for many years to come reason was dethroned from the eminence upon which the classical poets had placed it, and was put, as it should be in poetry, below imagination, in subordination to it, its handmaid and not its master. Where reason dominates, art is apt to be critical rather than creative, but when imagination is master, then art is creative. So in the early nineteenth century there dawned a great creative period rivalling that of the Elizabethans, and probably, if we omit the miracle of Shakespeare, even excelling it in the work of Wordsworth and Coleridge, of Shelley and Keats, and of Byron.

A very prominent feature of Elizabethan poetry is, not the individuality of the various poets, but the pervasive general Elizabethan quality, so that we have to know the various lyrists in particular very well before we can distinguish between them. The poetry of the metaphysicals, however, shows sharply marked differences of personality. Then came the relative impersonality of the classical poets, and, partly owing to their respect for conventions and forms, a common quality once more: the work of Pope, for example, is not readily distinguishable from that of those who helped him in translating Homer. Now in the poetry of the Romantic Revival individuality again became a hall-mark of each poet's work. Thus there is no confusing of Keats with Shelley, or of either with Byron, or of any with Wordsworth or Coleridge. Traits in common, of course, exist, but each of these five poets developed on his own lines, exemplifying the truth of the dictum of Keats that " the Genius of Poetry must work out its own salvation in a man."

Wordsworth lived long and wrote much, and is our greatest poetic interpreter of nature and of childhood. Coleridge, too soon silent as a poet, was a master of melody and a wizard in his evocation of the supernatural. Shelley, dead at thirty, was lit by a flame of revolutionary idealism and was keenly alive to the beauty of nature, and particularly to her colours and her music: his longer poems are full of loveliness, but they do not reach the certain immortality of his match-less lyrics. Keats is the poet of the rich sensuous beauty of the world, and one of our greatest masters of the Ode; his later poems and especially *Hyperion* show him as a deeper philosopher than Shelley and rouse our keen regret for his early death. Byron, lyrist, narrative poet, satirist, whose masterpiece is *Don Juan*, is regarded in Europe as our greatest poet next to Shakespeare and Milton—English critics are less generous to him. And lastly let us not forget Scott. He is not in poetry as great as these others, yet he had a true lyrical gift, and his narrative poems, with their enormous popularity, are splendid examples of the love of the picturesque and of the medieval which was a prominent trait of this great revival of the romantic spirit.

VICTORIAN POETRY.—The great romantic period lasted barely thirty years. In 1798 it had begun—by 1824 Byron, Shelley, and Keats were dead, Scott and Coleridge had deserted poetry, and Wordsworth's best work lay behind him. Now was the time for the exuberant creative genius to become more sober. Keats had scornfully remarked of the school of Pope that "they sway'd about upon a rocking-horse, and thought it Pegasus," and he and his fellows had ridden their true poetic steeds sometimes with abandon—now came Tennyson, who held the reins of his no less noble steed more tightly. So Tennyson followed the romantics, as Milton followed the Elizabethans; the variety and imagination of the romantics he kept, but he added the order and harmony of the classical spirit. In some ways Tennyson seems conventional, particularly when compared with Shelley, and indeed he is, in thought, representative of the best of Victorian thinking rather than an original or deep thinker, but in the art of poetry he is with Milton and Pope one of our greatest masters, a "lord of language," as he himself called Virgil.

Next to Tennyson the chief Victorian poets were Browning, Matthew Arnold, Dante Gabriel Rossetti, Christina Rossetti, Swinburne, and Francis Thompson. The strong healthy optimism of Browning has to many a greater appeal than the more hesitant philosophy of Tennyson, but, with his frequent grotesqueness and obscurity, he is below Tennyson as an artist. Matthew Arnold is nearer to Tennyson, with a sadness in much of his poetry, and a very conscious harmony in his verse. Dante Rossetti was one of the leaders of the " pre-Raphaelite " movement in art and poetry, which began in 1848, and which aimed at producing in poetry simple, melodious craftsmanship, and a pictorial style rich in colour and sensuous beauty. Swinburne is remarkable for his wonderful command over rich and elaborate metrical harmonies; unlike the other Victorians we have named, Swinburne shows an almost pagan worship of passion, and, far from being a typical Victorian like Tennyson, was in his sympathies an ardent revolutionary like Shelley. All the great Victorian poets possessed the lyrical faculty to a high degree.

MODERN POETRY.—Between Victorian and what we now call modern poetry there seems a great gap. But in literature change is seldom abrupt. The human spirit is never static and the poets are especially sensitive to change and often prelude in their poetry the atmosphere and values of the next age. Poems by Meredith like his " difficult " *Woods of Westermain*, and the spare, rugged, astringent verses of Hardy have a quality decidedly modern rather than Victorian; Browning's dramatic monologues present people speaking with a natural talking rhythm, caught between thought and emotion, feeling their way in the web of circumstance, like moderns—T. S. Eliot's *Alfred Prufrock* is far nearer to Browning's *Bishop Blougram* than to most of the figures of Victorian poetry. And further back, in America, was Edgar Allan Poe from whom largely derived the impulse to symbolism, which, passing through French poets like Mallarmé, was to help to produce an essential part of the technique of modern poetry.

For some thirty years there was an attempt to break away from Victorian poetic values. Above all, there was a reaction against Tennyson: it was held that he was shallow, pretty, complacent, and prostituted poetry to the debased puritanism of the selfrighteous, money-making middle class. So in the nineties arose a new poetry: the poets were æsthetes, with little to say, save, with fastidious artistry and a sentimental disillusionment, to lament how the charms of women and wine pass. Sick of the public nobleness of Tennysonian poetry they preferred plaintive sensuousness in a corner. These poets were the logical conclusion of the æstheticism of Dante Rossetti and the musical sensuousness of Swinburne, with the added influence of Pater's æsthetic theory and of the poetry of Baudelaire and Verlaine. The poets of the nineties left a few polished poems by Dowson and others, and the mournful beauty of Yeats's early poetry of Irish myth and legend.

In the nineties, of course, Meredith and Hardy were still writing; there was the religious poetry of Francis Thompson and Alice Meynell; A. E. Housman's *Shropshire Lad* came in 1896. And yet more sharply to remind us of the impossibility of neat classifications of poetry there was Kipling. His *Departmental Ditties* showed no signs of the century's poetry dying in a drawing-room, and he went on to sing with fresh and individual vigour of the courage and beauty and irony of life which he was proud to share with the common man.

In the early years of this century Masefield, too, wrote for the many, with his sea songs and his realistic tales, keeping poetry alive, modern, even startling. And in the years before 1914 there were many poets: Binyon, Lascelles Abercrombie, Noyes,

Chesterton, Gordon Bottomley, De la Mare and others. Then in 1912 came the first Georgian anthology, to go on to the fifth and last in 1922. It was "issued in the belief that English poetry is now again putting on a new strength and beauty." Rupert Brooke was outstanding at the start; at the end J. C. Squire led this rather self-conscious band who had set out to bring back into poetry the simple and natural. They could sing, but were little troubled by thought and the new industrialised world hardly existed for them. Of their number W. H. Davies and De la Mare were delightful and unique, Flecker a poet of promise, Drinkwater, Shanks and Freeman pleasant; only Blunden outgrew his Georgian limitations. And about 1912, too, the Imagists, Ezra Pound in America, T. E. Hulme in England, tried to purge poetry of effete romanticism by direct statement and new images and rhythms.

Then in 1917 modern poetry really began with T. S. Eliot's *Prufrock* volume. In witty, allusive, intellectual poetry he exposed the death-will he discerned in civilisation, his attack culminating in *The Waste Land* (1922). The French symbolists, the Imagists, the English metaphysicals, Jacobean dramatists, Dante, these and other influences combined in him to produce a new dynamic poetry. Steadily he has grown in poetic stature through *Ash Wednesday* to *Little Gidding* (1942). Alongside him in the twenties Edith Sitwell was a dazzling experimenter. Then by 1930 a new group of poets appeared, Auden, Macneice, Day Lewis, Stephen Spender, inspired by Eliot, and by Manley Hopkins and Wilfred Owen, but seeking to cure the Waste Land by the help of Marx and Freud instead of Eliot's later Catholicism. On their heels tread many young poets. But up to 1939 Yeats, developing to the last, towered up the one master poet of this century.

BALLADS.

WE owe our glorious heritage of ballads chiefly to anonymous wandering minstrels of the fourteenth fifteenth, and sixteenth centuries—a few belong to the seventeenth century. These men were the poets of the common people celebrating in song local stories and legends of war and love, outlawry and magic. Many ballads, no doubt, have been lost, but many were printed on rough broad-sheets in the sixteenth century, and others lived longer still on the lips of their singers and their audiences, till at last they were rescued into print. They are marked in a high degree by simplicity, naturalness and sincerity, and the heart is moved by them " more than with a trumpet." Ben Jonson said he would rather have written *Chevy-Chase* than all his works.

The Scotch ballads are on the whole considerably the finer; among the best of them, in addition to *Chevy Chase* and those given here, are *Clerk Saunders*, *The Queen's Marie*, *The Twa Corbies*, *The Ballad of Otterburn*, *Edom o'Gordon*, and *The Gay Goshawk*. Among the best English ballads are *The Nut-Brown Maid*, *The Children in the Wood*, and some of the many lays of Robin Hood.

Of the ballads below *Young Waters*, *The Bailiff's Daughter of Islington*, and *Sir Patrick Spens* are reprinted from Percy's *Reliques* (1765). The version of *Binnorie* contains some verses from others of the several forms of the ballad, but mainly follows the version in Scott's *Minstrelsy of the Scottish Border*. *The Wife of Usher's Well*, too, is printed from Scott's *Minstrelsy*. *Edward, Edward* is printed from Percy with some slight simplification of spelling.

EDWARD, EDWARD.

" Why does your brand sae drop wi' blude,
  Edward, Edward ?
Why does your brand sae drop wi' blude,
  And why sae sad gang ye, O ? "
" O I hae killed my hawk sae gude,
  Mither, mither :
O I hae killed my hawk sae gude,
  And I had nae mair but he, O."

" Your hawk's blude was never sae red,
  Edward, Edward.
Your hawk's blude was never sae red,
  My dear son, I tell thee, O."
" O I hae killed my red-roan steed,
  Mither, Mither :
O I hae killed my red-roan steed,
  That erst was sae fair and free, O."

" Your steed was auld, and ye hae got mair,
  Edward, Edward :
Your steed was auld, and ye hae got mair,
  Some other dule ye dree, O."
" O I hae killed my father dear,
  Mither, mither :
O I hae killed my father dear,
  Alas ! and wae is me, O."

" And whatten penance will ye dree for that,
  Edward, Edward ?
And whatten penance will ye dree for that ?
  My dear son, now tell me, O."
" I'll set my feet in yonder boat,
  Mither, mither :
I'll set my feet in yonder boat,
  And I'll fare over the sea, O."

" And what will ye do wi' your towers and your ha',
    Edward, Edward ?
  And what will ye do wi' your towers and your ha'
    That were sae fair to see, O ? "
" I'll let them stand till they doun fa',
    Mither, mither :
  I'll let them stand till they doun fa',
    For here never mair maun I be, O."

" And what will ye leave to your bairns and your wife,
    Edward, Edward ?
  And what will ye leave to your bairns and your wife,
    When ye gang over the sea, O ? "
" The warld's room, let them beg through life,
    Mither, mither :
  The warld's room, let them beg through life,
    For them never mair will I see, O."

" And what will ye leave to your ain mither dear,
    Edward, Edward ?
  And what will ye leave to your ain mither dear ?
    My dear son, now tell me, O."
" The curse of hell frae me sall ye bear,
    Mither, mither :
  The curse of hell frae me sall ye bear,
    Sic counsels ye gave to me, O."

THE WIFE OF USHER'S WELL.

There lived a wife at Usher's Well,
    And a wealthy wife was she :
She had three stout and stalwart sons,
    And sent them o'er the sea.

They hadna been a week from her,
   A week but barely ane,
When word came to the carline wife
   That her three sons were gane.

They hadna been a week from her,
   A week but barely three,
When word came to the carline wife
   That her sons she'd never see.

" I wish the wind may never cease,
   Nor fashes in the flood,
Till my three sons come hame to me,
   In earthly flesh and blood ! "

It fell about the Martinmas,
   When nights are lang and mirk,
The carline wife's three sons came home,
   And their hats were o' the birk.

It neither grew in syke nor ditch,
   Nor yet in ony sheugh;
But at the gates o' Paradise
   That birk grew fair eneugh. . . .

" Blow up the fire, my maidens !
   Bring water from the well !
For all my house shall feast this night,
   Since my three sons are well ! "

And she has made to them a bed,
   She's made it large and wide;
And she's ta'en her mantle her about;
   Sat down at the bed-side.

Up then crew the red, red cock,
   And up and crew the gray:
The eldest to the youngest said,
   "'Tis time we were away!"

The cock he hadna crawed but once,
   And clapped his wings at a',
When the youngest to the eldest said,
   "Brother, we must awa'."

"The cock doth craw, the day doth daw,
   The channerin' worm doth chide:
Gin we be miss'd out o' our place,
   A sair pain we maun bide.

"Fare ye weel, my mother dear!
   Fareweel to barn and byre!
And fare ye weel, the bonny lass,
   That kindles my mother's fire!"

BINNORIE.

There were twa sisters sat in a bower;
   Binnorie, O Binnorie!
There cam a knight to be their wooer
   By the bonnie mill-dams o' Binnorie.

He courted the eldest wi' glove and ring,
But he loved the youngest abune a' thing.

He courted the eldest wi' brotch and knife,
But he loved the youngest as his life.

The eldest she was vexèd sair,
And sair envièd her sister fair.

Into her bower she could not rest,
Wi' grief and spite she almost brast.

Upon a morning fair and clear,
She cried upon her sister dear:

" O sister, come to yon sea strand,
And see our father's ships come to land."

She's ta'en her by the lily hand,
And led her down to the river-strand.

The youngest stude upon a stane,
The eldest cam and pushed her in.

She took her by the middle sma',
And dashed her bonny back to the jaw.

" O sister, sister, reach your hand !
And ye shall be heir o' half my land:

" O sister, reach me but your glove !
And sweet William shall be your love."

" O sister, sister, save my life,
And I swear I'll never be nae man's wife."

Sometimes she sank, and sometimes she swam,
Until she cam to the miller's dam.

O out then cam the miller's son,
And saw the fair maid swimmin' in.

" O father, father, draw your dam !
Here's either a mermaid or a milk-white swan."

The miller hasted and drew his dam,
And there he found a drown'd womàn.

You couldna see her yellow hair
For gold and pearl that were so rare.

You couldna see her middle sma',
Her gowden girdle was sae braw.

You couldna see her lily feet,
Her gowden fringes were sae deep.

You couldna see her fingers white,
For gowden rings that were sae gryte.

And by there cam a harper fine,
That harpèd to the king at dine.

And when he did look that lady upon,
He sigh'd and made a heavy moan.

He's made a harp of her breast-bane
Whose sound wad melt a heart of stane.

He's ta'en three locks o' her yellow hair,
And wi' them strung his harp sae rare.

He brought it to her father's hall,
And there was the court assembled all.

He laid his harp upon a stane,
And straight it began to play alane.

" O yonder sits my father, the King,
And yonder sits my mother, the Queen;

And yonder stands my brother Hugh,
And by him my William, sweet and true."

But the last tune that the harp play'd then—
   Binnorie, O Binnorie !
Was " Woe to my sister, false Helèn ! "
   By the bonnie mill-dams of Binnorie.

NOTE.—The *Binnorie* refrain should be repeated in each verse.

YOUNG WATERS.

About Yule, quhen the wind blew cule,
    And the round tables began,
A' ! there is cum to our kings court
    Mony a well-favourd man.

The queen luikt owre the castle wa',
    Beheld baith dale and down,
And then she saw young Waters
    Cum riding to the town.

His footmen they did rin before,
    His horsemen rade behind,
Ane mantel of the burning gowd
    Did keip him frae the wind.

Gowden graith'd his horse before
    And siller shod behind,
The horse yong Waters rade upon
    Was fleeter than the wind.

But than spake a wylie lord,
    Unto the queen said he,
" O tell me quha's the fairest face
    Rides in the company."

" I've sene lord, and I've sene laird,
    And knights of high degree;
Bot a fairer face than young Watèrs
    Mine eyne did never see."

Out then spack the jealous king,
    (And an angry man was he)
" O, if he had been twice as fair,
    You micht have excepted me."

" You 're neither laird nor lord," she says,
  " Bot the king that wears the crown;
Ther is not a knight in fair Scotland
  Bot to thee maun bow down."

For a' that she could do or say,
  Appeasd he wad nae bee;
Bot for the words which she had said
  Young Waters he maun dee.

They hae taen young Waters, and
  Put fetters to his feet;
They hae taen young Waters, and
  Thrown him in dungeon deep.

" Aft have I ridden thro' Stirling town
  In the wind both and the weit;
Bot I neir rade thro' Stirling town
  Wi' fetters at my feet.

" Aft have I ridden thro' Stirling town
  In the wind both and the rain;
Bot I neir rade thro' Stirling town
  Neir to return again."

They hae taen to the heiding-hill
  His young son in his craddle,
And they hae taen to the heiding-hill,
  His horse both and his saddle.

They hae taen to the heiding-hill,
  His lady fair to see:
And for the words the Queen had spoke,
  Young Waters he did dee.

THE BAILIFF'S DAUGHTER OF ISLINGTON

There was a youthe, and a well-beloved youthe,
  And he was a squires son:
He loved the bayliffes daughter deare,
  That lived in Islington.

Yet she was coye and would not believe
  That he did love her soe,
Noe, nor at any time would she
  Any countenance to him showe.

But when his friendes did understand
  His fond and foolish minde,
They sent him up to faire London
  An apprentice for to binde.

And when he had been seven long yeares,
  And never his love could see:
" Many a teare have I shed for her sake,
  When she little thought of mee."

Then all the maids of Islington
  Went forth to sport and playe,
All but the bayliffes daughter deare;
  She secretly stole awaye.

She pulled off her gowne of greene,
  And put on ragged attire,
And to faire London she would go
  Her true love to enquire.

And as she went along the high road,
  The weather being hot and drye,
She sat her downe upon a green bank,
  And her true love came riding bye.

She started up, with a colour soe redd,
    Catching hold of his bridle-reine;
" One penny, one penny, kind sir," she sayd,
" Will ease me of much paine."

" Before I give you one penny, sweet-heart,
    Praye tell me where you were borne."
" At Islington, kind sir," sayd shee,
" Where I have had many a scorne."

" I prythee, sweet-heart, then tell to mee,
O tell me, whether you knowe
The bayliffes daughter of Islington."
" She is dead, sir, long agoe."

" If she be dead, then take my horse,
    My saddle and bridle also;
For I will into some farr countrye,
    Where noe man shall me knowe."

" O staye, O staye, thou goodlye youth,
    She standeth by thy side;
She is here alive, she is not dead,
    And readye to be thy bride."

" O, farewell griefe, and welcome joye,
    Ten thousand times therefore;
For nowe I have founde mine owne true love,
    Whom I thought I should never see more."

HELEN OF KIRCONNELL.

I wish I were where Helen lies;
Night and day on me she cries;
O, that I were where Helen lies
    On fair Kirconnell lea !

Curst be the heart that thought the thought,
And curst the hand that fired the shot,
When in my arms burd Helen dropt,
    And died to succour me !

O think na ye my heart was sair
When my Love dropt doun and spak nae mair !
I laid her doun wi' meikle care
    On fair Kirconnell lea.

As I went doun the water-side,
None but my foe to be my guide,
None but my foe to be my guide,
    On fair Kirconnell lea;

I lighted doun my sword to draw,
I hackèd him in pieces sma',
I hackèd him in pieces sma',
    For her sake that died for me.

O Helen fair, beyond compare !
I'll make a garland of thy hair
Shall bind my heart for evermair
    Until the day I die.

O that I were where Helen lies !
Night and day on me she cries:
Out of my bed she bids me rise,
    Says, " Haste and come to me ! "

O Helen fair ! O Helen chaste !
If I were with thee, I were blest,
Where thou lies low and takes thy rest
    On fair Kirconnell lea.

I wish my grave were growing green,
A winding-sheet drawn ower my een,
And I in Helen's arms lying,
   On fair Kirconnell lea.

I wish I were where Helen lies;
Night and day on me she cries;
And I am weary of the skies,
   For her sake that died for me.

SIR PATRICK SPENS.

The king sits in Dumferling toune,
   Drinking the bluid-reid wine:
" O whar will I get guid sailòr,
   To sail this schip of mine ? "

Up and spak an eldern knicht,
   Sat at the king's richt kne:
" Sir Patrick Spence is the best sailòr
   That sails upon the se."

The king has written a braid letter,
   And signed it wi' his hand,
And sent it to Sir Patrick Spence,
   Was walking on the sand.

The first line that Sir Patrick red,
   A loud lauch lauched he:
The next line that Sir Patrick red,
   The teir blinded his ee.

" O wha is this has don this deid,
   This ill deid don to me,
To send me out this time o' the yeir,
   To sail upon the se ?

" Mak haste, mak haste, my mirry men all,
  Our guid schip sails the morne."
" O say na sae, my master deir,
  For I feir a deadlie storme.

" Late late yestreen I saw the new moone
  Wi' the auld moone in hir arme;
And I feir, I feir, my deir mastèr,
  That we will cum to harme."

O our Scots nobles wer richt laith
  To weet their cork-heild schoon;
Bot lang owre a' the play wer playd,
  Thair hats they swam aboone.

O lang, lang may their ladies sit,
  Wi' their fans into their hand,
Or eir they se Sir Patrick Spence
  Cum sailing to the land.

O lang, lang may the ladies stand
  Wi' their gold kems in their hair,
Waiting for thair ain deir lords,
  For they'll se thame na mair.

Have ower, have ower to Aberdour,
  It's fiftie fadom deip:
And thair lies guid Sir Patrick Spence,
  Wi' the Scots lords at his feit.

SPENSER.

EDMUND SPENSER (1552–1599) is the moon in the heavens of Elizabethan poetry, Shakespeare being the sun. On publishing his *Shepherd's Calendar* in 1579 Spenser was hailed as "the new poet," and *The Faerie Queene* (1590–6), won him immortality. He was also a satirist, a sonneteer, and in his Marriage Songs, and his Hymns on Love and Beauty and their heavenly counterparts one of our supremely great lyrists. He lived an active official life, helping in administering Ireland in the troubled years 1580 to 1599.

TO IMMORTALISE HIS LOVE.

One day I wrote her name upon the strand,
But came the waves and washèd it away:
Again I wrote it with a second hand,
But came the tide, and made my pains his prey.
Vain man, said she, that dost in vain essay
A mortal thing so to immortalise,
For I myself shall like to this decay,
And eek my name be wipèd out likewise.
Not so, quod I, let baser things devise
To die in dust, but you shall live by fame:
My verse your virtues rare shall eternize,
And in the heavens write your glorious name.
Where when as death shall all the world subdue,
Our love shall live, and later life renew.

THE BOWER OF BLISS.

And in the midst of all a fountain stood,
Of richest substance that on earth might be,
So pure and shiny, that the silver flood
Through every channel running one might see;

Most goodly it with curious imagery
Was over-wrought, and shapes of naked boys,
Of which some seemed with lively jollity
To fly about, playing their wanton toys,
Whilst others did themselves embay in liquid joys.

And over all of purest gold was spread
A trail of ivy in his native hue;
For the rich metal was so colourèd,
That wight, who did not well avis'd it view,
Would surely deem it to be ivy true:
Low his lascivious arms adown did creep,
That themselves dipping in the silver dew
Their fleecy flowers they fearfully did steep,
Which drops of crystal seemed for wantoness to weep.

Infinite streams continually did well
Out of this fountain, sweet and fair to see,
The which into an ample laver fell,
And shortly grew to so great quantity,
That like a little lake it seemed to be;
Whose depth exceeded not three cubits height
That through the waves one might the bottom see,
All pav'd beneath with jaspar shining bright,
That seemed the fountain in that sea did sail upright.

*   *   *   *

Eftsoons they heard a most melodious sound,
Of all that mote delight a dainty ear,
Such as at once might not on living ground,
Save in this paradise, be heard elsewhere:
Right hard it was for wight, which did it hear,
To read what manner music that mote be;
For all that pleasing is to living ear
Was there consorted in one harmony;
Birds, voices, instruments, winds, waters, all agree.

The joyous birds, shrouded in cheerful shade,
Their notes unto the voice attempered sweet;
The angelical soft trembling voices made
To the instruments divine respondence meet;
The silver sounding instruments did meet
With the base murmur of the water's fall;
The water's fall with difference discreet,
Now soft, now loud, unto the wind did call;
The gentle warbling wind low answerèd to all.

    *   *   *   *

The whiles some one did chaunt this lovely lay;
Ah see, whoso fair thing dost fain to see,
In springing flower the image of thy day;
Ah see the virgin rose, how sweetly she
Doth first peep forth with bashful modesty,
That fairer seems the less ye see her may;
Lo see, soon after, how more bold and free
Her barèd bosom she doth broad display;
Lo see, soon after, how she fades, and falls away.

So passeth, in the passing of a day,
Of mortal life, the leaf, the bud, the flower;
Ne more doth flourish after first decay,
That erst was sought to deck both bed and bower
Of many a lady, and many a paramour!
Gather therefore the rose, whilst yet in prime,
For soon comes age, that will her pride deflower:
Gather the rose of love, whilst yet is time,
Whilst loving thou mayst lovèd be with equal crime.

                         (*The Faerie Queene*, II. xii.)

From his bridal-song EPITHALAMION.

Open the temple gates unto my love,
Open them wide that she may enter in,
And all the posts adorn as doth behove,

And all the pillars deck with garlands trim,
For to receive this Saint with honour due,
That cometh in to you.
With trembling steps and humble reverence,
She cometh in, before the Almighty's view—
Of her, ye virgins, learn obedience
When so ye come into those holy places,
To humble your proud faces:
Bring her up to the high altar, that she may
The sacred ceremonies there partake,
The which do endless matrimony make,
And let the roaring organs loudly play
The praises of the Lord in lively notes,
The whiles with hollow throats
The Choristers the joyous Anthem sing,
That all the woods may answer and their echo ring.

Behold whiles she before the altar stands
Hearing the holy priest that to her speaks
And blesseth her with his two happy hands,
How the red roses flush up in her cheeks,
And the pure snow with goodly vermeil stain,
Like crimson dyed in grain,
That even the Angels which continually
About the sacred Altar do remain
Forget their service and about her fly,
Oft peeping in her face that seems more fair,
The more they on it stare.
But her sad eyes, still fastened on the ground,
Are governed with goodly modesty,
That suffers not one look to glance awry,
Which may let in a little thought unsound.
Why blush ye, love, to give to me your hand,
The pledge of all our band?
Sing, ye sweet Angels, Alleluya sing,
That all the woods may answer and your echo ring.

Now all is done; bring home the bride again,
Bring home the triumph of our victory,
Bring home with you the glory of her gain,
With joyance bring her and with jollity.
Never had man more joyful day than this,
Whom heaven would heap with bliss.
Make feast therefore now all this livelong day,
This day for ever to me holy is,
Pour out the wine without restraint or stay,
Pour out not cups, but by the belly full,
Pour out to all that will,
And sprinkle all the posts and walls with wine,
That they may sweat, and drunken be withal.
Crown ye God Bacchus with a coronal,
And Hymen also crown with wreaths of vine,
And let the Graces dance unto the rest,
For they can do it best:
The whiles the maidens do their carol sing,
To which the woods shall answer and their echo ring.

PROTHALAMION.

Calm was the day, and through the trembling air
Sweet breathing Zephyrus did softly play,
A gentle spirit, that lightly did delay
Hot Titan's beams which then did glister fair;
When I (whom sullen care,
Through discontent of my long fruitless stay
In Prince's Court, and expectation vain
Of idle hopes, which still do fly away
Like empty shadows, did afflict my brain)
Walked forth to ease my pain
Along the shore of silver-streaming Thames,
Whose rutty bank, the which his river hems,
Was painted all with variable flowers,

And all the meads adorned with dainty gems
Fit to deck maidens' bowers,
And crown their paramours
Against the bridal day, which is not long:
   Sweet Thames ! run softly, till I end my song.

There, in a meadow, by the river's side,
A flock of Nymphs I chancèd to espy,
All lovely daughters of the flood thereby,
With goodly greenish locks, all loose untied,
As each had been a bride;
And each one had a little wicker basket,
Made of fine twigs entrailèd curiously,
In which they gathered flowers to fill their flasket,
And with fine fingers cropped full feateously
The tender stalks on high.
Of every sort which in that meadow grew
They gathered some; the violet, pallid blue,
The little daisy that at evening closes,
The virgin lily, and the primrose true,
With store of vermeil roses,
To deck their bridegrooms' posies
Against the bridal day, which was not long:
   Sweet Thames ! run softly, till I end my song.

With that I saw two swans of goodly hue
Come softly swimming down along the Lee;
Two fairer birds I yet did never see:
The snow, which doth the top of Pindus strew,
Did never whiter shew,
Nor Jove himself, when he a swan would be
For love of Leda, whiter did appear;
Yet Leda was (they say) as white as he,
Yet not so white as these, nor nothing near:
So purely white they were,

That even the gentle stream, the which them bare,
Seemed foul to them, and bade his billows spare
To wet their silken feathers, lest they might
Soil their fair plumes with water not so fair,
And mar their beauties bright,
That shone as heaven's light,
Against their bridal day, which was not long:
   Sweet Thames ! run softly, till I end my song.

Eftsoons the Nymphs, which now had flowers their fill,
Ran all in haste to see that silver brood,
As they came floating on the crystal flood;
Whom when they saw, they stood amazèd still,
Their wondering eyes to fill:
Them seemed they never saw a sight so fair,
Of fowls so lovely, that they sure did deem
Them heavenly born, or to be that same pair
Which through the sky draw Venus' silver team;
For sure they did not seem
To be begot of any earthly seed,
But rather angels, or of angels' breed;
Yet were they bred of summer's heat, they say,
In sweetest season, when each flower and weed
The earth did fresh array;
So fresh they seemed as day,
Even as their bridal day, which was not long:
   Sweet Thames ! run softly, till I end my song.

Then forth they all out of their baskets drew
Great store of flowers, the honour of the field,
That to the sense did fragrant odours yield,
All which upon those goodly birds they threw,
And all the waves did strew,
That like old Peneus' waters they did seem,
When down along by pleasant Tempe's shore,

Scattered with flowers, through Thessaly they stream,
That they appear, through lilies' plenteous store,
Like a bride's chamber floor.
Two of those Nymphs, meanwhile, two garlands bound
Of freshest flowers which in that mead they found,
The which presenting all in trim array,
Their snowy foreheads therewithal they crowned,
Whilst one did sing this lay,
Prepared against that day,
Against their bridal day, which was not long:
   Sweet Thames ! run softly, till I end my song.

" Ye gentle birds, the world's fair ornament,
And heaven's glory, whom this happy hour
Doth lead unto your lovers' blissful bower,
Joy may you have, and gentle hearts' content
Of your love's couplement !
And let fair Venus, that is Queen of love,
With her heart-quelling son upon you smile,
Whose smile, they say, hath virtue to remove
All love's dislike, and friendship's faulty guile
For ever to assoil.
Let endless peace your steadfast hearts accord,
And blessèd plenty wait upon your board;
And let your bed with pleasures chaste abound,
That fruitful issue may to you afford,
Which may your foes confound,
And make you joys redound
Upon your bridal day, which is not long:
   Sweet Thames ! run softly, till I end my song."

So ended she; and all the rest around
To her redoubled that her undersong,
Which said, their bridal day should not be long:
And gentle Echo from the neighbour ground

Their accents did resound.
So forth those joyous birds did pass along,
Adown the Lee, that to them murmured low,
As he would speak, but that he lacked a tongue,
Yet did by signs his glad affection show,
Making his stream run slow.
And all the fowl which in his flood did dwell
Gan flock about these twain, that did excel
The rest, so far as Cynthia doth shend
The lesser stars.   So they, enrangèd well,
Did on those two attend,
And their best service lend
Against their wedding day, which was not long:
   Sweet Thames ! run softly, till I end my song.

At length they all to merry London came,
To merry London, my most kindly nurse,
That to me gave this life's first native source:
Though from another place I take my name,
An house of ancient fame.
There when they came, whereas those bricky towers,
The which on Thames' broad aged back do ride,
Where now the studious lawyers have their bowers,
There whilom wont the Templar Knights to bide,
Till they decayed through pride;
Next whereunto there stands a stately place,
Where oft I gainèd gifts and goodly grace
Of that great lord, which therein wont to dwell,
Whose want too well now feels my friendless case;
But ah ! here fits not well
Old woes, but joys, to tell,
Against the bridal day, which is not long:
   Sweet Thames ! run softly, till I end my song.

Yet therein now doth lodge a noble peer,
Great England's glory and the world's wide wonder,

Whose dreadful name late through all Spain did thunder,
And Hercules' two pillars standing near
Did make to quake and fear:
Fair branch of honour, flower of chivalry,
That fillest England with thy triumph's fame,
Joy have thou of thy noble victory,
And endless happiness of thine own name
That promiseth the same;
That through thy prowess and victorious arms,
Thy country may be freed from foreign harms,
And great Elisa's glorious name may ring
Through all the world, filled with thy wide alarms,
Which some brave muse may sing
To ages following,
Upon the bridal day, which is not long:
   Sweet Thames ! run softly, till I end my song.

From those high towers this noble lord issuing,
Like radiant Hesper, when his golden hair
In the ocean billows he hath bathèd fair,
Descended to the river's open viewing,
With a great train ensuing.
Above the rest were goodly to be seen
Two gentle knights of lovely face and feature
Beseeming well the bower of any queen,
With gifts of wit and ornament of nature
Fit for so goodly stature:
That like the twins of Jove they seemed in sight,
Which deck the bauldrick of the heavens bright.
They two, forth pacing to the river's side,
Received those two fair brides, their love's delight,
Which at th' appointed tide,
Each one did make his bride,
Against their bridal day, which is not long:
   Sweet Thames ! run softly, till I end my song.

CHRIST TRUE LOVE'S EXAMPLE.

Most glorious Lord of life, that on this day
Didst make Thy triumph over death and sin,
And having harrowed hell didst bring away
Captivity thence captive us to win:
This joyous day, dear Lord, with joy begin,
And grant that we for whom Thou diddest die
Being with Thy dear blood clean washed from sin,
May live for ever in felicity;
And that Thy love we weighing worthily,
May likewise love Thee for the same again:
And for Thy sake that all like dear didst buy,
With love may one another entertain.
     So let us love, dear love, like as we ought,
     Love is the lesson which the Lord us taught.

RALEIGH.

SIR WALTER RALEIGH (1552 ?–1618) was a typical
Elizabethan in his manysidedness. As a courtier, he
was a favourite of Queen Elizabeth; as a man of
action, he was both soldier and sailor; as an explorer,
he promoted colonisation in America, the introduction
of tobacco and potatoes into this country being,
according to tradition, due to the attempts made under
his support to colonise Virginia; as a man of letters
he was a patron of Edmund Spenser, wrote poetry
much of which is lost, and began a *History of the World*
(1614) which he brought down to 130 B.C. He was
executed on an old charge of complicity in a plot
against James I., but really to appease Spanish anger
roused by his raid on a Spanish Settlement in South
America.

MY LOVE HATH LEFT ME.

As you came from the holy land
    Of Walsingham,
Met you not with my true love,
    By the way, as you came?

How shall I know your true love,
    That have met many one,
As I went to the holy land,
    That have come, that have gone?

She is neither white, nor brown,
    But as the heavens fair;
There is none hath a form so divine
    In the earth or the air.

Such a one did I meet, good sir,
    Such an angelic face,
Who like a queen, like a nymph, did appear
    By her gait, by her grace.

She hath left me here all alone,
    All alone, as unknown,
Who sometimes did me lead with herself,
    And me loved as her own.

What's the cause that she leaves you alone,
    And a new way doth take,
Who loved you once as her own,
    And her joy did you make?

I have loved her all my youth,
    But now am old, as you see:
Love likes not the falling fruit
    From the withered tree.

Know that Love is a careless child,
  And forgets promise past;
He is blind, he is deaf when he list,
  And in faith never fast.

His desire is a dureless content,
  And a trustless joy;
He is won with a world of despair,
  And is lost with a toy.

Of womenkind such indeed is the love,
  Or the word love abusèd,
Under which many childish desires
  And conceits are excusèd.

But true love is a durable fire,
  In the mind ever burning,
Never sick, never old, never dead,
  From itself never turning.

REPLY TO MARLOWE'S "THE PASSIONATE
SHEPHERD TO HIS LOVE."

If all the world and love were young,
And truth in every shepherd's tongue,
These pretty pleasures might me move
To live with thee and be thy love.

But time drives flocks from field to fold,
When rivers rage and rocks grow cold;
And Philomel becometh dumb;
The rest complains of cares to come.

The flowers do fade, and wanton fields
To wayward winter reckoning yields:
A honey tongue, a heart of gall,
Is fancy's spring, but sorrow's fall.

Thy gowns, thy shoes, thy beds of roses,
Thy cap, thy kirtle, and thy posies,
Soon break, soon wither, soon forgotten,—
In folly ripe, in reason rotten.

Thy belt of straw and ivy buds,
Thy coral clasps and amber studs,—
All those in me no means can move
To come to thee and be thy love.

But could youth last, and love still breed;
Had joys no date, nor age no need;
Then those delights my mind might move
To live with thee and be thy love.

THE CONCLUSION.

Even such is Time, which takes in trust
   Our youth, our joys, our all we have,
And pays us but with earth and dust;
   Who, in the dark and silent grave,
When we have wandered all our ways,
Shuts up the story of our days;
But from this earth, this grave, this dust
My God shall raise me up, I trust.

SIDNEY.

SIR PHILIP SIDNEY (1554–1586), courtier, diplomatist, soldier, and poet, was one of the noblest and most chivalrous of the Elizabethans. His sonnet sequence *Astrophel and Stella*, published in 1591, heralded a great outburst of sonneteering; his novel *Arcadia* is a medley of pastoral and chivalrous romance in the prose style of a poet; his *Apology for Poetry* is an impassioned defence of the art, and our first notable critical work. He died of a wound on the battlefield of Zutphen.

MY TRUE LOVE HATH MY HEART.

My true love hath my heart, and I have his,
By just exchange one for another given:
I hold his dear, and mine he cannot miss.
There never was a better bargain driven:
His heart in me keeps him and me in one,
My heart in him his thoughts and senses guides:
He loves my heart, for once it was his own,
I cherish his because in me it bides:
His heart his wound receivèd from my sight,
My heart was wounded with his wounded heart;
For as from me on him his heart did light,
So still methought in me his heart did smart.
    Both equal hurt, in this change sought our bliss;
    My true love hath my heart, and I have his.

LOVE LIKE A BOY.

In truth, O Love, with what a boyish kind
Thou dost proceed in thy most serious ways,
That when the heaven to thee his best displays
Yet of that best thou leav'st the best behind.
For, like a child that some fair book doth find,
With gilded leaves or coloured vellum plays,
Or, at the most, on some fair picture stays,
But never heeds the fruit of writer's mind:
So when thou saw'st in Nature's cabinet
Stella, thou straight look'st babies in her eyes,
In her cheek's pit thou didst thy pitfold set,
And in her breast bo-peep or couching lies,
    Playing and shining in each outward part;
    But, fool, seek'st not to get into her heart.

LEAVE ME, O LOVE.

Leave me, O Love ! which reachest but to dust,
And there, my mind, aspire to higher things;
Grow rich in that which never taketh rust:
Whatever fades, but fading pleasure brings.
Draw in thy beams, and humble all thy might
To that sweet yoke, where lasting freedoms be,
Which breaks the clouds, and opens forth the light,
That doth both shine and give us sight to see.
Oh, take fast hold ! Let that Light be thy guide
In this small course, which birth draws out to death,
And think how evil becometh him to slide
Who seeketh heaven, and comes of heavenly breath.
    Then farewell, world !   Thy uttermost I see.
    Eternal Love, maintain thy life in me.

WITH HOW SAD STEPS, O MOON.

With how sad steps, O Moon, thou climb'st the skies;
How silently; and with how wan a face !
What ! may it be, that even in heavenly place
That busy Archer his sharp arrows tries ?
Sure, if that long-with-love-acquainted eyes
Can judge of love, thou feel'st a lover's case;
I read it in thy looks; thy languisht grace
To me that feel the like, thy state descries.
Then, even of fellowship, O Moon, tell me,
Is constant love deem'd there but want of wit ?
Are beauties there as proud as here they be ?
Do they above love to be loved, and yet
    Those lovers scorn, whom that love doth possess ?
    Do they call *virtue* there—*ungratefulness !*

LYLY.

JOHN LYLY (1554 ?–1606) was a dramatist and a novelist. His plays are comedies, whose matter is drawn largely from classical history and mythology, and whose wit and charming heroines gave Shakespeare hints for his romantic love comedies like *As You Like It*. His novel was *Euphues,* which set a fashion of very ornate prose and so gave a word to our language. The plays contain some dainty lyrics.

CUPID AND MY CAMPASPE.

Cupid and my Campaspe played
At cards for kisses—Cupid paid.
He stakes his quiver, bow, and arrows,
His mother's doves, and team of sparrows;
Loses them too; then down he throws
The coral of his lip, the rose
Growing on's cheek (but none knows how);
With these the crystal of his brow,
And then the dimple of his chin—
All these did my Campaspe win.
At last he set her both his eyes—
She won and Cupid blind did rise.

    O Love, has she done this to thee ?
    What shall, alas ! become of me ?

PEELE.

GEORGE PEELE (1558 ?–1597) was, like Lyly, a "University Wit." He is remembered as a dramatist of the pre-Shakespearian group, but lives rather by a few lyrics. In *David and the Fair Bathsheba,* a Bible story dramatised, he wrote some very musical and poetical blank verse, and in *The Old Wives' Tale,* on which Milton drew for *Comus,* he achieved a lively medley of fairy-tale, magic, farce, and poetry.

FAIR AND FAIR.

Oenone. Fair and fair, and twice so fair,
　　　　As fair as any may be;
　　　　The fairest shepherd on our green,
　　　　A love for any lady.

Paris. Fair and fair, and twice so fair,
　　　　As fair as any may be;
　　　　Thy love is fair for thee alone,
　　　　And for no other lady.

Oenone. My love is fair, my love is gay,
　　　　As fresh as bin the flowers in May,
　　　　And of my love my roundelay,
　　　　My merry, merry, merry roundelay
　　　　Concludes with Cupid's curse:
　　　　They that do change old love for new,
　　　　Pray gods they change for worse!

Both together. They that do change old love for new,
　　　　Pray gods they change for worse!

Oenone. My love can pipe, my love can sing,
　　　　My love can many a pretty thing,
　　　　And of his lovely praises ring
　　　　My merry, merry, merry roundelays
　　　　Amen to Cupid's curse—
　　　　They that do change old love for new,
　　　　Pray gods they change for worse!

Both together. They that do change old love for new,
　　　　Pray gods they change for worse.

GREENE.

ROBERT GREENE (1560?–1592) was a typical Elizabethan bohemian man-of-letters, University-bred.
His *Friar Bacon and Friar Bungay* combines a story of
magic, inspired by Marlowe, with a delightful love
story of Prince Ned of Wales and a fair dairymaid,

who is our best heroine in drama before Shakespeare. This was his only real success in drama. He also wrote some pleasant prose romances, some pungent and personal pamphlets, and some delightful lyrics.

SEPHESTIA'S CRADLE SONG.

Weep not, my wanton, smile upon my knee;
When thou art old there's grief enough for thee.
　Mother's wag, pretty boy,
　Father's sorrow, father's joy;
　When thy father first did see
　Such a boy by him and me,
　He was glad, I was woe;
　Fortune changed made him so,
　When he left his pretty boy,
　Last his sorrow, first his joy.

Weep not, my wanton, smile upon my knee;
When thou art old there's grief enough for thee.
　Streaming tears that never stint,
　Like pearl-drops from a flint,
　Fell by course from his eyes,
　That one another's place supplies;
　Thus he grieved in every part,
　Tears of blood fell from his heart,
　When he left his pretty boy,
　Father's sorrow, father's joy.

Weep not, my wanton, smile upon my knee;
When thou art old there's grief enough for thee.
　The wanton smiled, father wept,
　Mother cried, baby leapt;
　More he crow'd, more we cried,
　Nature could not sorrow hide:
　He must go, he must kiss

Child and mother, baby bliss,
    For he left his pretty boy,
    Father's sorrow, father's joy.
Weep not, my wanton, smile upon my knee;
When thou art old there's grief enough for thee.

SOUTHWELL.

ROBERT SOUTHWELL (1561 ?–1595) was a Jesuit,
tortured and executed for his faith. His mystical
religious poetry stands out prominently amid Elizabethan poetry, from which the strain of intense
religious feeling is almost absent.

THE BURNING BABE.

As I in hoary winter's night
    Stood shivering in the snow,
Surprised I was with sudden heat
    Which made my heart to glow;
And lifting up a fearful eye
    To view what fire was near,
A pretty babe all burning bright
    Did in the air appear:
Who, scorchèd with excessive heat,
    Such floods of tears did shed,
As though his floods should quench his flames,
    Which with his tears were bred.
" Alas ! " quoth he, " but newly born,
    In fiery heats I fry,
Yet none approach to warm their hearts
    Or feel my fire but I."

" My faultless breast the furnace is,
    The fuel wounding thorns;
Love is the fire, and sighs the smoke,
    The ashes, shames and scorns;

The fuel Justice layeth on,
    And Mercy blows the coals;
The metal in this furnace wrought
    Are men's defilèd souls:
For which, as now on fire I am
    To work them to their good,
So will I melt into a bath,
    To wash them in my blood."
With this he vanished out of sight,
    And swiftly shrank away,
And straight I called unto my mind
    That it was Christmas day.

DANIEL.

SAMUEL DANIEL (1562–1619) was praised by Jonson for his " sweetness of ryming," and by another poet as " well-languaged Daniel." His longer poems such as the historical *Civil Wars* (1595–1609) maintain a constant high level of such sweet musical verse. He wrote a sonnet series *Delia*, but his true vein is philosophic not passionate, as his *Epistle* (see below) indicates.

CARE-CHARMER SLEEP.

Care-charmer Sleep, son of the sable Night,
Brother of Death, in silent darkness born,
Relieve my languish, and restore the light;
With dark forgetting of my care, return !
And let the day be time enough to mourn
The shipwreck of my ill-adventured youth;
Let waking eyes suffice to wail their scorn,
Without the torment of the night's untruth.
Cease, dreams, the images of day-desires,
To model forth the passions of the morrow:

Never let rising sun approve you liars,
To add more grief to aggravate my sorrow.
　　Still let me sleep, embracing clouds in vain,
　　And never wake to feel the day's disdain.

From the EPISTLE TO THE LADY MARGARET, COUNTESS OF CUMBERLAND.

He that of such a height hath built his mind,
And reared the dwelling of his thoughts so strong,
As neither fear nor hope can shake the frame
Of his resolvèd powers; nor all the wind
Of vanity or malice pierce to wrong
His settled peace, or to disturb the same:
What a fair seat hath he, from whence he may
The boundless wastes and wilds of man survey ! . . .

This concord, madam, of a well-tuned mind
Hath been so set by that all-working hand
Of heaven that, though the world hath done his worst
To put it out by discords most unkind,
Yet doth it still in perfect union stand
With God and man; nor ever will be forced
From that most sweet accord, but still agree,
Equal in fortune's inequality. . . .

CONSTABLE.

HENRY CONSTABLE (1562–1613) was one of the many poets who published sonnet sequences after Sidney's *Astrophel and Stella* set the fashion. His *Diana* first appeared in 1592, and was re-issued with additional poems in 1594. The love is probably imaginary.

DIAPHENIA.

Diaphenia, like the daffadowndilly,
White as the sun, fair as the lily,
Heigh ho, how I do love thee !
I do love thee as my lambs
Are belovèd of their dams;
How blest were I if thou wouldst prove me.

Diaphenia, like the spreading roses,
That in thy sweets all sweets encloses,
Fair sweet, how I do love thee !
I do love thee as each flower
Loves the sun's life-giving power;
For, dead, thy breath to life might move me.

Diaphenia, like to all things blessèd,
When all thy praises are expressèd,
Dear joy, how I do love thee !
As the birds do love the spring,
Or the bees their careful king:
Then in requite, sweet virgin, love me !

DRAYTON.

MICHAEL DRAYTON (1563–1631), like Daniel, wrote
a long historical poem, *The Barons' Wars* (1596–1603),
good in narrative and descriptive power, but without
the full genius which makes a long poem live. His
Polyolbion, descriptive of Britain's surface and history,
is similarly overweighted. His sonnet series *Idea*,
however, contains the undying sonnet below, his
Ballad of Agincourt burns with martial fire, and his
Nymphidia is a dainty tale of fairyland.

SINCE THERE'S NO HELP.

Since there's no help, come, let us kiss and part—
Nay, I have done: you get no more of me;
And I am glad, yea, glad with all my heart,
That thus so cleanly I myself can free.
Shake hands for ever, cancel all our vows,
And when we meet at any time again,
Be it not seen in either of our brows
 That we one jot of former love retain.
Now at the last gasp of Love's latest breath,
When, his pulse failing, Passion speechless lies,
When Faith is kneeling by his bed of death,
And Innocence is closing up his eyes,
   Now, if thou wouldst, when all have given him over,
   From death to life thou mightst him yet recover.

QUEEN MAB SETS OUT.

Her chariot ready straight is made,
Each thing therein is fitting laid,
That she by nothing might be stayed,
   For nought must her be letting;
Four nimble gnats the horses were,
Their harnesses of gossamer,
Fly Cranion her charioteer
   Upon the coach-box getting.

Her chariot of a snail's fine shell,
Which for the colours did excel,
The fair Queen Mab becoming well,
   So lively was the limning;
The seat the soft wool of the bee,
The cover, gallantly to see,
The wing of a pied butterflee;
   I trow 'twas simple trimming.

The wheels composed of crickets' bones,
And daintily made for the nonce,
For fear of rattling on the stones
   With thistle-down they shod it;
For all her maidens much did fear
If Oberon had chanced to hear
That Mab his Queen should have been there,
   He would not have abode it.

She mounts her chariot with a trice,
Nor would she stay, for no advice,
Until her maids that were so nice
   To wait on her were fitted;
But ran herself away alone,
Which when they heard, there was not one
But hasted after to be gone,
   As she had been diswitted.

Hop and Mop and Drop so clear,
Pip and Trip and Skip that were
To Mab, their sovereign, ever dear,
   Her special maids of honour;
Fib and Tib and Pink and Pin,
Tick and Quick and Jill and Jin,
Tit and Nit and Wap and Win,
   The train that wait upon her.

Upon a grasshopper they got
And, what with amble and with trot,
For hedge nor ditch they sparèd not,
   But after her they hie them;
A cobweb over them they throw,
To shield the wind if it should blow,
Themselves they wisely could bestow
   Lest any should espy them.

               (From *Nymphidia*.)

BALLAD OF AGINCOURT.

Fair stood the wind for France,
When we our sails advance,
Nor now to prove our chance
    Longer will tarry;
But putting to the main,
At Caux, the mouth of Seine,
With all his martial train,
    Landed King Harry.

And taking many a fort,
Furnished in warlike sort,
Marcheth tow'rds Agincourt
    In happy hour;
Skirmishing day by day,
With those that stopp'd his way,
Where the French gen'ral lay
    With all his power.

Which in his height of pride,
King Henry to deride,
His ransom to provide
    To the king sending,
Which he neglects the while,
As from a nation vile,
Yet with an angry smile
    Their fall portending.

And turning to his men,
Quoth our brave Henry then,
Though they to one be ten,
    Be not amazèd.
Yet have we well begun,
Battles so bravely won,
Have ever to the sun
    By fame been raisèd.

And for myself (quoth he),
This my full rest shall be,
England ne'er mourn for me,
   Nor more esteem me.
Victor I will remain,
Or on this earth lie slain,
Never shall she sustain
   Loss to redeem me.

Poitiers and Cressy tell,
When most their pride did swell,
Under our swords they fell :
   No less our skill is,
Than when our grandsire-great,
Claiming the regal seat,
By many a warlike feat
   Lopp'd the French lilies.

The Duke of York so dread
The eager vaward led;
With the main Henry sped,
   Amongst his hench-men.
Exeter had the rear,
A braver man not there,
O Lord, how hot they were
   On the false Frenchmen !

They now to fight are gone,
Armour on armour shone,
Drum now to drum did groan,
   To hear was wonder;
That with the cries they make,
The very earth did shake,
Trumpet to trumpet spake,
   Thunder to thunder.

Well it thine age became,
O noble Erpingham,
Which didst the signal aim
    To our hid forces;
When from a meadow by,
Like a storm suddenly,
The English archery
    Struck the French horses.

With Spanish yew so strong,
Arrows a cloth-yard long,
That like to serpents stung,
    Piercing the weather;
None from his fellow starts,
But playing manly parts,
And like true English hearts,
    Stuck close together.

When down their bows they threw,
And forth their bilbos drew,
And on the French they flew,
    Not one was tardy;
Arms were from shoulders sent,
Scalps to the teeth were rent,
Down the French peasants went,
    Our men were hardy.

This while our noble king,
His broad sword brandishing,
Down the French host did ding,
    As to o'erwhelm it,
And many a deep wound lent,
His arms with blood besprent,
And many a cruel dent
    Bruisèd his helmet.

Gloucester, that duke so good,
Next of the royal blood,
For famous England stood,
    With his brave brother;
Clarence, in steel so bright,
Though but a maiden knight,
Yet in that furious fight
    Scarce such another.

Warwick in blood did wade,
Oxford the foe invade,
And cruel slaughter made,
    Still as they ran up;
Suffolk his axe did ply,
Beaumont and Willoughby
Bare them right doughtily,
    Ferrers and Fanhope.

Upon Saint Crispin's day
Fought was this noble fray,
Which fame did not delay
    To England to carry;
O when shall English men,
With such acts fill a pen,
Or England breed again
    Such a King Harry?

MARLOWE.

CHRISTOPHER MARLOWE (1564-1593) was our greatest
dramatist before Shakespeare. *Tamburlaine*, *Dr.
Faustus*, and *The Jew of Malta* are great poetic
tragedies. His last play *Edward II.* is often considered
superior to Shakespeare's *Richard II.* In non-dramatic
poetry he wrote *The Passionate Shepherd to his Love*,
and *Hero and Leander*, completed by Chapman.

THE PASSIONATE SHEPHERD TO HIS LOVE.

Come live with me and be my love,
And we will all the pleasures prove
That hills and valleys, dale and field
And all the craggy mountains yield.

There will we sit upon the rocks
And see the shepherds feed their flocks,
By shallow rivers, to whose falls
Melodious birds sing madrigals.

There will I make thee beds of roses
And a thousand fragrant posies;
A cap of flowers, and a kirtle
Embroider'd all with leaves of myrtle;

A gown made of the finest wool,
Which from our pretty lambs we pull;
Fair-linèd slippers for the cold,
With buckles of the purest gold;

A belt of straw and ivy buds
With coral clasps and amber studs:
And if these pleasures may thee move
Come live with me and be my love.

Thy silver dishes for thy meat
As precious as the gods do eat,
Shall on an ivory table be
Prepared each day for thee and me.

Thy shepherd swains shall dance and sing
For thy delight each May-morning.
If these delights thy mind may move,
Then live with me and be my love.

From FAUSTUS.

Ah, Faustus,
Now hast thou but one bare hour to live,
And then thou must be damned perpetually !
Stand still, you ever-moving spheres of heaven,
That time may cease, and midnight never come;
Fair Nature's eye, rise, rise again, and make
Perpetual day; or let this hour be but
A year, a month, a week, a natural day,
That Faustus may repent and save his soul !
O lente, lente currite, noctis equi !
The stars move still, time runs, the clock will strike,
The devil will come, and Faustus must be damned.
O, I'll leap up to my God !—Who pulls me down ?—
See, see, where Christ's blood streams in the firma-
    ment !
One drop would save my soul, half a drop: ah, my
    Christ !—
Ah, rend not my heart for naming of my Christ !
Yet will I call on Him: O, spare me, Lucifer !—
Where is it now ? 'tis gone: and see, where God
Stretcheth out His arm, and bends His ireful brows !
Mountains and hills, come, come, and fall on me,
And hide me from the heavy wrath of God !
No, no !
Then will I headlong run into the earth:
Earth, gape ! O, no, it will not harbour me !
You stars that reigned at my nativity,
Whose influence hath allotted death and hell,
Now draw up Faustus, like a foggy mist,
Into the entrails of yon labouring clouds,
That, when you vomit forth into the air,
My limbs may issue from your smoky mouths,
So that my soul may but ascend to heaven !

From TAMBURLAINE.

If all the pens that ever poets held
Had fed the feeling of their masters' thoughts,
And every sweetness that inspir'd their hearts,
Their minds and muses on admirèd themes;
If all the heavenly quintessence they 'still
From their immortal flowers of poesy,
Wherein, as in a mirror, we perceive
The highest reaches of a human wit;
If these had made one poem's period
And all combin'd in beauty's worthiness,
Yet should there hover in their restless heads
One thought, one grace, one wonder, at the least,
Which into words no virtue could digest.

SHAKESPEARE.

WILLIAM SHAKESPEARE (1564–1616) is our one unchallenged world-figure in literature. Of his life we know little, but it is enough that we have Ben Jonson's tribute: " I loved the man, and do honour his memory on this side idolatry as much as any."   He was not only a dramatist, but also an actor, and the two occupations earned him a comfortable fortune. His supreme greatness as a playwright tends to make us forget that he is our greatest poet too: the plays overflow with poetry and abound with lyrics, but in addition we have the narrative poems *Venus and Adonis* and *The Rape of Lucrece*, and the Sonnets.

Moreover, while compelling the admiration of the whole world, Shakespeare remains essentially English; in his history plays he has dramatised England's story from the time of Richard II. to that of Henry VIII., looking back also to the time of King John, and therein we find a true Englishman's love for this our " other Eden, demi-paradise."

Again, great as he is, Shakespeare is not always, nor perhaps even ever, the master-genius, who leaves us nothing to do but admire his works. Instead, we see him at every stage of his development—from the young man rewriting the plays of others, until, through practice, he rises to the tragic heights of *King Lear*, and then writes his last in a quieter vein of philosophic romance with *The Tempest* and *A Winter's Tale*. Thus, while being " not for an age, but for all time," his plays are for youth as well as for maturity, and as we grow mature so do the plays grow in meaning for us.

Shakespeare, says Carlyle, "is the grandest thing we have yet done. . . . This King Shakespeare, does not he shine, in crowned sovereignty, over us all, as the noblest, gentlest, yet strongest of rallying-signs; *in*destructible. . . .? We can fancy him as radiant aloft over all the Nations of Englishmen, a thousand years hence."

COME HITHER.

Under the greenwood tree
Who loves to lie with me,
And turn his merry note
Unto the sweet bird's throat,
Come hither, come hither, come hither !
Here shall he see
No enemy
But winter and rough weather.

Who doth ambition shun,
And loves to live i' the sun,
Seeking the food he eats,
And pleas'd with what he gets,
Come hither, come hither, come hither !
Here shall he see
No enemy
But winter and rough weather.

COME BUY.

Lawn as white as driven snow;
Cyprus black as e'er was crow;
Cloves as sweet as damask roses;
Masks for faces and for noses;
Bugle-bracelet, necklace-amber;
Perfume for a lady's chamber;
Golden quoifs and stomachers,
For my lads to give their dears;
Pins and poking-sticks of steel;
What maids lack from head to heel:
Come buy of me, come; come buy, come buy;
Buy lads, or else your lasses cry:
Come buy.

COME UNTO THESE YELLOW SANDS.

Come unto these yellow sands,
    And then take hands:
Curtsied when you have and kiss'd—
    The wild waves whist—
Foot it featly here and there;
And, sweet sprites, the burden bear.
    Hark, hark!
    Bow—wow.
    The watch-dogs bark:
    Bow—wow.
    Hark, hark! I hear
The strain of strutting Chanticleer
Cry Cock-a-diddle-dow.

BEAUTY BEYOND PRAISE.

When in the chronicle of wasted time
I see descriptions of the fairest wights,
And beauty making beautiful old rime
In praise of ladies dead and lovely knights,

Then, in the blazon of sweet beauty's best,
Of hand, of foot, of lip, of eye, of brow,
I see their antique pen would have express'd
Even such a beauty as you master now.
So all their praises are but prophecies
Of this our time, all you prefiguring;
And, for they look'd but with divining eyes,
They had not skill enough your worth to sing:
 For we, which now behold these present days,
 Have eyes to wonder, but lack tongues to praise.

I'LL LIVE IN THIS POOR RIME.

Not mine own fears, nor the prophetic soul
Of the wide world dreaming on things to come,
Can yet the lease of my true love control,
Suppos'd as forfeit to a confin'd doom.
The mortal moon hath her eclipse endured,
And the sad augurs mock their own presage;
Incertainties now crown themselves assured,
And peace proclaims olives of endless age.
Now with the drops of this most balmy time
My love looks fresh, and Death to me subscribes,
Since, spite of him, I'll live in this poor rime,
While he insults o'er dull and speechless tribes:
 And thou in this shalt find thy monument,
 When tyrants' crests and tombs of brass are spent.

WHO IS SYLVIA?

Who is Sylvia? what is she,
That all her swains commend her?
Holy, fair, and wise is she;
The heaven such grace did lend her,
That she might admiréd be.

Is she kind as she is fair?
For beauty lives with kindness.
Love doth to her eyes repair,
To help him of his blindness,
And, being helped, inhabits there.

Then to Sylvia let us sing,
That Sylvia is excelling:
She excels each mortal thing
Upon the dull earth dwelling:
To her let us garlands bring.

LOVE.

A lover's eyes will gaze an eagle blind;
A lover's ear will hear the lowest sound,
When the suspicious head of theft is stopp'd:
Love's feeling is more soft and sensible
Than are the tender horns of cockled snails:
Love's tongue proves dainty Bacchus gross in taste.
For valour, is not Love a Hercules,
Still climbing trees in the Hesperides?
Subtle as Sphinx; as sweet and musical
As bright Apollo's lute, strung with his hair;
And when Love speaks, the voice of all the gods
Makes heaven drowsy with the harmony.
Never durst poet touch a pen to write
Until his ink were tempered with Love's sighs;
O! then his lines would ravish savage ears,
And plant in tyrants mild humility.
From women's eyes this doctrine I derive:
They sparkle still the right Promethean fire;
They are the books, the arts, the academes,
That show, contain, and nourish all the world;
Else none at all in aught proves excellent.

                                (Love's Labour's Lost, IV. iii.)

O, MISTRESS MINE.

O mistress mine ! where are you roaming ?
O stay and hear ! your true love's coming,
That can sing both high and low:
Trip no further, pretty sweeting;
Journeys end in lovers meeting,
Every wise man's son doth know.

What is love ? 'tis not hereafter;
Present mirth hath present laughter;
What's to come is still unsure:
In delay there lies no plenty;
Then come kiss me, sweet and twenty,
Youth's a stuff will not endure.

LOVE'S NOT TIME'S FOOL.

Let me not to the marriage of true minds
Admit impediments.   Love is not love
Which alters when it alteration finds,
Or bends with the remover to remove:
O, no ! it is an ever-fixèd mark,
That looks on tempests and is never shaken;
It is the star to every wandering bark,
Whose worth's unknown, although his height be
    taken.
Love's not Time's fool, though rosy lips and cheeks
Within his bending sickle's compass come;
Love alters not with his brief hours and weeks,
But bears it out even to the edge of doom.
    If this be error, and upon me proved,
    I never writ, nor no man ever loved.

LOVE'S DUET.

Jul. Wilt thou be gone? it is not yet near day:
It was the nightingale, and not the lark,
That pierc'd the fearful hollow of thine ear;
Nightly she sings on yon pomegranate tree:
Believe me, love, it was the nightingale.

Rom. It was the lark, the herald of the morn,
No nightingale: look, love, what envious streaks
Do lace the severing clouds in yonder east:
Night's candles are burnt out, and jocund day
Stands tiptoe on the misty mountain tops:
I must be gone and live, or stay and die.

Jul. Yon light is not daylight, I know it, I:
It is some meteor that the sun exhales,
To be to thee this night a torch-bearer,
And light thee on thy way to Mantua:
Therefore stay yet; thou need'st not to be gone.

Rom. Let me be ta'en, let me be put to death;
I am content, so thou wilt have it so.
I'll say yon grey is not the morning's eye,
'Tis but the pale reflex of Cynthia's brow;
Nor that is not the lark, whose notes do beat
The vaulty heaven so high above our heads:
I have more care to stay than will to go:
Come, death, and welcome! Juliet wills it so.
How is't, my soul? let's talk; it is not day.

Jul. It is, it is; hie hence, be gone, away!
It is the lark that sings so out of tune,
Straining harsh discords and unpleasing sharps.
Some say the lark makes sweet division;
This doth not so, for she divideth us:
Some say the lark and loathèd toad change eyes;
O! now I would they had chang'd voices too,
Since arm from arm that voice doth us affray,
Hunting thee hence with hunts-up to the day.

O ! now be gone; more light and light it grows.

   Rom. More light and light; more dark and dark our
     woes.   (*Romeo and Juliet*, III. v.)

SWEET LOVERS LOVE THE SPRING.

It was a lover and his lass.
   With a hey, and a ho, and a hey nonino,
That o'er the green corn-field did pass
   In the spring time, the only pretty ring time,
When birds do sing, hey ding a ding, ding:
   Sweet lovers love the spring.

Between the acres of the rye,
   With a hey, and a ho, and a hey nonino,
These pretty country folks would lie,
   In the spring time, etc.

This carol they began that hour,
   With a hey, and a ho, and a hey nonino,
How that life was but a flower
   In the spring time, etc.

And therefore take the present time,
   With a hey, and a ho, and a hey nonino,
For love is crownèd with the prime
   In the spring time, the only pretty ring time,
When birds do sing, hey ding a ding, ding:
   Sweet lovers love the spring.

DAFFODIL TIME.

When daffodils begin to peer,
   With heigh ! the doxy over the dale,
Why, then comes in the sweet of the year;
   For the red blood reigns in the winter's pale.

The white sheet bleaching on the hedge,
  With heigh ! the sweet birds, O, how they sing !
Doth set my pugging tooth on edge;
  For a quart of ale is a dish for a king.

The lark, that tirra-lyra chants,
  With heigh ! with heigh ! the thrush and the jay,
Are summer songs for me and my aunts,
  While we lie tumbling in the hay.

O, FOR FLOWERS.

                    O Proserpina !
For the flowers now that frighted thou let'st fall
From Dis's waggon ! daffodils,
That come before the swallow dares, and take
The winds of March with beauty; violets dim,
But sweeter than the lids of Juno's eyes
Or Cytherea's breath; pale primroses
That die unmarried ere they can behold
Bright Phoebus in his strength, a malady
Most incident to maids; bold oxlips and
The crown imperial; lilies of all kinds,
The flower-de-luce being one.   O ! these I lack
To make you garlands of, and my sweet friend,
To strew him o'er and o'er !
                    (*The Winter's Tale*, IV. iii.)

BRIGHT DAWN—GREY DAY.

Full many a glorious morning have I seen
Flatter the mountain-tops with sovereign eye,
Kissing with golden face the meadows green,
Gilding pale streams with heavenly alchemy;
Anon permit the basest clouds to ride

With ugly rack on his celestial face,
And from the forlorn world his visage hide,
Stealing unseen to west with this disgrace:
Even so my sun one early morn did shine
With all-triumphant splendour on my brow;
But out, alack ! he was but one hour mine,
The region cloud hath mask'd him from me now.
  Yet him for this my love no whit disdaineth;
  Suns of the world may stain when heaven's sun
    staineth.

QUEEN MAB.

She is the fairies' midwife, and she comes
In shape no bigger than an agate-stone
On the fore-finger of an alderman,
Drawn with a team of little atomies
Athwart men's noses as they lie asleep:
Her waggon-spokes made of long spinners' legs;
The cover, of the wings of grasshoppers;
The traces, of the smallest spider's web;
The collars, of the moonshine's watery beams;
Her whip of cricket's bone; the lash, of film;
Her waggoner, a small grey-coated gnat,
Not half so big as a round little worm
Prick'd from the lazy finger of a maid;
Her chariot is an empty hazel-nut,
Made by the joiner squirrel or old grub,
Time out o' mind the fairies' coach-makers.
And in this state she gallops night by night
Through lovers' brains, and then they dream of love;
O'er courtiers' knees, that dream on curtsies straight;
O'er lawyers' fingers, who straight dream on fees;
O'er ladies' lips, who straight on kisses dream;
Which oft the angry Mab with blisters plagues,
Because their breaths with sweetmeats tainted are.

Sometimes she gallops o'er a courtier's nose
And then dreams he of smelling out a suit;
And sometimes comes she with a tithe-pig's tail,
Tickling a parson's nose as a' lies asleep,
Then dreams he of another benefice;
Sometimes she driveth o'er a soldier's neck,
And then dreams he of cutting foreign throats,
Of breaches, ambuscadoes, Spanish blades,
Of healths five fathom deep; and then anon
Drums in his ear, at which he starts and wakes;
And, being thus frighted, swears a prayer or two,
And sleeps again.   This is that very Mab . .

(Romeo and Juliet, I. iv.)

MOONLIGHT.

How sweet the moonlight sleeps upon this bank !
Here will we sit, and let the sounds of music
Creep in our ears: soft stillness and the night
Become the touches of sweet harmony.
Sit, Jessica: look how the floor of heaven
Is thick inlaid with patines of bright gold:
There's not the smallest orb which thou behold'st
But in his motion like an angel sings,
Still quiring to the young-eyed cherubins;
Such harmony is in immortal souls;
But whilst this muddy vesture of decay
Doth grossly close it in, we cannot hear it.

(The Merchant of Venice, V. i.)

ARIEL'S SONGS.

(1)

Where the bee sucks there suck I:
In a cowslip's bell I lie;
There I couch when owls do cry.
On the bat's back I do fly,

After summer merrily.
Merrily, merrily shall I live now
Under the blossom that hangs on the bough.

(2)

Full fathom five thy father lies;
   Of his bones are coral made;
Those are pearls that were his eyes:
   Nothing of him that doth fade
But doth suffer a sea-change
Into something rich and strange.
Sea-nymphs hourly ring his knell:
               Ding-dong.
Hark ! now I hear them: Ding-dong, bell.

TIME.

Time hath, my lord, a wallet at his back,
Wherein he puts alms for oblivion,
A great-siz'd monster of ingratitudes:
Those scraps are good deeds past; which are devour'd
As fast as they are made, forgot as soon
As done: perséverance, dear my lord,
Keeps honour bright: to have done, is to hang
Quite out of fashion, like a rusty mail
In monumental mockery.   Take the instant way;
For honour travels in a strait so narrow
Where one but goes abreast: keep, then, the path;
For emulation hath a thousand sons
That one by one pursue: if you give way,
Or hedge aside from the direct forthright,
Like to an enter'd tide they all rush by
And leave you hindmost;
Or, like a gallant horse fall'n in first rank,
Lie there for pavement to the abject rear,

O'errun and trampled on: then what they do in present
Though less than yours in past, must o'ertop yours;
For time is like a fashionable host,
That slightly shakes his parting guest by the hand,
And with his arms outstretch'd, as he would fly,
Grasps in the comer: welcome ever smiles,
And farewell goes out sighing. O ! let not virtue seek
Remuneration for the thing it was;
For beauty, wit,
High birth, vigour of bone, desert in service,
Love, friendship, charity, are subjects all
To envious and calumniating time.
One touch of nature makes the whole world kin,
That all with one consent praise new-born gawds,
Though they are made and moulded of things past,
And give to dust that is a little gilt
More laud than gilt o'er-dusted.

(Troilus and Cressida, III. iii.)

SONG.

Blow, blow, thou winter wind,
    Thou art not so unkind
       As man's ingratitude;
    Thy tooth is not so keen
    Because thou art not seen,
       Although thy breath be rude.
Heigh ho ! sing heigh ho ! unto the green holly:
Most friendship is feigning, most loving mere folly:
    Then, heigh ho ! the holly !
    This life is most jolly.

Freeze, freeze, thou bitter sky,
    Thou dost not bite so nigh
       As benefits forgot:

> Though thou the waters warp,
> Thy sting is not so sharp
> As friend remember'd not.
Heigh ho ! sing heigh ho ! unto the green holly:
Most friendship is feigning, most loving mere folly:
> Then, heigh ho ! the holly !
> This life is most jolly.

(As You Like It.)

AY, BUT TO DIE.

Ay, but to die, and go we know not where;
To lie in cold obstruction and to rot;
This sensible warm motion to become
A kneaded clod; and the delighted spirit
To bathe in fiery floods, or to reside
In thrilling region of thick-ribbèd ice;
To be imprison'd in the viewless winds,
And blown with restless violence round about
The pendent world; or to be worse than worst
Of those that lawless and uncertain thoughts
Imagine howling: 'tis too horrible !
The weariest and most loathèd worldly life
That age, ache, penury, and imprisonment
Can lay on nature is a paradise
To what we fear of death.

(Measure for Measure, III. i.)

CLEOPATRA IN HER BARGE.

The barge she sat in, like a burnish'd throne,
Burn'd on the water; the poop was beaten gold,
Purple the sails, and so perfumèd that
The winds were love-sick with them; the oars were
  silver,
Which to the tune of flutes kept stroke, and made

The water which they beat to follow faster,
As amorous of their strokes.   For her own person,
It beggar'd all description; she did lie
In her pavilion—cloth-of-gold of tissue—
O'er-picturing that Venus where we see
The fancy outwork nature; on each side her
Stood pretty-dimpled boys, like smiling Cupids,
With divers-colour'd fans, whose wind did seem
To glow the delicate cheeks which they did cool,
And what they undid did.

> (*Antony and Cleopatra*, II. ii.)

ON DOVER CLIFFS.

> How fearful

And dizzy 'tis to cast one's eyes so low !
The crows and choughs that wing the midway air
Show scarce so gross as beetles: half way down
Hangs one that gathers samphire, dreadful trade !
Methinks he seems no bigger than his head:
The fishermen, that walk upon the beach,
Appear like mice; and yond tall anchoring bark,
Diminish'd to her cock—her cock, a buoy
Almost too small for sight: the murmuring surge,
That on the unnumber'd idle pebble chafes,
Cannot be heard so high.   I'll look no more;
Lest my brain turn, and the deficient sight
Topple down headlong.

> (*King Lear*, IV. vi.)

ENGLAND.

This royal throne of kings, this sceptered isle,
This earth of majesty, this seat of Mars,
This other Eden, demi-paradise,
This fortress built by Nature for herself

Against infection and the hand of war,
This happy breed of men, this little world,
This precious stone set in the silver sea,
Which serves it in the office of a wall,
Or as a moat defensive to a house,
Against the envy of less happier lands,
This blessed plot, this earth, this realm, this England.

(*Richard II.*, II. i.)

LIFE'S PAGEANT.

Our revels now are ended. These our actors,
As I foretold you, were all spirits and
Are melted into air, into thin air:
And, like the baseless fabric of this vision,
The cloud-capp'd towers, the gorgeous palaces,
The solemn temples, the great globe itself,
Yea, all which it inherit, shall dissolve
And, like this insubstantial pageant faded,
Leave not a rack behind. We are such stuff
As dreams are made on, and our little life
Is rounded with a sleep.

(*The Tempest*, IV. i.)

CAMPION.

THOMAS CAMPION (1567?–1619) was both musician
and poet. His sweet graceful lyrics in their various
measures leave hardly a note of the typical Elizabethan
lyre untouched: in his *Books of Airs* there are all the
themes—love, with its joys and jealousies; courtly
lovers and country lovers, the poet with his Helen,
Jack with his Joan; the song of birds, the gaiety of
flowers, the whisper of fairyland; the transitoriness of
pleasure; the sadness of death.

CHERRY RIPE.

There is a garden in her face
Where roses and white lilies blow;
A heavenly paradise is that place
Wherein all pleasant fruits do flow.
  There cherries grow which none may buy,
  Till " Cherry Ripe " themselves do cry.

Those cherries fairly do enclose
Of orient pearl a double row,
Which when her lovely laughter shows,
They look like rose-buds filled with snow;
  Yet them nor peer nor prince can buy,
  Till " Cherry Ripe " themselves do cry.

Her eyes like angels watch them still,
Her brows like bended bows do stand,
Threatening with piercing frowns to kill
All that attempt with eye or hand
  Those sacred cherries to come nigh,
  Till " Cherry Ripe " themselves do cry.

MY SWEETEST LESBIA.

My sweetest Lesbia, let us live and love,
And though the sager sort our deeds reprove,
Let us not weigh them.   Heaven's great lamps do dive
Into their west, and straight again revive;
But, soon as once set is our little light,
Then must we sleep one ever-during night.

If all would lead their lives in love like me,
Then bloody swords and armour should not be;

No drum nor trumpet peaceful sleeps should move,
Unless alarm came from the camp of Love.
But fools do live and waste their little light,
And seek with pain their ever-during night.

When timely death my life and fortune ends,
Let not my hearse be vext with mourning friends;
But let all lovers, rich in triumph, come
And with sweet pastimes grace my happy tomb:
And, Lesbia, close up thou my little light,
And crown with love my ever-during night.

ROSE-CHEEKED LAURA.

Rose-cheeked Laura, come;
Sing thou smoothly with thy beauty's
Silent music, either other
          Sweetly gracing.

Lovely forms do flow
From consent divinely framèd;
Heaven is music, and thy beauty's
          Birth is heavenly.

These dull notes we sing
Discords need for helps to grace them,
Only beauty purely loving
          Knows no discord,

But still moves delight,
Like clear springs renewed by flowing,
Ever perfect, ever in them-
          Selves eternal.

LOVE, AND NEVER FEAR.

Never love unless you can
Bear with all the faults of man:
Men sometimes will jealous be,
Though but little cause they see;
And hang the head, as discontent,
And speak what straight they will repent.

Men that but one saint adore,
Make a show of love to more:
Beauty must be scorned in none,
Though but truly served in one:
For what is courtship, but disguise?
True hearts may have dissembling eyes.

Men, when their affairs require,
Must a while themselves retire,
Sometimes hunt, and sometimes hawk,
And not ever sit and talk.
If these and such like you can bear,
Then like, and love, and never fear.

WOTTON.

Sir Henry Wotton (1568–1639), after a busy life as
a diplomat in the course of which he was three times
ambassador to Venice, became Provost of Eton in 1624.
His best poems are the two here given, and apart from
them he lives in our literature by his letter to Milton,
which the latter printed as an introduction to *Comus*.

OF A HAPPY LIFE.

How happy is he born and taught
    That serveth not another's will;
Whose armour is his honest thought,
    And simple truth his utmost skill;

Whose passions not his masters are;
  Whose soul is still prepared for death,
Untied unto the world by care
  Of public fame or private breath;

Who envies none that chance doth raise,
  Nor vice; who never understood
How deepest wounds are given by praise;
  Nor rules of state, but rules of good;

Who hath his life from rumours freed;
  Whose conscience is his strong retreat;
Whose state can neither flatterers feed,
  Nor ruin make oppressors great;

Who God doth late and early pray
  More of his grace than gifts to lend;
And entertains the harmless day
  With a religious book or friend:

This man is freed from servile bands
  Of hope to rise or fear to fall:
Lord of himself, though not of lands,
  And, having nothing, yet hath all.

ON HIS MISTRESS, THE QUEEN OF BOHEMIA.

You meaner beauties of the night,
  That poorly satisfy our eyes
More by your number, than your light;
  You common people of the skies,
  What are you when the Moon shall rise?

Ye violets that first appear,
  By your pure purple mantles known,

Like the proud virgins of the year,
    As if the Spring were all your own;
    What are you when the Rose is blown?

Ye curious chaunters of the wood,
    That warble forth dame Nature's lays,
Thinking your passions understood
    By your weak accents: what's your praise,
    When Philomel her voice shall raise?

So when my mistress shall be seen
    In sweetness of her looks and mind;
By virtue first, then choice, a Queen;
    Tell me, if she was not design'd
    Th' eclipse and glory of her kind?

DEKKER.

THOMAS DEKKER (1570?–1641?) was a dramatist of
the second rank, and a pamphleteer with a healthy relish
for realistic description, as in his *Seven Deadly Sins of
London* (1606). He touched perfection only in his
lyrics.

O, SWEET CONTENT.

Art thou poor, yet hast thou golden slumbers?
    O, sweet content!
Art thou rich, yet is thy mind perplexed?
    O, punishment!
Dost thou laugh to see how fools are vexed
To add to golden numbers golden numbers?
    O, sweet content! O, sweet, O sweet content!
    Work apace, apace, apace, apace;
    Honest labour bears a lovely face;
    Then hey nonny nonny, hey nonny nonny!

Canst drink the waters of the crispèd spring ?
    O, sweet content !
Swim'st thou in wealth, yet sink'st in thine own tears ?
    O, punishment !
Then he that patiently want's burden bears,
No burden bears, but is a king, a king !
    O, sweet content ! O, sweet, O, sweet content !
        Work apace, apace, apace, apace;
        Honest labour bears a lovely face;
        Then hey nonny nonny, hey nonny nonny !

LULLABY.

Golden slumbers kiss your eyes,
Smiles awake you when you rise.
Sleep, pretty wantons, do not cry,
And I will sing a lullaby:
Rock them, rock them, lullaby.

Care is heavy, therefore sleep you;
You are care, and care must keep you.
Sleep, pretty wantons, do not cry,
And I will sing a lullaby:
Rock them, rock them, lullaby.

JONSON.

BEN JONSON (1573 ?–1637), with *Every Man in his Humour* (1598), introduced the " comedy of humours," a satirical analysis of contemporary types. The three masterpieces *Volpone* (1605), *Epicoene*, and *The Alchemist* followed. In tragedy he largely failed, his admiration for classical tragedy making his plays stiff and cumbrous. For many years, in collaboration with Inigo Jones, he wrote masques for the Court of James I. As a lyrist he inspired many followers, of whom Herrick was chief.

HYMN TO DIANA.

Queen and huntress, chaste and fair,
  Now the sun is laid to sleep,
Seated in thy silver chair,
    State in wonted manner keep;
      Hesperus entreats thy light,
      Goddess excellently bright.

Earth, let not thy envious shade
  Dare itself to interpose;
Cynthia's shining orb was made
    Heaven to clear when day did close:
      Bless us then with wishèd sight,
      Goddess excellently bright.

Lay thy bow of pearl apart,
  And thy crystal shining quiver;
Give unto the flying hart
    Space to breath, how short soever:
      Thou that mak'st a day of night,
      Goddess excellently bright.

TO CELIA.

Drink to me only with thine eyes,
  And I will pledge with mine,
Or leave a kiss but in the cup,
  And I'll not look for wine.
The thirst, that from the soul doth rise,
  Doth ask a drink divine:
But might I of Jove's nectar sup,
  I would not change for thine.

I sent thee late a rosy wreath,
　　Not so much honouring thee,
As giving it a hope that there
　　It could not withered be.
But thou thereon didst only breathe,
　　And sent'st it back to me:
Since when it grows, and smells, I swear,
　　Not of itself, but thee.

A WITCHES' CHARM.

The owl is abroad, the bat and the toad,
　　And so is the cat-a-mountain;
The ant and the mole sit both in a hole,
　　And the frog peeps out o' the fountain.
The dogs they do bay, and the timbrels play,
　　The spindle is now a-turning;
The moon it is red, and the stars are fled,
　　But all the sky is a-burning:
The ditch is made, and our nails the spade,
With pictures full of wax and of wool:
Their livers I stick with needles quick;
There lacks but the blood to make up the flood.
Quickly, dame, then bring your part in!
Spur, spur upon little Martin!
Merrily, merrily, make him sail,
A worm in his mouth and a thorn in his tail,
Fire above, and fire below,
With a whip in your hand to make him go!
　　(O now she's come!
　　Let all be dumb.)

SIMPLICITY.

Still to be neat, still to be drest,
As you were going to a feast;

Still to be powder'd, still perfum'd:
Lady, it is to be presumed,
Though art's hid causes are not found,
All is not sweet, all is not sound.

Give me a look, give me a face,
That makes simplicity a grace;
Robes loosely flowing, hair as free:
Such sweet neglect more taketh me
Than all th' adulteries of art;
They strike mine eyes, but not my heart.

DONNE.

JOHN DONNE (1573–1631) was a rebel from the
Elizabethan poetic conventions. Their smoothness
and naturalness irked him, and he indulged himself
in the irregular, and the unexpected, in subtlety and
intensity. Too often this revolt led to the marring of
poems which yet had much beauty, but often he
achieved true beauty all the finer for its fresh sincerity
of thought and feeling. His early lyrics were of love,
his later were religious. From 1621 he was Dean of
St. Paul's.

BREAK OF DAY

Stay, O sweet, and do not rise;
The light that shines comes from thine eyes;
The day breaks not; it is my heart,
Because that you and I must part.
  Stay, or else my joys will die
  And perish in their infancy.

THE SUN RISING.

Busy old fool, unruly Sun,
  Why dost thou thus,
Through windows, and through curtains, call on us?

Must to thy motions lovers' seasons run?
   Saucy pedantic wretch, go chide
   Late school-boys and sour prentices,
  Go tell court-huntsmen that the king will ride,
  Call country ants to harvest offices;
Love, all alike, no season knows nor clime,
Nor hours, days, months, which are the rags of time.

   Thy beams so reverend and strong
   Why shouldst thou think?
I could eclipse and cloud them with a wink,
But that I would not lose her sight so long.
   If her eyes have not blinded thine,
   Look, and to-morrow late tell me,
  Whether both the Indias of spice and mine
  Be where thou left'st them, or lie here with me.
Ask for those kings whom thou saw'st yesterday,
And thou shalt hear, " All here in one bed lay."

   She is all states, and all princes I;
   Nothing else is;
Princes do but play us; compared to this,
All honour's mimic, all wealth alchemy.
   Thou, Sun, art half as happy as we,
   In that the world's contracted thus;
  Thine age asks ease, and since thy duties be
  To warm the world, that's done in warming us.
Shine here to us, and thou art everywhere;
This bed thy centre is, these walls thy sphere.

GO AND CATCH A FALLING STAR.

  Go and catch a falling star,
   Get with child a mandrake root,
  Tell me where all past years are,
   Or who cleft the devil's foot.

Teach me to hear mermaids singing,
    Or to keep off envy's stinging,
            And find
            What wind
Serves to advance an honest mind.

If thou be'st born to strange sights,
    Things invisible to see,
Ride ten thousand days and nights,
    Till age snow white hairs on thee,
Thou, when thou return'st, wilt tell me
    All strange wonders that befell thee,
            And swear
            No where
Lives a woman true and fair.

If thou find'st one, let me know;
    Such a pilgrimage were sweet.
Yet do not, I would not go,
    Though at next door we might meet.
Though she were true when you met her,
    And last till you write your letter,
            Yet she
            Will be
False, ere I come, to two or three.

THE ANNIVERSARY.

All kings, and all their favourites,
    All glory of honours, beauties, wits,
The sun itself, which makes time, as they pass,
Is elder by a year now than it was
When thou and I first one another saw.
All other things to their destruction draw,

Only our love hath no decay;
This no to-morrow hath, nor yesterday;
Running it never runs from us away,
But truly keeps his first, last, everlasting day.

Two graves must hide thine and my corse;
If one might, death were no divorce.
Alas ! as well as other princes, we
(Who prince enough in one another be)
Must leave at last in death these eyes and ears,
Oft fed with true oaths, and with sweet salt tears;
But souls where nothing dwells but love
(All other thoughts being inmates) then shall prove
This or a love increasèd there above,
When bodies to their graves, souls from their
    graves remove.

And then we shall be throughly blest;
But we no more than all the rest.
Here upon earth we're kings, and none but we
Can be such kings, nor of such subjects be.
Who is so safe as we ? where none can do
Treason to us, except one of us two.
True and false fears let us refrain,
Let us live nobly, and live, and add again
Years and years unto years, till we attain
To write threescore; this is the second of our
    reign.

DEATH, BE NOT PROUD.

Death, be not proud, though some have callèd thee
Mighty and dreadful, for thou art not so:
For those, whom thou think'st thou dost overthrow,
Die not, poor Death; nor yet canst thou kill me.

From rest and sleep, which but thy pictures be,
Much pleasure, then from thee much more must flow;
And soonest our best men with thee do go,
Rest of their bones and souls' delivery.
Thou'rt slave to Fate, Chance, kings, and desperate
    men,
And dost with poison, war, and sickness dwell;
And poppy or charms can make us sleep as well
And better than thy stroke; why swell'st thou then?
    One short sleep past, we wake eternally,
      And Death shall be no more: Death, thou shalt die.

A HYMN TO GOD THE FATHER.

I.

Wilt Thou forgive that sin where I begun,
    Which was my sin, though it were done before?
Wilt Thou forgive that sin, through which I run,
    And do run still, though still I do deplore?
    When Thou hast done, Thou hast not done,
      For I have more.

II.

Wilt Thou forgive that sin which I have won
    Others to sin, and made my sin their door?
Wilt Thou forgive that sin which I did shun
    A year or two, but wallowed in a score?
    When Thou hast done, Thou hast not done,
      For I have more.

III.

I have a sin of fear, that when I have spun
    Thy last thread, I shall perish on the shore;

But swear by Thyself, that at my death Thy Son
  Shall shine as He shines now, and heretofore;
  And, having done that, Thou hast done;
    I fear no more.

BATTER MY HEART.

Batter my heart, three-personed God; for you
As yet but knock, breathe, shine, and seek to mend.
That I may rise and stand, o'erthrow me and bend
Your force to break, blow, burn and make me new.
I, like an usurped town, to another due,
Labour to admit you, but oh, to no end;
Reason, your viceroy in me, me should defend,
But is captived and proves weak or untrue.
Yet dearly I love you and would be loved fain,
But am betrothed unto your enemy:
Divorce me, untie or break that knot again,
Take me to you, imprison me, for I,
Except you enthrall me, never shall be free,
Nor ever chaste, except you ravish me.

FLETCHER.

JOHN FLETCHER (1579–1625), after leaving Cambridge, began at least as early as 1607 to write for the
stage. For some ten years he collaborated with
Francis Beaumont (1584–1616), and their plays were
in the front rank of popularity: among the best of
these products of collaboration were *Philaster*, *The
Maid's Tragedy*, and *The Knight of the Burning Pestle*.
After Beaumont's death Fletcher wrote several other
plays. The plays of these two dramatists, like those
of most dramatists of their day, contain a number of
charming lyrics.

THE RIVER-GOD'S SONG.

Do not fear to put thy feet
Naked in the river, sweet;
Think not leech, or newt, or toad,
Will bite thy foot, when thou hast trod;
Nor let the water rising high,
As thou wad'st in, make thee cry
And sob; but ever live with me,
And not a wave shall trouble thee!

FOLDING THE FLOCKS.

Shepherds all, and maidens fair,
Fold your flocks up; for the air
'Gins to thicken, and the sun
Already his great course hath run.
See the dew-drops how they kiss
Every little flower that is;
Hanging on their velvet heads,
Like a rope of crystal beads,
See the heavy clouds low falling,
And bright Hesperus down calling
The dead Night from underground;
At whose rising, mists unsound,
Damps and vapours, fly apace,
Hovering o'er the wanton face
Of these pastures, where they come
Striking dead both bud and bloom:
Therefore from such danger lock
Every one his lovéd flock;
And let your dogs lie loose without,
Lest the wolf come as a scout
From the mountains, and ere day
Bear a lamb or kid away;
Or the crafty, thievish fox

Break upon your simple flocks.
To secure yourself from these
Be not too secure in ease;
So shall you good shepherds prove,
And deserve your master's love.
Now, good night ! may sweetest slumbers
And soft silence fall in numbers
On your eye-lids ! so farewell;
—Thus I end my evening's knell.

SLEEP.

Care-charming Sleep, thou easer of all woes,
Brother to Death, sweetly thyself dispose
On this afflicted prince; fall like a cloud,
In gentle showers; give nothing that is loud,
Or painful to his slumbers; easy, light,
And as a purling stream, thou son of Night
Pass by his troubled senses; sing his pain,
Like hollow murmuring wind or silver rain;
Into this prince gently, oh, gently slide,
And kiss him into slumbers like a bride.

GOD LYAEUS.

God Lyaeus, ever young,
Ever honour'd, ever sung,
Stain'd with blood of lusty grapes,
In a thousand lusty shapes
Dance upon the mazer's brim,
In the crimson liquor swim;
From thy plenteous hand divine
Let a river run with wine:
    God of youth, let this day here
    Enter neither care nor fear.

MELANCHOLY.

Hence, all you vain delights,
As short as are the nights
    Wherein you spend your folly !
There's nought in this life sweet,
If man were wise to see't,
    But only melancholy—
    Oh, sweetest melancholy !

Welcome, folded arms, and fixèd eyes,
A sight that piercing mortifies,
A look that's fasten'd to the ground,
A tongue chain'd up, without a sound !

Fountain-heads, and pathless groves,
Places which pale passion loves !
Moonlight walks, when all the fowls
Are warmly housed, save bats and owls !
    A midnight bell, a parting groan !
      These are the sounds we feed upon;
Then stretch our bones in a still gloomy valley;
Nothing's so dainty sweet as lovely melancholy.

TRUE IN DEATH.

Lay a garland on my hearse
    Of the dismal yew;
Maidens, willow branches bear;
    Say, I died true.

My love was false, but I was firm
    From my hour of birth.
Upon my buried body lie
    Lightly, gentle earth !

DRUMMOND.

WILLIAM DRUMMOND (1585–1649) was a Scot. After leaving Edinburgh University he visited London and the Continent, but in 1610 on his father's death settled for the rest of his life on his estate at Hawthornden near Edinburgh. His poetry was mostly written between 1610 and 1630; in beauty and idealism it resembles that of the Elizabethans, but also shows slightly the new metaphysical style. Drummond's best prose is his *Cypress Grove*, a meditation on death, and he has also left us a record of Ben Jonson's conversation with him on a visit in 1618–19.

PHOEBUS, ARISE.

Phoebus, arise !
And paint the sable skies
With azure, white, and red:
Rouse Memnon's mother from her Tithon's bed
That she may thy career with roses spread:
The nightingales thy coming eachwhere sing:
Make an eternal Spring !
Give life to this dark world which lieth dead;
Spread forth thy golden hair
In larger locks than thou wast wont before
And emperor-like decore
With diadem of pearl thy temples fair:
Chase hence the ugly night
Which serves but to make dear thy glorious light.

—This is that happy morn,
That day, long-wishéd day
Of all my life so dark,
(If cruel stars have not my ruin sworn
And fates my hopes betray),
Which, purely white, deserves
An everlasting diamond should it mark.

This is the morn should bring unto this grove
My Love, to hear and recompense my love.
Fair King, who all preserves,
But show thy blushing beams,
And thou two sweeter eyes
Shalt see than those which by Penéus' streams
Did once thy heart surprize.
Now, Flora, deck thyself in fairest guise:
If that ye winds would hear
A voice surpassing far Amphion's lyre,
Your stormy chiding stay;
Let Zephyr only breathe,
And with her tresses play,
Kissing sometimes those purple ports of death.
—The winds all silent are,
And Phoebus in his chair
Ensaffroning sea and air
Makes vanish every star:
Night like a drunkard reels
Beyond the hills, to shun his flaming wheels:
The fields with flowers are deck'd in every hue,
The clouds with orient gold spangle their blue;
Here is the pleasant place—
And everything, save Her, who all should grace.

SLEEP.

Sleep, Silence' child, sweet father of soft rest,
Prince, whose approach peace to all mortals brings,
Indifferent host to shepherds and to kings,
Sole comforter of minds with grief opprest;
Lo, by thy charming rod all breathing things
Lie slumbering, with forgetfulness possesst,
And yet o'er me to spread thy drowsy wings
Thou spares, alas ! who cannot be thy guest.

Since I am thine, O come, but with that face
To inward light which thou art wont to show,
With feignèd solace ease a true-felt woe;
Or if, deaf god, thou do deny that grace,
  Come as thou wilt, and what thou wilt, bequeath:
  I long to kiss the image of my death.

SAINT JOHN BAPTIST.

The last and greatest herald of heaven's King,
Girt with rough skins, hies to the desert wild,
Among that savage brood the woods forth bring,
Which he than man more harmless found and mild:
His food was locusts, and what young doth spring,
With honey that from virgin hives distill'd;
Parched body, hollow eyes, some uncouth thing
Made him appear long since from earth exil'd.
There burst he forth: " All ye, whose hopes rely
On God, with me amidst these deserts mourn;
Repent, repent, and from old errors turn."
Who listen'd to his voice, obey'd his cry ?
    Only the echoes, which he made relent,
    Rung from their marble caves " Repent, repent."

HERRICK.

ROBERT HERRICK (1591–1674) was a Devonshire
clergyman of Royalist sympathies. His love lyrics to
his Celias and Dianemes are numerous and graceful;
in addition he sang the beauties of the countryside
and particularly of flowers, often praised good wine,
and described the doings of the fairies. His religious
poems have a naïve charm, but none of Donne's
passion of soul. In poetic craftsmanship Herrick was
a true " Son of Ben."

TO THE VIRGINS, TO MAKE MUCH OF TIME.

Gather ye rose-buds while ye may,
  Old Time is still a-flying;
And this same flower that smiles to-day,
  To-morrow will be dying.

The glorious lamp of heaven, the sun,
  The higher he's a-getting,
The sooner will his race be run,
  And nearer he's to setting.

That age is best, which is the first,
  When youth and blood are warmer;
But being spent, the worse, and worst
  Times, still succeed the former.

Then be not coy, but use your time,
  And while ye may, go marry;
For having lost but once your prime.
  You may for ever tarry.

TO DIANEME.

Sweet, be not proud of those two eyes
Which starlike sparkle in their skies;
Nor be you proud that you can see
All hearts your captives, yours yet free:
Be you not proud of that rich hair
Which wantons with the lovesick air;
Whenas that ruby which you wear,
Sunk from the tip of your soft ear,
Will last to be a precious stone
When all your world of beauty's gone.

TO DAFFODILS.

Fair Daffodils, we weep to see
　　You haste away so soon:
As yet the early-rising sun
　　Has not attained his noon.
　　　　Stay, stay,
　　Until the hasting day
　　　　Has run
　　But to the even-song;
And, having pray'd together, we
　　Will go with you along.

We have short time to stay, as you,
　　We have as short a Spring!
As quick a growth to meet decay
　　As you, or any thing.
　　　　We die,
　　As your hours do, and dry
　　　　Away
　　Like to the Summer's rain;
Or as the pearls of morning's dew
　　Ne'er to be found again.

TO CARNATIONS.

Stay while ye will, or go;
　　And leave no scent behind ye:
Yet, trust me, I shall know
　　The place where I can find ye:

Within my Lucia's cheek,
　　Whose livery ye wear,
Play ye at hide and seek,
　　I'm sure to find ye there.

THE MAD MAID'S SONG.

Good morrow to the day so fair;
  Good morning, sir, to you;
Good morrow to mine own torn hair,
  Bedabbled with the dew.

Good morning to this primrose too;
  Good morrow to each maid
That will with flowers the tomb bestrew
  Wherein my love is laid.

Ah! woe is me, woe, woe is me,
  Alack, and well-a-day!
For pity, sir, find out that bee
  Which bore my love away.

I'll seek him in your bonnet brave;
  I'll seek him in your eyes;
Nay, now I think they've made his grave
  I' th' bed of strawberries.

I'll seek him there; I know, ere this,
  The cold, cold earth doth shake him;
But I will go, or send a kiss
  By you, sir, to awake him.

Pray hurt him not; though he be dead,
  He knows well who do love him;
And who with green turfs rear his head,
  And who do rudely move him.

He's soft and tender, pray take heed,
  With bands of cowslips bind him,
And bring him home; but 'tis decreed,
  That I shall never find him.

OBERON'S FEAST.

A little mushroom table spread,
After short prayers, they set on bread;
A moon-parcht grain of purest wheat,
With some small glit'ring grit, to eat
His choice bits with; then in a trice
They make a feast less great than nice.
But all this while his eye is serv'd,
We must not think his ear was starv'd:
But that there was in place to stir
His spleen, the chirring grasshopper;
The merry cricket, puling fly,
The piping gnat for minstralcy.
And now, we must imagine first,
The elves present to quench his thirst
A pure seed-pearl of infant dew,
Brought and besweetened in a blue
And pregnant violet; which done,
His kitling eyes begin to run
Quite through the table, where he spies
The horns of papery butterflies,
Of which he eats, and tastes a little
Of that we call the cuckoo's spittle.
A little fuz-ball pudding stands
By, yet not blessèd by his hands,
That was too coarse; but then forthwith
He ventures boldly on the pith
Of sugared rush, and eats the sag
And well bestrutted bee's sweet bag:
Glading his palate with some store
Of emits' eggs; what would he more ?
But beards of mice, a newt's stew'd thigh,
A bloated earwig, and a fly;
With the red-capt worm, that's shut
Within the concave of a nut

Brown as his tooth.   A little moth,
Late fattened in a piece of cloth:
With withered cherries; mandrakes' ears;
Moles' eyes; to these, the slain-stag's tears:
The unctuous dewlaps of a snail;
The broke-heart of a nightingale
O'er-come in music; with a wine,
Ne'er ravisht from the flattering vine,
But gently prest from the soft side
Of the most sweet and dainty bride,
Brought in a dainty daisy, which
He fully quaffs up to bewitch
His blood to height; this done, commended
Grace by his priest; *The feast is ended.*

A THANKSGIVING TO GOD FOR HIS HOUSE.

Lord, thou hast given me a cell
　　Wherein to dwell;
A little house, whose humble roof
　　Is weatherproof,
Under the spars of which I lie
　　Both soft and dry;
Where Thou, my chamber for to ward,
　　Hast set a guard
Of harmless thoughts, to watch and keep
　　Me while I sleep.
Low is my porch, as is my fate,
　　Both void of state;
And yet the threshold of my door
　　Is worn by th' poor,
Who thither come and freely get
　　Good words or meat.
Like as my parlour, so my hall
　　And kitchen's small:

A little buttery, and therein
    A little bin,
Which keeps my little loaf of bread
    Unchipped, unflead;
Some brittle sticks of thorn or briar
    Make me a fire;
Close by whose living coal I sit,
    And glow like it.
Lord, I confess too, when I dine,
    The pulse is Thine,
And all those other bits that be
    There placed by Thee;
The worts, the purslane, and the mess
    Of water-cress,
Which of thy kindness Thou hast sent;
    And my content
Makes those, and my belovèd beet,
    To be more sweet.
'Tis Thou that crown'st my glittering hearth
    With guiltless mirth,
And giv'st me wassail bowls to drink,
    Spiced to the brink.
Lord, 'tis Thy plenty-dropping hand
    That soils my land,
And giv'st me, for my bushel sown,
    Twice ten for one:
Thou mak'st my teeming hen to lay
    Her egg each day;
Besides my healthful ewes to bear
    Me twins each year;
The while the conduits of my kine
    Run cream, for wine.
All these, and better Thou dost send
    Me, to this end,
That I should render, for my part,
    A thankful heart.

Which, fired with incense, I resign,
 As wholly Thine;
But the acceptance, that must be,
 My Christ, by Thee.

TO HIS SAVIOUR, A CHILD: A PRESENT BY A CHILD.

Go, pretty child, and bear this flower
Unto thy little Saviour;
And tell Him, by that bud now blown,
He is the Rose of Sharon known.
When thou hast said so, stick it there
Upon His bib or stomacher;
And tell Him, for good handsel too,
That thou hast brought a whistle new,
Made of a clean straight oaten reed,
To charm His cries at time of need.
Tell Him, for coral, thou hast none,
But if thou hadst, He should have one;
But poor thou art, and known to be
Even as moneyless as He.
Lastly, if thou canst win a kiss
From those mellifluous lips of His;
Then never take a second on,
To spoil the first impression.

HERBERT.

GEORGE HERBERT (1593–1632) began as a courtier, but ended as " holy Mr. Herbert," the saintly vicar of Bemerton, near Salisbury. His poems are all religious, and breathe a serene piety, a deep spirituality, human sympathy, and gentle humour. In style he belongs to the " metaphysical " school of Donne.

CHURCH-MUSIC.

Sweetest of sweets, I thank you: when displeasure
    Did through my body wound my mind,
You took me thence; and in your house of pleasure
    A dainty lodging me assign'd.

Now I in you without a body move,
    Rising and falling with your wings:
We both together sweetly live and love,
    Yet say sometimes, *God help poor Kings*.

VIRTUE.

Sweet day, so cool, so calm, so bright,
    The bridal of the earth and sky,
The dew shall weep thy fall to-night;
        For thou must die.

Sweet rose, whose hue angry and brave
Bids the rash gazer wipe his eye,
Thy root is ever in its grave,
        And thou must die.

Sweet spring, full of sweet days and roses,
A box where sweets compacted lie,
My music shows ye have your closes,
        And all must die.

Only a sweet and virtuous soul,
Like season'd timber, never gives;
But though the whole world turn to coal,
        Then chiefly lives.

THE PULLEY.

When God at first made man,
Having a glass of blessings standing by,
" Let us," said He, " pour on him all we can;
Let the world's riches, which dispersèd lie,
    Contract into a span."

So strength first made a way,
Then beauty flow'd, then wisdom, honour, pleasure;
When almost all was out, God made a stay,
Perceiving that, alone of all His treasure,
    Rest in the bottom lay.

" For if I should," said He,
" Bestow this jewel also on My creature,
He would adore My gifts in stead of Me,
And rest in Nature, not the God of Nature:
    So both should losers be.

Yet let him keep the rest,
But keep them with repining restlessness;
Let him be rich and weary, that at least,
If goodness lead him not, yet weariness
    May toss him to My breast."

DISCIPLINE.

Throw away thy rod,
Throw away thy wrath:
    O my God,
Take the gentle path.

For my heart's desire
Unto Thine is bent:
    I aspire
To a full consent.

Not a word or look
I affect to own,
        But by book,
And Thy book alone.

Though I fail, I weep:
Though I halt in pace,
        Yet I creep
To the throne of grace.

Then let wrath remove;
Love will do the deed:
        For with love
Stony hearts will bleed.

Love is swift of foot;
Love's a man of war,
        And can shoot,
And can hit from far.

Who can 'scape his bow?
That which wrought on Thee,
        Brought Thee low,
Needs must work on me.

Throw away Thy rod;
Though Man frailties hath,
        Thou art God:
Throw away Thy wrath.

PRAYER.

Prayer, the church's banquet, angel's age,
God's breath in man returning to his birth . . .
Church-bells beyond the stars heard, the soul's blood,
The land of spices, something understood.

CAREW.

THOMAS CAREW (1595 ?–1639 ?) was a courtier of Charles I.'s court, who wrote some masques, and occasional songs. The finished ease and grace of his versification proclaims him of " the tribe of Ben," and the light artificiality of his sentiments and the trifling things which occasion his songs are typical of the Cavalier lyrists.

A SONG.

Ask me no more where Jove bestows,
When June is past, the fading rose;
For in your beauty's orient deep
These flowers, as in their causes, sleep.

Ask me no more whither do stray
The golden atoms of the day;
For in pure love heaven did prepare
Those powders to enrich your hair.

Ask me no more whither doth haste
The nightingale, when May is past;
For in your sweet dividing throat
She winters, and keeps warm her note.

Ask me no more where those stars 'light,
That downwards fall in dead of night;
For in your eyes they sit, and there
Fixèd become, as in their sphere.

Ask me no more if east or west
The phoenix builds her spicy nest;
For unto you at last she flies,
And in your fragrant bosom dies.

MILTON.

JOHN MILTON (1608-1674) is one of our most learned and most widely-read poets. Giving up his early intention of entering the Church, he devoted himself after leaving Cambridge to further studies and to the writing of a few but almost perfect poems. The *Hymn on the Morning of Christ's Nativity* he wrote at Cambridge; *L'Allegro and Il Penseroso*, *Comus*, his masque, and *Lycidas* his elegy, were composed between 1632 and 1637. In the Civil War his passionate love of liberty placed him on the side of Parliament; in prose pamphlets of occasional splendour and constant vigour he argued for reform in the Church, pleaded for freedom of conscience (and in *Areopagitica* for freedom of the Press), and defended the execution of Charles I. At the Restoration, after a short imprisonment, he retired to the country and gave himself up to the achievement of the great literary work he had for years meditated. *Paradise Lost* (1667) is our greatest long poem, excelling all in majesty of conception and sustained magnificence of execution; in part it is not only Milton's " justification of the ways of God to man," but the expression of Milton's political idealism baffled and disillusioned by the fall of the Commonwealth. *Paradise Regained* and his lyrical drama *Samson Agonistes* appeared in 1671.

CHRIST'S TRIUMPHANT NATIVITY.

Peor and Baälïm
Forsake their temples dim,
With that twice-battered God of Palestine;
And moonèd Ashtaroth,
Heaven's queen and mother both,
Now sits not girt with tapers' holy shine:
The Libyc Hammon shrinks his horn;
In vain the Tyrian maids their wounded Thammuz mourn.

And sullen Moloch, fled,
Hath left in shadows dread

His burning idol all of blackest hue;
　　　　In vain with cymbals' ring
　　　　They call the grisly king,
　　In dismal dance about the furnace blue;
The brutish gods of Nile as fast,
Isis, and Orus, and the dog Anubis, haste.

　　　　Nor is Osiris seen
　　　　In Memphian grove or green,
　　Trampling the unshowered grass with lowings loud;
　　　　Nor can he be at rest
　　　　Within his sacred chest;
　　Nought but profoundest Hell can be his shroud;
In vain, with timbrelled anthems dark,
The sable-stolèd sorcerers bear his worshipped ark.

　　　　He feels from Juda's land
　　　　The dreaded Infant's hand;
　　The rays of Bethlehem blind his dusky eyn;
　　　　Nor all the gods beside
　　　　Longer dare abide,
　　Not Typhon huge ending in snaky twine:
Our Babe, to show his Godhead true,
Can in his swaddling bands control the damnèd crew.
　　　　　　(*Hymn on the Morning of Christ's Nativity.*)

AT A SOLEMN MUSIC.

Blest pair of Sirens, pledges of Heaven's joy,
Sphere-born harmonious Sisters, Voice and Verse!
Wed your divine sounds, and mixt power employ,
Dead things with inbreathed sense able to pierce;
And to our high-raised phantasy present
That undisturbèd Song of pure concent
Aye sung before the sapphire-colour'd throne
　　　　To Him that sits thereon,

With saintly shout and solemn jubilee;
Where the bright Seraphim in burning row
Their loud uplifted angel-trumpets blow;
And the Cherubic host in thousand quires
Touch their immortal harps of golden wires,
With those just Spirits that wear victorious palms,
      Hymns devout and holy psalms
      Singing everlastingly:
That we on earth, with undiscording voice
May rightly answer the melodious noise;
As once we did, till disproportion'd sin
Jarr'd against nature's chime, and with harsh din
Broke the fair music that all creatures made
To their great Lord, whose love their motion sway'd
In perfect diapason, whilst they stood
In first obedience, and their state of good.
O may we soon again renew that Song,
And keep in tune with Heaven, till God ere long
To his celestial consort us unite,
To live with him, and sing in endless morn of light !

L'ALLEGRO.

Hence, loathéd Melancholy,
  Of Cerberus and blackest Midnight born
In Stygian cave forlorn
  'Mongst horrid shapes, and shrieks, and sights
    unholy !
Find out some uncouth cell
  Where brooding Darkness spreads his jealous wings,
And the night-raven sings;
  There under ebon shades, and low-brow'd rocks,
As ragged as thy locks,
  In dark Cimmerian desert ever dwell.
  But come, thou goddess fair and free,

In heaven yclept Euphrosyne,
And by men heart-easing Mirth;
Whom lovely Venus at a birth
With two sister Graces more
To ivy-crownéd Bacchus bore;
Or whether (as some sager sing)
The frolic wind that breathes the spring,
Zephyr, with Aurora playing,
As he met her once a-Maying—
There on beds of violets blue
And fresh-blown roses wash'd in dew
Fill'd her with thee, a daughter fair,
So buxom, blithe, and debonair.

Haste thee, Nymph, and bring with thee
Jest, and youthful Jollity,
Quips, and cranks, and wanton wiles,
Nods, and becks, and wreathéd smiles
Such as hang on Hebe's cheek,
And love to live in dimple sleek;
Sport that wrinkled Care derides,
And Laughter holding both his sides.
Come, and trip it as you go
On the light fantastic toe;
And in thy right hand lead with thee
The mountain-nymph, sweet Liberty;
And, if I give thee honour due,
Mirth, admit me of thy crew,
To live with her, and live with thee
In unreprovéd pleasures free;
To hear the lark begin his flight,
And, singing, startle the dull night
From his watch-tower in the skies,
Till the dappled dawn doth rise;
Then to come, in spite of sorrow,
And at my window bid good-morrow
Through the sweetbriar, or the vine,

Or the twisted eglantine:
While the cock with lively din
Scatters the rear of darkness thin,
And to the stack, or the barn-door,
Stoutly struts his dames before:
Oft listening how the hounds and horn
Cheerly rouse the slumbering morn,
From the side of some hoar hill,
Through the high wood echoing shrill;
Sometime walking, not unseen,
By hedge-row elms, on hillocks green,
Right against the eastern gate
Where the great Sun begins his state
Robed in flames and amber light,
The clouds in thousand liveries dight;
While the ploughman, near at hand,
Whistles o'er the furrow'd land,
And the milkmaid singeth blithe,
And the mower whets his scythe,
And every shepherd tells his tale
Under the hawthorn in the dale.
Straight mine eye hath caught new pleasures
Whilst the landscape round it measures;
Russet lawns, and fallows gray,
Where the nibbling flocks do stray;
Mountains, on whose barren breast
The labouring clouds do often rest;
Meadows trim with daisies pied,
Shallow brooks, and rivers wide;
Towers and battlements it sees
Bosom'd high in tufted trees,
Where perhaps some beauty lies,
The cynosure of neighbouring eyes.
  Hard by, a cottage chimney smokes
From betwixt two aged oaks,
Where Corydon and Thyrsis, met,

Are at their savoury dinner set
Of herbs, and other country messes
Which the neat-handed Phyllis dresses;
And then in haste her bower she leaves
With Thestylis to bind the sheaves;
Or, if the earlier season lead,
To the tann'd haycock in the mead.
 Sometimes with secure delight
The upland hamlets will invite,
When the merry bells ring round,
And the jocund rebecks sound
To many a youth and many a maid
Dancing in the chequer'd shade;
And young and old come forth to play
On a sunshine holy-day,
Till the live-long day-light fail:
Then to the spicy nut-brown ale,
With stories told of many a feat,
How faery Mab the junkets eat:
She was pinch'd, and pull'd, she said;
And he, by friar's lantern led,
Tells how the drudging Goblin sweat
To earn his cream-bowl duly set,
When in one night, ere glimpse of morn,
His shadowy flail hath thresh'd the corn
That ten day-labourers could not end;
Then lies him down the lubber fiend,
And, stretch'd out all the chimney's length,
Basks at the fire his hairy strength;
And crop-full out of doors he flings,
Ere the first cock his matin rings.
 Thus done the tales, to bed they creep,
By whispering winds soon lull'd asleep.
 Tower'd cities please us then,
And the busy hum of men,
Where throngs of knights and barons bold,

In weeds of peace, high triumphs hold,
With store of ladies, whose bright eyes
Rain influence, and judge the prize
Of wit or arms, while both contend
To win her grace, whom all commend.
There let Hymen oft appear
In saffron robe, with taper clear,
And pomp, and feast, and revelry,
With mask, and antique pageantry;
Such sights as youthful poets dream
On summer eves by haunted stream.
Then to the well-trod stage anon,
If Jonson's learned sock be on,
Or sweetest Shakespeare, Fancy's child,
Warble his native wood-notes wild.

    And ever against eating cares
Lap me in soft Lydian airs
Married to immortal verse,
Such as the meeting soul may pierce
In notes, with many a winding bout
Of linkéd sweetness long drawn out
With wanton heed and giddy cunning,
The melting voice through mazes running,
Untwisting all the chains that tie
The hidden soul of harmony;
That Orpheus' self may heave his head
From golden slumber, on a bed
Of heap'd Elysian flowers, and hear
Such strains as would have won the ear
Of Pluto, to have quite set free
His half-regain'd Eurydice.

    These delights if thou canst give,
Mirth, with thee I mean to live.

IL PENSEROSO.

Hence, vain deluding Joys,
　　The brood of Folly without father bred !
How little you bestead
　　Or fill the fixéd mind with all your toys !
Dwell in some idle brain,
　　And fancies fond with gaudy shapes possess,
As thick and numberless
　　As the gay motes that people the sunbeams,
Or likest hovering dreams,
　　The fickle pensioners of Morpheus' train.

　　But hail, thou goddess sage and holy,
Hail, divinest Melancholy !
Whose saintly visage is too bright
To hit the sense of human sight,
And therefore to our weaker view
O'erlaid with black, staid Wisdom's hue;
Black, but such as in esteem
Prince Memnon's sister might beseem,
Or that starr'd Ethiop queen that strove
To set her beauty's praise above
The sea-nymphs, and their powers offended:
Yet thou art higher far descended:
Thee bright-hair'd Vesta, long of yore,
To solitary Saturn bore;
His daughter she; in Saturn's reign
Such mixture was not held a stain:
Oft in glimmering bowers and glades
He met her, and in secret shades
Of woody Ida's inmost grove,
While yet there was no fear of Jove.
　　Come, pensive Nun, devout and pure,
Sober, steadfast, and demure,
All in a robe of darkest grain

Flowing with majestic train,
And sable stole of cypress lawn
Over thy decent shoulders drawn:
Come, but keep thy wonted state,
With even step, and musing gait,
And looks commercing with the skies,
Thy rapt soul sitting in thine eyes:
There, held in holy passion still,
Forget thyself to marble, till
With a sad leaden downward cast
Thou fix them on the earth as fast:
And join with thee calm Peace, and Quiet,
Spare Fast, that oft with gods doth diet,
And hears the Muses in a ring
Aye round about Jove's altar sing:
And add to these retired Leisure
That in trim gardens takes his pleasure:—
But first and chiefest, with thee bring
Him that yon soars on golden wing
Guiding the fiery-wheeléd throne,
The cherub Contemplatión;
And the mute Silence hist along,
'Less Philomel will deign a song
In her sweetest saddest plight
Smoothing the rugged brow of Night,
While Cynthia checks her dragon yoke
Gently o'er the accustomed oak.
—Sweet bird, that shunn'st the noise of folly,
Most musical, most melancholy !
Thee, chauntress, oft, the woods among
I woo, to hear thy even-song;
And missing thee, I walk unseen
On the dry smooth-shaven green,
To behold the wandering Moon
Riding near her highest noon,
Like one that had been led astray

Through the heaven's wide pathless way,
And oft, as if her head she bow'd,
Stooping through a fleecy cloud.
    Oft, on a plat of rising ground
I hear the far-off curfew sound
Over some wide-water'd shore,
Swinging slow with sullen roar:
Or, if the air will not permit,
Some still removéd place will fit,
Where glowing embers through the room
Teach light to counterfeit a gloom;
Far from all resort of mirth,
Save the cricket on the hearth,
Or the bellman's drowsy charm
To bless the doors from nightly harm.
    Or let my lamp at midnight hour
Be seen in some high lonely tower,
Where I may oft out-watch the Bear
With thrice-great Hermes, or unsphere
The spirit of Plato, to unfold
What worlds or what vast regions hold
The immortal mind, that hath forsook
Her mansion in this fleshy nook:
And of those demons that are found
In fire, air, flood, or under ground,
Whose power hath a true consent
With planet, or with element.
Sometime let gorgeous Tragedy
In scepter'd pall come sweeping by,
Presenting Thebes, or Pelops' line,
Or the tale of Troy divine;
Or what (though rare) of later age
Ennobled hath the buskin'd stage.
    But, O sad Virgin, that thy power
Might raise Musaeus from his bower,
Or bid the soul of Orpheus sing

Such notes as, warbled to the string,
Drew iron tears down Pluto's cheek
And made Hell grant what Love did seek !
Or call up him that left half-told
The story of Cambuscan bold,
Of Camball, and of Algarsife,
And who had Canacé to wife,
That own'd the virtuous ring and glass;
And of the wondrous horse of brass
On which the Tartar king did ride:
And if aught else great bards beside
In sage and solemn tunes have sung
Of turneys, and of trophies hung,
Of forests, and enchantments drear,
Where more is meant than meets the ear.

   Thus, Night, oft see me in thy pale career,
Till civil-suited Morn appear,
Not trick'd and frounced as she was wont
With the Attic boy to hunt,
But kerchieft in a comely cloud
While rocking winds are piping loud,
Or usher'd with a shower still,
When the gust hath blown his fill,
Ending on the rustling leaves
With minute drops from off the eaves.
And when the sun begins to fling
His flaring beams, me, goddess, bring
To archéd walks of twilight groves,
And shadows brown, that Sylvan loves,
Of pine, or monumental oak,
Where the rude axe, with heavéd stroke,
Was never heard the nymphs to daunt
Or fright them from their hallow'd haunt.
There in close covert by some brook
Where no profaner eye may look,
Hide me from day's garish eye,

While the bee with honey'd thigh
That at her flowery work doth sing,
And the waters murmuring,
With such consort as they keep
Entice the dewy-feather'd Sleep;
And let some strange mysterious dream
Wave at his wings in airy stream
Of lively portraiture display'd,
Softly on my eyelids laid:
And, as I wake, sweet music breathe
Above, about, or underneath,
Sent by some spirit to mortals good,
Or the unseen Genius of the wood,
    But let my due feet never fail
To walk the studious cloister's pale
And love the high-embowéd roof,
With antique pillars massy proof
And storied windows richly dight
Casting a dim religious light:
There let the pealing organ blow
To the full-voiced quire below
In service high and anthems clear,
As may with sweetness, through mine ear,
Dissolve me into ecstasies,
And bring all Heaven before mine eyes.
    And may at last my weary age
Find out the peaceful hermitage,
The hairy gown and mossy cell
Where I may sit and rightly spell
Of every star that heaven doth shew,
And every herb that sips the dew;
Till old experience do attain
To something like prophetic strain.

    These pleasures, Melancholy, give,
And I with thee will choose to live.

THE SONG OF COMUS.

The star that bids the shepherd fold
Now the top of heaven doth hold;
And the gilded car of day
His glowing axle doth allay
In the steep Atlantic stream;
And the slope sun his upward beam
Shoots against the dusky pole;
Pacing toward the other goal
Of his chamber in the east.
Meanwhile welcome joy and feast,
Midnight shout and revelry,
Tipsy dance and jollity.
Braid your locks with rosy twine,
Dropping odours, dropping wine.
Rigour now is gone to bed,
And Advice with scrupulous head,
Strict Age, and sour Severity,
With their grave saws, in slumber lie.
We, that are of purer fire,
Imitate the starry choir,
Who, in their nightly watchful spheres,
Lead in swift round the months and years.
The sounds and seas, with all their finny drove,
Now to the moon in wavering morrice move;
And on the tawny sands and shelves
Trip the pert fairies and the dapper elves.
By dimpled brook and fountain brim,
The wood-nymphs, decked with daisies trim,
Their merry wakes and pastimes keep.
What hath night to do with sleep?
Night hath better sweets to prove;
Venus now wakes, and wakens Love.
Come, let us our rites begin,
'Tis only daylight that makes sin,

Which these dun shades will ne'er report.
Hail, Goddess of nocturnal sport,
Dark-veiled Cotytto, to whom the secret flame
Of midnight torches burns; mysterious dame
That ne'er art called, but when the dragon womb
Of Stygian darkness spets her thickest gloom,
And makes one blot of all the air !
Stay thy cloudy ebon chair,
Wherein thou ridest with Hecat', and befriend
Us thy vowed priests, till utmost end
Of all thy dues be done, and none left out;
Ere the blabbing eastern scout,
The nice Morn on the Indian steep,
From her cabined loophole peep,
And to the tell-tale sun descry
Our concealed solemnity.
Come, knit hands, and beat the ground,
In a light fantastic round.

FLOWERS FOR LYCIDAS.

Return, Alpheus; the dread voice is past
That shrunk thy streams; return Sicilian Muse,
And call the vales, and bid them hither cast
Their bells and flowerets of a thousand hues.
Ye valleys low, where the mild whispers use
Of shades, and wanton winds, and gushing brooks,
On whose fresh lap the swart star sparely looks,
Throw hither all your quaint enamelled eyes,
That on the green turf suck the honeyed showers,
And purple all the ground with vernal flowers.
Bring the rathe primrose that forsaken dies,
The tufted crow-toe, and pale jessamine,
The white pink, and the pansy freaked with jet,
The glowing violet,
The musk rose, and the well-attired woodbine,

With cowslips wan that hang the pensive head,
And every flower that sad embroidery wears;
Bid amaranthus all his beauty shed,
And daffodillies fill their cups with tears,
To strew the laureate hearse where Lycid lies.
For so, to interpose a little ease,
Let our frail thoughts dally with false surmise,
Ay me ! whilst thee the shores and sounding seas
Wash far away, where'er thy bones are hurled;
Whether beyond the stormy Hebrides,
Where thou perhaps under the whelming tide
Visit'st the bottom of the monstrous world;
Or whether thou, to our moist vows denied,
Sleep'st by the fable of Bellerus old,
Where the great Vision of the guarded mount
Looks toward Namancos and Bayona's hold.

EVE TO ADAM.

With thee conversing, I forget all time,
All seasons, and their change; all please alike.
Sweet is the breath of Morn, her rising sweet,
With charm of earliest birds; pleasant the Sun,
When first on this delightful land he spreads
His orient beams, on herb, tree, fruit, and flower,
Glistering with dew; fragrant the fertile Earth
After soft showers; and sweet the coming-on
Of grateful Evening mild; then silent Night,
With this her solemn bird, and this fair Moon,
And these the gems of Heaven, her starry train:
But neither breath of Morn, when she ascends
With charm of earliest birds; nor rising Sun
On this delightful land; nor herb, fruit, flower,
Glistering with dew; nor fragrance after showers;
Nor grateful Evening mild; nor silent Night,

With this her solemn bird; nor walk by moon,
Or glittering starlight without thee is sweet.

(Paradise Lost, IV., 639–656.)

THE FEAST IN THE WILDERNESS.

He spake no dream; for, as his words had end,
Our Saviour, lifting up his eyes, beheld,
In ample space under the broadest shade,
A table richly spread in regal mode,
With dishes piled and meats of noblest sort
And savour—beasts of chase, or fowl of game,
In pastry built, or from the spit, or boiled,
Grisamber-steamed; all fish, from sea or shore,
Freshet or purling brook, of shell or fin,
And exquisitest name, for which was drained
Pontus, and Lucrine bay, and Afric coast.
Alas ! how simple, to these cates compared,
Was that crude apple that diverted Eve !
And at a stately sideboard, by the wine,
That fragrant smell diffused, in order stood
Tall stripling youths rich-clad, of fairer hue
Than Ganymed or Hylas; distant more,
Under the trees now tripped, now solemn stood,
Nymphs of Diana's train, and Naiades
With fruits and flowers from Amalthea's horn,
And ladies of the Hesperides, that seemed
Fairer than feigned of old, or fabled since
Of faery damsels met in forest wide
By knights of Logres, or of Lyones,
Lancelot, or Pelleas, or Pellenore.
And all the while harmonious airs were heard
Of chiming strings or charming pipes; and winds
Of gentlest gale Arabian odours fanned
From their soft wings, and Flora's earliest smells.

(Paradise Regained, II., 337–365.)

ON HIS BEING ARRIVED AT THE AGE OF TWENTY-THREE.

How soon hath Time, the subtle thief of youth,
   Stolen on his wing my three-and-twentieth year !
   My hasting days fly on with full career,
But my late spring no bud or blossom shew'th.
Perhaps my semblance might deceive the truth
   That I to manhood am arrived so near;
   And inward ripeness doth much less appear,
That some more timely-happy spirits endu'th.
   Yet, be it less or more, or soon or slow,
It shall be still in strictest measure even
   To that same lot, however mean or high,
Toward which Time leads me, and the will of Heaven;
   All is, if I have grace to use it so,
   As ever in my great Task-Master's eye.

ON HIS BLINDNESS.

When I consider how my light is spent
   Ere half my days in this dark world and wide,
   And that one talent which is death to hide
   Lodged with me useless, though my soul more bent
To serve therewith my Maker, and present
   My true account, lest He, returning, chide;
   " Dost God exact day-labour, light denied ? "
I fondly ask.   But Patience, to prevent
That murmur, soon replies: " God doth not need
   Either man's work, or his own gifts.   Who best
   Bear his mild yoke, they serve him best.   His state
Is kingly; thousands at his bidding speed,
   And post o'er land and ocean without rest;
   They also serve who only stand and wait."

ON HIS DECEASED WIFE.

Methought I saw my late espousèd saint
   Brought to me like Alcestis from the grave,
   Whom Jove's great son to her glad husband gave,
   Rescued from death by force, though pale and faint.
Mine, as whom washed from spot of child-bed taint
   Purification in the old law did save,
   And such, as yet once more I trust to have
   Full sight of her in Heaven without restraint,
Came vested all in white, pure as her mind.
   Her face was veiled; yet to my fancied sight
   Love, sweetness, goodness, in her person shined
So clear as in no face with more delight.
   But, oh ! as to embrace me she inclined,
   I waked, she fled, and day brought back my night.

ON THE LATE MASSACRE IN PIEDMONT.

Avenge, O Lord, thy slaughtered saints, whose bones
   Lie scattered on the Alpine mountains cold;
   Even them who kept thy truth so pure of old,
   When all our fathers worshipped stocks and stones,
Forget not; in thy book record their groans
   Who were thy sheep, and in their ancient fold
   Slain by the bloody Piemontese, that rolled
   Mother with infant down the rocks.   Their moans
The vales redoubled to the hills, and they
   To heaven.   Their martyred blood and ashes sow
   O'er all the Italian fields, where still doth sway
The triple tyrant; that from these may grow
   A hundredfold, who having learnt thy way
   Early may fly the Babylonian woe.

ALL IS BEST.

All is best, though we oft doubt
What the unsearchable dispose
Of Highest Wisdom brings about,
And ever best found in the close.
Oft He seems to hide His face,
But unexpectedly returns,
And to His faithful champion hath in place
Bore witness gloriously; whence Gaza mourns,
And all that band them to resist
His uncontrollable intent.
His servants He, with new acquist
Of true experience from this great event,
With peace and consolation hath dismissed,
And calm of mind, all passion spent.

(Samson Agonistes.)

SUCKLING.

Sir John Suckling (1609–1642) was, like Carew,
one of the Cavalier poets of Charles I.'s reign. His
poems are elegant trifles, now and then slightly
cynical; best known is his *Ballad upon a Wedding*.

WHY SO PALE?

Why so pale and wan, fond lover?
   Prithee, why so pale?
Will, when looking well can't move her,
   Looking ill prevail?
   Prithee, why so pale?

Why so dull and mute, young sinner?
   Prithee, why so mute?
Will, when speaking well can't win her,
   Saying nothing do't?
   Prithee, why so mute?

Quit, quit, for shame ! this will not move,
    This cannot take her;
If of herself she will not love,
    Nothing can make her:
    The Devil take her !

From A BALLAD UPON A WEDDING.

The maid (and thereby hangs a tale),
For such a maid no Whitsun-ale
    Could ever yet produce:
No grape, that's kindly ripe, could be
So round, so plump, so soft as she,
    Nor half so full of juice.

Her finger was so small, the ring
Would not stay on, which they did bring,
    It was too wide a peck:
And to say truth (for out it must)
It looked like the great collar (just)
    About our young colt's neck.

Her feet beneath her petticoat,
Like little mice, stole in and out,
    As if they feared the light:
But O she dances such a way !
No sun upon an Easter-day
    Is half so fine a sight.

Her cheeks so rare a white was on,
No daisy makes comparison,
    (Who sees them is undone),
For streaks of red were mingled there,
Such as are on a Catherine pear
    The side that's next the sun.

Her lips were red, and one was thin,
Compar'd to that was next her chin
   (Some bee had stung it newly);
But, Dick, her eyes so guard her face,
I durst no more upon them gaze
   Than on the sun in July.

CRASHAW.

RICHARD CRASHAW (1613 ?–1649) was ejected by the Puritans from a Fellowship at Cambridge, and entered the Roman Church. Most of his poems appeared in 1646 as *Steps to the Temple*, and *Delights of the Muses*: the first burn at times with the purest glow of mystical ardour, at others are marred by the grotesque " conceits " of the metaphysicals; the second class shows him as a son of Ben and a Cavalier, singing lightly of love.

TO SAINT TERESA.

O thou undaunted daughter of desires !
By all thy dower of lights and fires;
By all the eagle in thee, all the dove;
By all thy lives and deaths of love;
By thy large draughts of intellectual day,
And by thy thirsts of love more large than they;
By all thy brim-fill'd bowls of fierce desire;
By thy last morning's draught of liquid fire;
By the full kingdom of that final kiss
That seized thy parting soul, and seal'd thee His;
By all the Heaven thou hast in Him
(Fair sister of the seraphim)
By all of Him we have in thee;
Leave nothing of myself in me.
Let me so read thy life, that I
Unto all life of mine may die.

From WISHES TO HIS SUPPOSED MISTRESS

Whoe'er she be,
That not impossible She
That shall command my heart and me;

Where'er she lie,
Lock'd up from mortal eye
In shady leaves of destiny:

Till that ripe birth
Of studied Fate stand forth,
And teach her fair steps to our earth :

Till that divine
Idea take a shrine
Of crystal flesh, through which to shine:

—Meet you her, my Wishes,
Bespeak her to my blisses,
And be ye call'd my absent kisses.

I wish her beauty
That owes not all his duty
To gaudy tire, or glist'ring shoe-tie:

Something more than
Taffata or tissue can,
Or rampant feather, or rich fan. . . .

A face that's best
By its own beauty drest,
And can alone commend the rest.

A face made up
Out of no other shop
Than what Nature's white hand sets ope. . . .

A well-tamed heart,
For whose more noble smart
Love may be long choosing a dart. . . .

Days, that need borrow
No part of their good morrow
From a fore-spent night of sorrow:

Days, that in spite
Of darkness by the light
Of a clear mind are day all night. . . .

Life, that dares send
A challenge to his end,
And when it comes, say, " Welcome, friend."

Sydnaean showers
Of sweet discourse, whose powers
Can crown old Winter's head with flowers.

Soft silken hours,
Open suns, shady bowers;
'Bove all, nothing within that lours.

Whate'er delight
Can make day's forehead bright
Or give down to the wings of night. . . .

I wish her store
Of worth may leave her poor
Of wishes; and I wish—no more.

—Now, if Time knows
That Her, whose radiant brows
Weave them a garland of my vows;

Her that dares be
What these lines wish to see:
I seek no further, it is She. . . .

Such worth as this is
Shall fix my flying wishes,
And determine them to kisses.

Let her full glory,
My fancies, fly before ye;
Be ye my fictions:—but her story.

THE NIGHTINGALE.

Her supple breast thrills out
Sharp airs, and staggers in a warbling doubt
Of dallying sweetness, hovers o'er her skill,
And folds in wav'd notes with a trembling bill
The pliant series of her slippery song;
Then starts she suddenly into a throng
Of short thick sobs, whose thundering volleys float
And roll themselves over her lubric throat
In panting murmurs 'stilled out of her breast,
That ever-bubbling spring, the sugared nest
Of her delicious soul, that there does lie
Bathing in streams of liquid melody . . .
In that sweet soil it seems a holy choir,
Founded to th' name of great Apollo's lyre;
Whose silver roof rings with the sprightly notes
Of sweet-lipped angel-imps, that swill their throats
In cream of morning Helicon. . . .

And while she thus discharges a shrill peal
Of flashing airs, she qualifies their zeal
With the cool epode of a graver note,
Thus high, thus low, as if her silver throat
Would reach the brazen note of War's hoarse bird.
Her little soul is ravished, and so poured
Into loose ecstasies, that she is placed
Above herself, Music's enthusiast !

(*Music's Duel.*)

LOVELACE.

RICHARD LOVELACE (1618–1658) spent his fortune in the service of Charles I. against the Parliament, fought, was imprisoned, and died in poverty. He published *Lucasta* in 1649, and in the two poems below, by which alone he is remembered, he enshrines the very essence of the chivalrous spirit.

TO ALTHEA FROM PRISON.

When Love with unconfinèd wings,
  Hovers within my gates,
And my divine Althea brings
  To whisper at the grates;
When I lie tangled in her hair,
  And fettered to her eye,
The birds that wanton in the air
  Know no such liberty.

When flowing cups run swiftly round
  With no allaying Thames,
Our careless heads with roses bound,
  Our hearts with loyal flames;
When thirsty grief in wine we steep,
  When healths and draughts go free,
Fishes that tipple in the deep
  Know no such liberty.

When, like committed linnets, I
  With shriller throat shall sing
The sweetness, mercy, majesty,
  And glories of my King;
When I shall voice aloud how good
  He is, how great should be,
Enlargèd winds that curl the flood
  Know no such liberty.

Stone walls do not a prison make,
    Nor iron bars a cage;
Minds innocent and quiet take
    That for a hermitage;
If I have freedom in my love,
    And in my soul am free,
Angels alone that soar above
    Enjoy such liberty.

TO LUCASTA ON GOING TO THE WARS.

Tell me not, sweet, I am unkind,
    That from the nunnery
Of thy chaste breast and quiet mind
    To war and arms I fly.

True, a new mistress now I chase,
    The first foe in the field,
And with a stronger faith embrace
    A sword, a horse, a shield.

Yet this inconstancy is such
    As you, too, shall adore:
I could not love thee, dear, so much,
    Loved I not honour more.

COWLEY.

ABRAHAM COWLEY (1618–1667) began as a Spenserian, soon became a metaphysical, took to irregular so-called Pindaric Odes, and ended as a poet of the new school of correctness, polish, and restraint. Among his best lyrics are graceful love songs, humorous pieces, drinking songs, and an elegy or so, such as that on Crashaw.

THE CHRONICLE.

Margarita first possessed,
If I remember well, my breast;
  Margarita, first of all !
    But when a while the wanton maid
    With my restless heart had played,
  Martha took the flying ball.

Martha soon did it resign
To the beauteous Catherine.
  Beauteous Catherine gave place
    (Though loath and angry she to part
    With the possession of my heart)
  To Eliza's conquering face.

Eliza till this hour might reign,
Had she not evil counsels ta'en.
  Fundamental laws she broke,
    And still new favourites she chose,
    Till up in arms my passions rose,
  And cast away her yoke.

Mary then and gentle Anne
Both to reign at once began.
  Alternately they swayed;
    And sometimes Mary was the fair,
    And sometimes Anne the crown did wear;
  And sometimes both I obeyed.

Another Mary then arose
And did rigorous laws impose;
  A mighty tyrant she.
    Long, alas, should I have been
    Under that iron-sceptered Queen,
  Had not Rebecca set me free.

When fair Rebecca set me free,
'Twas then a golden time with me.
　　But soon those pleasures fled,
　　　　For the gracious Princess died
　　　　In her youth and beauty's pride,
　　And Judith reigned in her stead.

One month, three days, and half an hour,
Judith held the sovereign power;
　　Wondrous beautiful her face!
　　　　But so weak and small her wit
　　　　That she to govern was unfit,
　　And so Susanna took her place.

But when Isabella came,
Armed with a resistless flame
　　And th' artillery of her eye,
　　　　Whilst she proudly marched about
　　　　Greater conquests to find out,
　　She beat out Susan by the by. . . .

Gentle Henrietta then,
And a third Mary next began;
　　Then Joan, and Jane, and Audria;
　　　　And then a pretty Thomasine,
　　　　And then another Catherine,
　　And then a long *et cetera* . . .

But I will briefer with them be,
Since few of them were long with me.
　　A higher and a nobler strain
　　　　My present Empress does claim:
　　　　Heleonora, first o' th' name,
　　Whom God grant long to reign.

MARVELL.

ANDREW MARVELL (1621–1678) was a friend of
Milton, and at one time his colleague in serving the
Commonwealth. He wrote verse satires and political
pamphlets, but on that side lives only by his *Horatian
Ode Upon Cromwell's Return From Ireland.* His
unique gift is his deep feeling for Nature, rare at any
time and almost unknown in the literature of his own
day.

THOUGHTS IN A GARDEN.

How vainly men themselves amaze
To win the palm, the oak, or bays,
And their uncessant labours see
Crown'd from some single herb or tree,
Whose short and narrow-vergèd shade
Does prudently their toils upbraid;
While all the flowers and trees do close
To weave the garlands of repose !

Fair Quiet, have I found thee here,
And Innocence thy sister dear ?
Mistaken long, I sought you then
In busy companies of men:
Your sacred plants, if here below,
Only among the plants will grow;
Society is all but rude
To this delicious solitude.

No white nor red was ever seen
So amorous as this lovely green.
Fond lovers, cruel as their flame,
Cut in these trees their mistress' name:
Little, alas ! they know or heed
How far these beauties hers exceed !
Fair trees ! wheres'e'er your barks I wound,
No name shall but your own be found.

When we have run our passions' heat,
Love hither makes his best retreat:
The gods, that mortal beauty chase,
Still in a tree did end their race;
Apollo hunted Daphne so
Only that she might laurel grow;
And Pan did after Syrinx speed
Not as a nymph, but for a reed.

What wondrous life is this I lead!
Ripe apples drop about my head;
The luscious clusters of the vine
Upon my mouth do crush their wine;
The nectarine and curious peach
Into my hands themselves do reach;
Stumbling on melons, as I pass,
Ensnared with flowers, I fall on grass.

Meanwhile the mind, from pleasure less,
Withdraws into its happiness;
The mind, that ocean where each kind
Does straight its own resemblance find;
Yet it creates, transcending these,
Far other worlds, and other seas,
Annihilating all that's made
To a green thought in a green shade.

Here at the fountain's sliding foot,
Or at some fruit tree's mossy root,
Casting the body's vest aside,
My soul into the boughs does glide;
There, like a bird, it sits and sings,
There whets and combs its silver wings,
And, till prepared for longer flight,
Waves in its plumes the various light.

Such was that happy garden-state
While man there walk'd without a mate:
After a place so pure and sweet,
What other help could yet be meet!
But 'twas beyond a mortal's share
To wander solitary there:
Two paradises 'twere in one,
To live in Paradise alone.

How well the skilful gardener drew
Of flowers and herbs this dial new!
Where, from above, the milder sun
Does through a fragrant zodiac run:
And, as it works, th' industrious bee
Computes its time as well as we.
How could such sweet and wholesome hours
Be reckon'd, but with herbs and flowers!

BERMUDAS.

Where the remote Bermudas ride,
In the ocean's bosom unespied,
From a small boat, that rowed along,
The listening winds received this song.

" What should we do but sing His praise,
That led us through the watery maze
Unto an isle so long unknown,
And yet far kinder than our own?
Where He the huge sea-monsters wracks,
That lift the deep upon their backs,
He lands us on a grassy stage,
Safe from the storms, and prelates' rage:
He gave us this eternal Spring,
Which here enamels everything,

And sends the fowls to us in care,
On daily visits through the air:
He hangs in shades the orange bright,
Like golden lamps in a green night,
And does in the pomegranates close
Jewels more rich than Ormus shows:
He makes the figs our mouths to meet,
And throws the melons at our feet:
But apples plants of such a price,
No tree could ever bear them twice.
With cedars chosen by His hand
From Lebanon He stores the land;
And makes the hollow seas that roar
Proclaim the ambergris on shore.
He cast (of which we rather boast)
The Gospel's pearl upon our coast;
And in these rocks for us did frame
A temple where to sound His name.
Oh ! let our voice His praise exalt,
Till it arrive at Heaven's vault,
Whieh, thence (perhaps) rebounding, may
Echo beyond the Mexique Bay ! "

Thus sung they, in the English boat
A holy and a cheerful note,
And all the way, to guide their chime,
With falling oars they kept the time.

VAUGHAN.

HENRY VAUGHAN (1622–1695) was a doctor in
Brecknockshire. In his idealisation of childhood and
his spiritual interpretation of Nature he anticipates
the poetry of Wordsworth. His best work is contained
in *Silex Scintillans* (1650, 55). He owed his religious
outlook, he admitted, to George Herbert.

THE RETREAT.

Happy those early days, when I
Shined in my Angel-infancy.
Before I understood this place
Appointed for my second race,
Or taught my soul to fancy aught
But a white celestial thought;
When yet I had not walked above
A mile or two from my first love,
And looking back, at that short space,
Could see a glimpse of His bright face:
When on some gilded cloud or flower
My gazing soul would dwell an hour,
And in those weaker glories spy
Some shadows of eternity:
Before I taught my tongue to wound
My conscience with a sinful sound,
Or had the black art to dispense
A several sin to every sense,
But felt through all this fleshly dress
Bright shoots of everlastingness.

O how I long to travel back,
And tread again that ancient track !
That I might once more reach that plain,
Where first I left my glorious train;
From whence the enlightened spirit sees
That shady City of Palm-trees.
But ah ! my soul with too much stay
Is drunk, and staggers in the way !
Some men a forward motion love,
But I by backward steps would move;
And when this dust falls to the urn,
In that state I came, return.

THEY ARE ALL GONE.

They are all gone into the world of light !
    And I alone sit lingering here;
Their very memory is fair and bright,
    And my sad thoughts doth clear.

It glows and glitters in my cloudy breast,
    Like stars upon some gloomy grove,
Or those faint beams in which this hill is drest
    After the sun's remove.

I see them walking in an air of glory,
    Whose light doth trample on my days:
My days which are at best but dull and hoary,
    Mere glimmering and decays.

O holy Hope ! and high Humility,
    High as the heavens above!
These are your walks, and you have show'd them me,
    To kindle my cold love.

Dear, beauteous Death ! the jewel of the Just,
    Shining nowhere but in the dark;
What mysteries do lie beyond thy dust,
    Could man outlook that mark !

He that hath found some fledged bird's nest may
    know,
    At first sight, if the bird be flown;
But what fair well or grove he sings in now,
    That is to him unknown.

And yet, as angels in some brighter dreams
    Call to the soul, when man doth sleep:

So some strange thoughts transcend our wonted
   themes,
   And into glory peep. . . .

O Father of eternal life, and all
   Created glories under Thee !
Resume Thy spirit from this world of thrall
   Into true liberty. . . .

THE WATER-FALL.

With what deep murmurs through time's silent stealth
Doth thy transparent, cool and watery wealth
      Here flowing fall,
      And chide, and call,
As if his liquid, loose Retinue stayed
Lingering, and were of this steep place afraid,
      The common pass
      Where, clear as glass,
      All must descend
      Not to an end:
But quickened by this deep and rocky grave,
Rise to a longer course more bright and brave.

   Dear stream ! dear bank, where often I
   Have sate, and pleas'd my pensive eye,
   Why, since each drop of thy quick store
   Runs thither, whence it flow'd before,
   Should poor souls fear a shade or night,
   Who came (sure) from a sea of light ?
   Or since those drops are all sent back
   So sure to thee, that none doth lack,
   Why should frail flesh doubt any more
   That what God takes, he'll not restore ?
   O useful Element and clear !

My sacred wash and cleanser here,
My first consigner unto those
Fountains of life, where the Lamb goes ?
What sublime truths, and wholesome themes,
Lodge in thy mystical, deep streams !
Such as dull man can never find
Unless that spirit lead his mind,
Which first upon thy face did move,
And hatch'd all with his quickening love.
As this loud brook's incessant fall
In streaming rings restagnates all,
Which reach by course the bank, and then
Are no more seen, just so pass men.
O my invisible estate,
My glorious liberty, still late !
Thou art the Channel my soul seeks,
Not this with Cataracts and Creeks.

THE WORLD.

I saw Eternity the other night
Like a great Ring of pure and endless light,
    All calm, as it was bright;
And round beneath it, Time in hours, days, years,
        Driv'n by the spheres,
Like a vast shadow mov'd, in which the world
        And all her train were hurl'd.
The doting lover in his quaintest strain
        Did there complain;
Near him, his lute, his fancy, and his flights,
        Wit's sour delights,
With gloves, and knots the silly snares of pleasure,
        Yet his dear treasure,
All scatter'd lay, while he his eyes did pour
        Upon a flower.

The darksome States-man hung with weights and woe
Like a thick midnight-fog mov'd there so slow,
    He did not stay, nor go;
Condemning thoughts like sad eclipses scowl
      Upon his soul,
And clouds of crying witnesses without
      Pursued him with one shout.
Yet digg'd the mole, and, lest his ways be found,
      Worked under ground,
Where he did clutch his prey; but one did see
      That policy;
Churches and altars fed him; perjuries
      Were gnats and flies;
It rain'd about him blood and tears; but he
      Drank them as free.

The fearful miser on a heap of rust
Sat pining all his life there, did scarce trust
    His own hands with the dust,
Yet would not place one piece above, but lives
    In fear of thieves.
Thousands there were as frantic as himself,
    And hugg'd each one his pelf;
The down-right epicure plac'd heav'n in sense,
    And scorn'd pretence;
While others, slipped into a wide excess,
    Said little less;
The weaker sort slight, trivial wares enslave,
    Who think them brave,
And poor, despisèd truth sat counting by
    Their victory.

Yet some, who all this while did weep and sing,
And sing and weep, soar'd up into the Ring;
    But most would use no wing.

" O fools," said I, " thus to prefer dark night
    Before true light !
To live in grots and caves, and hate the day,
    Because it shows the way,
The way, which from this dead and dark abode
    Leads up to God,
A way where you might tread the Sun, and be
    More bright than he ! "
But as I did their madness so discuss
    One whisper'd thus,
" This ring the Bride-groom did for none provide,
    But for his bride."

DRYDEN.

JOHN DRYDEN (1631–1700), " glorious John," held his court as acknowledged literary king for many years at Will's coffee-house. He was the master satirist, and the greatest critic of his day, its leading reasoner in verse, and one of its outstanding drama-tists. The satiric portraits in *Absalom and Achitophel* (1681–2) are among his best work, but to-day we prefer to listen to the stirring music of his Odes. He commanded the van of the classical school, but in the overflowing vitality of his creative genius he reminds us of the Elizabethans.

REASON.

Dim as the borrowed beams of moon and stars
To lonely, weary, wandering travellers
Is Reason to the soul: and as on high
These rolling fires discover but the sky,
Not light us here, so Reason's glimmering ray
Was lent, not to assure our doubtful way,

But guide us upward to a better day.
And as these nightly tapers disappear
When day's bright lord ascends our hemisphere,
So pale grows Reason at Religion's sight,
So dies, and so dissolves in supernatural light.
Religio Laici.

CHARACTER OF BUCKINGHAM.

Some of their chiefs were princes of the land;
In the first rank of these did Zimri stand,
A man so various that he seemed to be
Not one, but all mankind's epitome:
Stiff in opinions, always in the wrong,
Was everything by starts and nothing long;
But in the course of one revolving moon
Was chymist, fiddler, statesman, and buffoon;
Then all for women, painting, rhyming, drinking,
Besides ten thousand freaks that died in thinking.
Blest madman, who could every hour employ
With something new to wish or to enjoy!
Railing and praising were his usual themes,
And both, to show his judgment, in extremes:
So over violent or over civil
That every man with him was God or Devil.
In squandering wealth was his peculiar art;
Nothing went unrewarded but desert.
Beggared by fools whom still he found too late,
He had his jest, and they had his estate.
He laughed himself from Court; then sought relief
By forming parties, but could ne'er be chief:
For spite of him, the weight of business fell
On Absalom and wise Achitophel;
Thus wicked but in will, of means bereft,
He left not faction, but of that was left.
(Absalom and Achitophel.)

A SONG FOR ST. CECILIA'S DAY, 1687.

From harmony, from heavenly harmony
   This universal frame began:
  When Nature underneath a heap
    Of jarring atoms lay,
   And could not heave her head,
The tuneful voice was heard from high—
  " Arise, ye more than dead ! "
Then cold and hot and moist and dry
   In order to their stations leap,
    And Music's power obey.
From harmony, from heavenly harmony
   This universal frame began:
   From harmony to harmony
Through all the compass of the notes it ran,
The diapason closing full in Man.

What passion cannot music raise and quell ?
   When Jubal struck the chorded shell,
  His listening brethren stood around,
   And, wondering, on their faces fell
  To worship that celestial sound:
Less than a god they thought there could not dwell
   Within the hollow of that shell,
   That spoke so sweetly and so well.
What passion cannot Music raise and quell ?

    The trumpet's loud clangour
     Excites us to arms,
   With shrill notes of anger
    And mortal alarms.
  The double double double beat
    Of the thundering drum
   Cries, " Hark ! the foes come !
Charge, charge, 'tis too late to retreat ! "

The soft complaining flute
In dying notes discovers
The woes of hopeless lovers,
Whose dirge is whispered by the warbling lute.

Sharp violins proclaim
Their jealous pangs and desperation,
Fury, frantic indignation;
Depth of pains and height of passion,
For the fair, disdainful dame.

But Oh ! what art can teach,
What human voice can reach,
The sacred organ's praise ?
Notes inspiring holy love,
Notes that wing their heavenly ways
To mend the choirs above !

Orpheus could lead the savage race,
And trees unrooted left their place,
Sequacious of the lyre;
But bright Cecilia raised the wonder higher:
When to her organ vocal breath was given,
An angel heard, and straight appeared,
Mistaking Earth for Heaven.

Grand Chorus.

As from the power of sacred lays
The spheres began to move,
And sung the great Creator's praise
To all the blessed above;
So when the last and dreadful hour
This crumbling pageant shall devour,
The trumpet shall be heard on high,
The dead shall live, the living die,
And Music shall untune the sky.

SEDLEY.

Sɪʀ Cʜᴀʀʟᴇs Sᴇᴅʟᴇʏ (1639 ?–1701) was one of the wittiest of Charles II.'s courtiers, " the Mob of Gentlemen," in Pope's phrase, " who wrote with Ease . . . like twinkling stars the Miscellanies o'er." In addition to his graceful songs he wrote some plays, but these have long been forgotten.

CHILD AND MAIDEN.

Ah, Chloris ! could I now but sit
   As unconcern'd as when
Your infant beauty could beget
   No happiness or pain !
When I the dawn used to admire,
   And praised the coming day,
I little thought the rising fire
   Would take my rest away.

Your charms in harmless childhood lay
   Like metals in a mine;
Age from no face takes more away
   Than youth conceal'd in thine.
But as your charms insensibly
   To their perfection prest,
So love as unperceived did fly,
   And center'd in my breast.

My passion with your beauty grew,
   While Cupid at my heart
Still as his mother favour'd you
   Threw a new flaming dart:
Each gloried in their wanton part;
   To make a lover, he
Employ'd the utmost of his art—
   To make a beauty, she.

PHYLLIS.

Phyllis is my only joy,
    Faithless as the winds or seas,
Sometimes cunning, sometimes coy,
    Yet she never fails to please:
        If with a frown
        I am cast down,
        Phyllis, smiling
        And beguiling,
Makes me happier than before.

Though alas ! too late I find
    Nothing can her fancy fix;
Yet the moment she is kind
    I forgive her all her tricks,
        Which though I see,
        I can't get free:
        She deceiving,
        I believing,
What need lovers wish for more ?

PRIOR.

MATTHEW PRIOR (1664–1721), while a youth, won the patronage of the Earl of Dorset, who sent him to Cambridge. He held various diplomatic posts, and was at one time ambassador at Paris. His heavier verse such as *Solomon* is quite eclipsed by that in his lighter vein of graceful compliment and humour which constitutes a collection of elegant lyrics sufficient to refute any charge that our Augustan period was deficient in the lyrical gift. " Prior, Sir," said Dr. Johnson, " is a lady's poet."

A LETTER TO THE HONOURABLE LADY MISS MARGARET CAVENDISH HOLLES-HARLEY.

My noble, lovely little Peggy,
Let this, my first epistle, beg ye,
At dawn of morn and close of even,
To lift your heart and hands to heaven.
In double beauty say your prayer:
Our Father first—then *Notre Père*:
And, dearest child, along the day,
In every thing you do and say,
Obey and please my lord and lady,
So God shall love, and angels aid ye.
 If to these precepts you attend,
 No second letter need I send,
 And so I rest your constant friend.

A SONG.

If wine and music have the power
To ease the sickness of the soul;
Let Phoebus every string explore,
And Bacchus fill the sprightly bowl.
Let them their friendly aid employ,
To make my Cloe's absence light;
And seek for pleasure, to destroy
The sorrows of this livelong night.
But she to-morrow will return.
 Venus, be thou to-morrow great;
Thy myrtles strow, thy odours burn,
And meet thy fav'rite nymph in state.
Kind goddess, to no other powers
Let us to-morrow's blessings own:
Thy darling loves shall guide the hours,
And all the day be thine alone.

FOR MY OWN MONUMENT.

As doctors give physic by way of prevention,
　　Mat, alive and in health, of his tombstone took care;
For delays are unsafe, and his pious intention
　　May haply be never fulfill'd by his heir.

Then take Mat's word for it, the sculptor is paid,
　　That the figure is fine, pray believe your own eye;
Yet credit but lightly what more may be said,
　　For we flatter ourselves, and teach marble to lie.

Yet counting as far as to fifty his years,
　　His virtues and vices were as other men's are;
High hopes he conceiv'd, and he smother'd great fears,
　　In life party-colour'd, half pleasure, half care.

Nor to business a drudge, nor to faction a slave,
　　He strove to make interest and freedom agree;
In public employments industrious and grave,
　　And alone with his friends, lord, how merry was he!

Now in equipage stately, now humbly on foot,
　　Both fortunes he tried, but to neither would trust;
And whirl'd in the round, as the wheel turn'd about,
　　He found riches had wings, and knew man was but
　　　　dust.

This verse, little-polish'd, though mighty sincere,
　　Sets neither his titles nor merit to view;
It says that his relics collected lie here,
　　And no mortal yet knows too if this may be true.

Fierce robbers there are that invest the highway,
　　So Mat may be killed, and his bones never found;
False witness at court, and fierce tempests at sea,
　　So Mat may yet chance to be hang'd, or be drown'd.

If his bones lie in earth, roll in sea, fly in air,
    To fate we must yield, and the thing is the same,
And if passing thou giv'st him a smile, or a tear,
    He cares not—yet prithee be kind to his fame.

POPE.

ALEXANDER POPE (1688–1744) was the true founder of literature as a profession in England—rejecting patrons, he made a comfortable fortune and won independence by the money he obtained from his poetry, largely from his great version of Homer. His little lyric *Solitude* he wrote while a boy; later he almost confined himself to satirical, mock-heroic and didactic poetry. His mock-heroic *Rape of the Lock* is his supreme achievement; *The Essay on Man* is full of epigrammatic verses which are still constantly quoted; as a satirist he stands with Dryden above all other English satirists, though unfortunately, perhaps, distinguished by a vein of malice. In constant perfection of artistry he is almost unrivalled.

SOLITUDE.

Happy the man, whose wish and care
A few paternal acres bound,
Content to breathe his native air
        In his own ground.

Whose herds with milk, whose fields with bread,
Whose flocks supply him with attire;
Whose trees in summer yield him shade,
        In winter fire.

Blest, who can unconcern'dly find
Hours, days, and years slide soft away
In health of body, peace of mind,
         Quiet by day,

Sound sleep by night; study and ease
Together mix'd, sweet recreation,
And innocence, which most does please
         With meditation.

Thus let me live, unseen, unknown;
Thus unlamented let me die;
Steal from the world, and not a stone
         Tell where I lie.

THE SOUND AN ECHO TO THE SENSE.

'Tis not enough no harshness gives offence,
The sound must seem an Echo to the sense:
Soft is the strain when Zephyr gently blows,
And the smooth stream in smoother numbers flows;
But when loud surges lash the sounding shore,
The hoarse, rough verse should like the torrent roar;
When Ajax strives some rock's vast weight to throw,
The line too labours, and the words move slow;
Not so, when swift Camilla scours the plain,
Flies o'er the unbending corn, and skims along the main.
Hear how Timotheus' varied lays surprise,
And bid alternate passions fall and rise !
While, at each change, the son of Libyan Jove
Now burns with glory, and then melts with love,
Now his fierce eyes with sparkling fury glow,
Now sighs steal out, and tears begin to flow:
Persians and Greeks like turns of Nature found,
And the world's victor stood subdu'd by Sound !

The pow'r of Music all our hearts allow,
And what Timotheus was, is DRYDEN now.

(*An Essay on Criticism.*)

THE NYMPH AT HER TOILET.

And now, unveil'd, the Toilet stands display'd,
Each silver Vase in mystic order laid.
First, rob'd in white, the Nymph intent adores,
With head uncover'd, the Cosmetic pow'rs.
A heav'nly image in the glass appears,
To that she bends, to that her eyes she rears;
Th' inferior Priestess, at her altar's side,
Trembling begins the sacred rites of Pride.
Unnumber'd treasures ope at once, and here
The various off'rings of the world appear;
From each she nicely culls with curious toil,
And decks the Goddess with the glitt'ring spoil.
This casket India's glowing gems unlocks,
And all Arabia breathes from yonder box.
The Tortoise here and Elephant unite,
Transform'd to combs, the speckled, and the white.
Here files of pins extend their shining rows,
Puffs, Powders, Patches, Bibles, Billet-doux.
Now awful Beauty puts on all its arms;
The fair each moment rises in her charms,
Repairs her smiles, awakens ev'ry grace,
And calls forth all the wonders of her face;
Sees by degrees a purer blush arise,
And keener lightnings quicken in her eyes.
The busy Sylphs surround their darling care,
These set the head, and those divide the hair,
Some fold the sleeve, whilst others plait the gown;
And Betty's prais'd for labours not her own.

(*The Rape of the Lock*, Canto I.)

SPORUS, THAT THING OF SILK.

Pope. Let Sporus tremble.

        Arbuthnot. What ? that thing of silk,
Sporus, that mere white curd of Ass's milk ?
Satire or sense, alas ! can Sporus feel ?
Who breaks a butterfly upon a wheel ?
P. Yet let me flap this bug with gilded wings,
This painted child of dirt, that stinks and stings;
Whose buzz the witty and the fair annoys,
Yet wit ne'er tastes, and beauty ne'er enjoys:
So well-bred spaniels civilly delight
In mumbling of the game they dare not bite.
Eternal smiles his emptiness betray,
As shallow streams run dimpling all the way.
Whether in florid impotence he speaks,
And, as the prompter breathes, the puppet squeaks;
Or at the ear of Eve, familiar Toad,
Half froth, half venom, spits himself abroad,
In puns, or politics, or tales or lies,
Or spite, or smut, or rhymes, or blasphemies.
His wit all see-saw, between that and this,
Now high, now low, now master up, now miss,
And he himself one vile Antithesis.
Amphibious thing ! that acting either part,
The trifling head or the corrupted heart,
Fop at the toilet, flatt'rer at the board,
Now trips a Lady, and now struts a Lord.
Eve's tempter thus the Rabbins have exprest,
A Cherub's face, a reptile all the rest;
Beauty that shocks you, parts that none will trust;
Wit that can creep, and pride that licks the dust.
             (Epistle to Dr. Arbuthnot.)

THE CONSUMMATION OF DULNESS.

In vain, in vain—the all-composing Hour
Resistless falls: the Muse obeys the Power.
She comes! she comes! the sable Throne behold
Of *Night* primeval and of *Chaos* old!
Before her, *Fancy's* gilded clouds decay,
And all its varying Rain-bows die away.
Wit shoots in vain its momentary fires,
The meteor drops, and in a flash expires.
As one by one, at dread Medea's strain,
The sickening stars fade off th' ethereal plain;
As Argus' eyes by Hermes' wand opprest,
Closed one by one to everlasting rest;
Thus at her felt approach, and secret might,
Art after *Art* goes out, and all is Night.
See skulking *Truth* to her old cavern fled,
Mountains of casuistry heap'd o'er her head!
Philosophy, that lean'd on Heav'n before,
Shrinks to her second cause, and is no more.
Physic of *Metaphysic* begs defence,
And *Metaphysic* calls for aid on *Sense*!
See *Mystery* to *Mathematics* fly!
In vain! they gaze, turn giddy, rave and die.
Religion blushing veils her sacred fires,
And unawares *Morality* expires.
For *public* Flame, nor *private*, dares to shine;
Nor *human* Spark is left, nor glimpse *divine*!
Lo! thy dread Empire, CHAOS! is restor'd;
Light dies before thy uncreating word;
Thy hand, great Anarch! lets the curtain fall,
And universal Darkness buries All.

(*The Dunciad.*)

DYER.

JOHN DYER (1700–1758), born in Carmarthenshire, first studied painting, then entered the Church. His longest poems, *The Fleece* and *The Ruins of Rome*, are too full of heavy reflection and moralising. *Grongar Hill* (1726), however, is purely charming; indeed, this landscape, a clear, bright little water-colour in verse sketched with a painter's eye for colour and form, is the most delightful landscape in our poetry between Milton, whose *L'Allegro* clearly influenced it, and Wordsworth, whose sonnet on Dyer prophesies that the poem will endure as " long as the thrush shall pipe on Grongar Hill."

GRONGAR HILL.*

Silent nymph, with curious eye !
Who, the purple evening, lie
On the mountain's lonely van,
Beyond the noise of busy man,
Painting fair the form of things,
While the yellow linnet sings;
Or the tuneful nightingale
Charms the forest with her tale;
Come with all thy various hues,
Come, and aid thy sister Muse;
Now while Phoebus riding high
Gives lustre to the land and sky !
Grongar Hill invites my song,
Draw the landscape bright and strong;
Grongar, in whose mossy cells
Sweetly-musing Quiet dwells;
Grongar, in whose silent shade
For the modest Muses made,
So oft I have, the even still,
At the fountain of a rill,
Sate upon a flowery bed,

* Slightly shortened.

With my hand beneath my head;
And strayed my eyes o'er Towy's flood,
Over mead and over wood,
From house to house, from hill to hill,
'Till Contemplation had her fill.

About his chequered sides I wind,
And leave his brooks and meads behind . . .
Now I gain the mountain's brow,
What a landscape lies below!
No clouds, no vapours intervene,
But the gay, the open scene
Does the face of Nature show,
In all the hues of heaven's bow!
And, swelling to embrace the light,
Spreads around beneath the sight.
Old castles on the cliffs arise,
Proudly towering in the skies!
Rushing from the woods, the spires
Seem from hence ascending fires! . . .

Below me trees unnumbered rise,
Beautiful in various dyes:
The gloomy pine, the poplar blue,
The yellow beech, the sable yew,
The slender fir that taper grows,
The sturdy oak with broad-spread boughs.
And beyond the purple grove,
Haunt of Phillis, queen of love!
Gaudy as the opening dawn,
Lies a long and level lawn,
On which a dark hill, steep and high,
Holds and charms the wandering eye!
Deep are his feet in Towy's flood,
His sides are clothed with waving wood,
And ancient towers crown his brow,
That cast an awful look below. . . .

And see the rivers how they run,
Through woods and meads; in shade and sun,
Sometimes swift, sometimes slow,
Wave succeeding wave, they go
A various journey to the deep,
Like human life to endless sleep. . . .

Ever charming, ever new,
When will the landscape tire the view !
The fountain's fall, the river's flow,
The woody valleys, warm and low;
The windy summit, wild and high,
Roughly rushing on the sky !
The pleasant seat, the ruined tower,
The naked rock, the shady bower;
The town and village, dome and farm,
Each give each a double charm,
As pearls upon an Ethiop's arm. . . .

O may I with myself agree,
And never covet what I see:
Content me with an humble shade,
My passions tamed, my wishes laid. . . .

Now, even now, my joys run high,
As on the mountain-turf I lie;
While the wanton Zephyr sings,
And in the vale perfumes his wings;
While the waters murmur deep;
While the shepherd charms his sheep;
While the birds unbounded fly,
And with music fill the sky,
Now, even now, my joys run high. . . .

Grass and flowers Quiet treads,
On the meads, and mountain-heads,
Along with Pleasure, close allied,

Each by each other's side:
And often, by the murmuring rill,
Hears the thrush, while all is still,
Within the groves of Grongar Hill.

THOMSON.

JAMES THOMSON (1700–1748), after studying at
Edinburgh University, went to London where, in 1726,
he published *Winter*, the first of his four poems on
the Seasons. These blank verse poems owed a good
deal to Milton, and their true descriptions of Nature
stand out in contrast to the Augustan reflections and
moralising with which they are mingled, while the
great Hymn later added as a conclusion preludes the
note of Wordsworth. In spite of the new note (and,
perhaps, because of it, too) these poems were very
well-received, and they were praised by Pope. In *The
Castle of Indolence* Thomson caught Spenser's tune
and style better than any other poet of the eighteenth
century.

LAND OF DROWSYHEAD.

In lowly dale, fast by a river's side,
With woody hill o'er hill encompass'd round,
A most enchanting wizard did abide,
Than whom a fiend more fell is no where found.
It was, I ween, a lovely spot of ground;
And there a season atween June and May,
Half prankt with Spring, with Summer half embrown'd,
A listless climate made, where, sooth to say,
No living wight could work, ne cared even to play.

Was nought around but images of rest,
Sleep-soothing groves, and quiet lawns between
And flowery beds that slumb'rous influence kest
From poppies breath'd and beds of pleasant green,
Where never yet was creeping creature seen.

Meantime unnumber'd glittering streamlets play'd,
And hurled everywhere their waters sheen,
That, as they bicker'd through the sunny glade,
Though restless still themselves, a lulling murmur made.

Join'd to the prattle of the purling rills
Were heard the lowing herds along the vale,
And flocks loud bleating from the distant hills,
And vacant shepherds piping in the dale;
And now and then sweet Philomel would wail,
Or stock-doves 'plain amid the forest deep,
That drowsy rustled to the sighing gale;
And still a coil the grasshopper did keep;
Yet all these sounds yblent inclinèd all to sleep.

Full in the passage of the vale, above,
A sable, silent, solemn, forest stood,
Where nought but shadowy forms were seen to move,
As idless fancy'd in her dreaming mood;
And up the hills, on either side, a wood
Of blackening pines, ay waving to and fro,
Sent forth a sleepy horror through the blood;
And where this valley winded out, below
The murmuring main was heard, and scarcely heard, to
    flow.

A pleasing land of drowsyhead it was,
Of dreams that wave before the half-shut eye,
And of gay castles in the clouds that pass,
For ever flushing round a summer sky;
There eke the soft delights, that witchingly,
Instil a wanton sweetness through the breast,
And the calm pleasures, always hover'd nigh;
But whate'er smack'd of noyance or unrest
Was far, far off expell'd from this delicious nest.
                    (*The Castle of Indolence.*)

GRAY.

THOMAS GRAY (1716–1771) from 1739 to 1741 travelled through France and Italy, but thereafter he settled for the rest of his life in Cambridge. He was a studious, somewhat melancholy man, but possessed of a vein of humour and the gift of friendship, and his letters are a delightful revelation of his personality. His poetic output was limited, and on it he expended the utmost care; thus he wrote very little that was weak, and at his best his touch was so sure that of *The Elegy* Dr. Johnson could say, " had Gray written often thus, it had been vain to blame, and useless to praise him "—and he wrote more often thus than Dr. Johnson thought.

ON A FAVOURITE CAT, DROWNED IN A TUB OF GOLD FISHES.

'Twas on a lofty vase's side,
Where China's gayest art had dyed
The azure flowers that blow,
Demurest of the tabby kind
The pensive Selima, reclined,
Gazed on the lake below.

Her conscious tail her joy declared:
The fair round face, the snowy beard,
The velvet of her paws,
Her coat that with the tortoise vies,
Her ears of jet, and emerald eyes—
She saw, and purr'd applause.

Still had she gazed, but 'midst the tide
Two angel forms were seen to glide,
The Genii of the stream:
Their scaly armour's Tyrian hue
Through richest purple to the view
Betray'd a golden gleam.

The hapless Nymph with wonder saw:
A whisker first, and then a claw
With many an ardent wish
She stretch'd, in vain, to reach the prize—
What female heart can gold despise?
What Cat's averse to fish?

Presumptuous maid! with looks intent
Again she stretch'd, again she bent,
Nor knew the gulf between—
Malignant Fate sat by and smiled—
The slippery verge her feet beguiled;
She tumbled headlong in!

Eight times emerging from the flood
She mew'd to every watery God
Some speedy aid to send—
No Dolphin came, no Nereid stirr'd,
Nor cruel Tom nor Susan heard—
A favourite has no friend!

From hence, ye Beauties! undeceived
Know one false step is ne'er retrieved,
And be with caution bold:
Not all that tempts your wandering eyes
And heedless hearts, is lawful prize,
Nor all that glisters, gold!

ELEGY WRITTEN IN A COUNTRY CHURCHYARD.

The curfew tolls the knell of parting day,
  The lowing herd wind slowly o'er the lea,
The ploughman homeward plods his weary way,
  And leaves the world to darkness and to me.

Now fades the glimmering landscape on the sight,
   And all the air a solemn stillness holds,
Save where the beetle wheels his droning flight,
   And drowsy tinklings lull the distant folds;

Save that from yonder ivy-mantled tower
   The moping owl does to the moon complain
Of such as, wand'ring near her secret bower,
   Molest her ancient solitary reign.

Beneath those rugged elms, that yew-tree's shade,
   Where heaves the turf in many a mould'ring heap,
Each in his narrow cell for ever laid,
   The rude Forefathers of the hamlet sleep.

The breezy call of incense-breathing Morn,
   The swallow twitt'ring from the straw-built shed,
The cock's shrill clarion, or the echoing horn,
   No more shall rouse them from their lowly bed.

For them no more the blazing hearth shall burn,
   Or busy housewife ply her evening care;
No children run to lisp their sire's return,
   Or climb his knees the envied kiss to share.

Oft did the harvest to their sickle yield,
   Their furrow oft the stubborn glebe has broke;
How jocund did they drive their team afield !
   How bowed the woods beneath their sturdy stroke !

Let not Ambition mock their useful toil,
   Their homely joys, and destiny obscure;
Nor Grandeur hear with a disdainful smile,
   The short and simple annals of the poor.

The boast of heraldry, the pomp of power,
  And all that beauty, all that wealth e'er gave,
Awaits alike th' inevitable hour.
  The paths of glory lead but to the grave.

Nor you, ye Proud, impute to these the fault,
  If Mem'ry o'er their tomb no trophies raise,
Where thro' the long-drawn aisle and fretted vault
  The pealing anthem swells the note of praise.

Can storied urn or animated bust
  Back to its mansion call the fleeting breath?
Can Honour's voice provoke the silent dust,
  Or Flatt'ry soothe the dull cold ear of Death?

Perhaps in this neglected spot is laid
  Some heart once pregnant with celestial fire;
Hands, that the rod of empire might have swayed,
  Or waked to ectasy the living lyre.

But Knowledge to their eyes her ample page
  Rich with the spoils of time did ne'er unroll;
Chill Penury repressed their noble rage,
  And froze the genial current of the soul.

Full many a gem, of purest ray serene,
  The dark unfathomed caves of ocean bear:
Full many a flower is born to blush unseen,
  And waste its sweetness on the desert air.

Some village-Hampden, that with dauntless breast
  The little tyrant of his fields withstood;
Some mute inglorious Milton here may rest,
  Some Cromwell guiltless of his country's blood.

Th' applause of listening senates to command,
  The threats of pain and ruin to despise,
To scatter plenty o'er a smiling land,
  And read their history in a nation's eyes,

Their lot forbad; nor circumscribed alone
  Their growing virtues, but their crimes confined;
Forbad to wade through slaughter to a throne,
  And shut the gates of mercy on mankind,

The struggling pangs of conscious truth to hide,
  To quench the blushes of ingenuous shame,
Or heap the shrine of Luxury and Pride
  With incense kindled at the Muse's flame.

Far from the madding crowd's ignoble strife
  Their sober wishes never learned to stray;
Along the cool sequestered vale of life
  They kept the noiseless tenor of their way.

Yet ev'n these bones from insult to protect
  Some frail memorial still erected nigh,
With uncouth rhymes and shapeless sculpture decked,
  Implores the passing tribute of a sigh.

Their name, their years, spelt by th' unlettered Muse,
  The place of fame and elegy supply;
And many a holy text around she strews,
  That teach the rustic moralist to die.

For who, to dumb Forgetfulness a prey,
  This pleasing anxious being e'er resigned,
Left the warm precincts of the cheerful day,
  Nor cast one longing ling'ring look behind?

On some fond breast the parting soul relies,
    Some pious drops the closing eye requires;
Ev'n from the tomb the voice of Nature cries,
    Ev'n in our ashes live their wonted fires.

For thee, who mindful of th' unhonoured Dead
    Dost in these lines their artless tale relate;
If chance, by lonely Contemplation led,
    Some kindred spirit shall inquire thy fate,

Haply some hoary-headed swain may say,
    " Oft have we seen him at the peep of dawn
Brushing with hasty steps the dews away
    To meet the sun upon the upland lawn.

" There at the foot of yonder nodding beech,
    That wreathes its old fantastic roots so high,
His listless length at noontide would he stretch,
    And pore upon the brook that babbles by.

" Hard by yon wood, now smiling as in scorn,
    Mutt'ring his wayward fancies he would rove,
Now drooping, woeful wan, like one forlorn,
    Or crazed with care, or crossed in hopeless love.

" One morn I missed him on the customed hill,
    Along the heath, and near his fav'rite tree;
Another came; nor yet beside the rill,
    Nor up the lawn, nor at the wood was he;

" The next with dirges due in sad array
    Slow thro' the church-way path we saw him borne,—
Approach and read (for thou canst read) the lay
    Graved on the stone beneath yon aged thorn."

THE EPITAPH.

HERE rests his head upon the lap of Earth
    A Youth to Fortune and to Fame unknown.
Fair Science frowned not on his humble birth,
    And Melancholy marked him for her own.

Large was his bounty, and his soul sincere,
    Heav'n did a recompence as largely send ;
He gave to Mis'ry all he had, a tear,
    He gained from Heav'n ('twas all he wished) a friend.

No farther seek his merits to disclose,
    Or draw his frailties from their dread abode,
(There they alike in trembling hope repose,)
    The bosom of his Father and his God.

COLLINS.

WILLIAM COLLINS (1721–1759), a friend of Dr. Johnson and Thomson, was little appreciated in his own day, his volume of *Odes* (1746) coming still-born from the press, but it is now recognised that he had an even finer ear and a more essentially lyrical note than his contemporary Gray. His *Ode to Evening* is a rare triumph in the difficult form of the unrhymed lyric. Next to this Ode his finest poem is probably his *Ode to the Passions*.

ODE WRITTEN IN 1746.

How sleep the brave, who sink to rest
By all their country's wishes blest !
When Spring, with dewy fingers cold,
Returns to deck their hallow'd mould,
She there shall dress a sweeter sod
Than Fancy's feet have ever trod.

By fairy hands their knell is rung,
By forms unseen their dirge is sung:
There Honour comes, a pilgrim gray,
To bless the turf that wraps their clay;
And Freedom shall awhile repair
To dwell a weeping hermit there !

ODE TO EVENING.

If aught of oaten stop, or pastoral song,
May hope, chaste Eve, to soothe thy modest ear,
  Like thy own solemn springs,
  Thy springs and dying gales;

O nymph reserved, while now the bright-haired sun
Sits in yon western tent, whose cloudy skirts,
  With braid ethereal wove,
  O'erhang his wavy bed;

Now air is hushed, save where the weak-eyed bat
With short shrill shriek flits by on leathern wing,
  Or where the beetle winds
  His small but sullen horn,

As oft he rises 'midst the twilight path
Against the pilgrim borne in heedless hum:
  Now teach me, maid composed,
  To breathe some softened strain,

Whose numbers, stealing through thy darkening vale
May not unseemly with its stillness suit:
  As, musing slow, I hail
  Thy genial loved return !

For when thy folding-star arising shows
His paly circlet, at his warning lamp
  The fragrant hours, and elves
  Who slept in buds the day,

And many a nymph, who wreathes her brows with sedge,
And sheds the freshening dew, and, lovelier still,
  The pensive pleasures sweet,
  Prepare thy shadowy car;

Then lead, calm votaress, where some sheety lake
Cheers the lone heath, or some time-hallow'd pile,
  Or upland fallows grey
  Reflect its last cool gleam.

Or, if chill blustering winds or driving rain
Prevent my willing feet, be mine the hut,
  That from the mountain's side
  Views wilds and swelling floods,

And hamlets brown, and dim-discovered spires;
And hears their simple bell, and marks o'er all
  Thy dewy fingers draw
  The gradual dusky veil.

While Spring shall pour his showers, as oft he wont,
And bathe thy breathing tresses, meekest Eve;
  While Summer loves to sport
  Beneath thy lingering light;

While sallow Autumn fills thy lap with leaves:
Or Winter, yelling through the troublous air,
  Affrights thy shrinking train,
  And rudely rends thy robes;

So long, regardful of thy quiet rule,
Shall Fancy, Friendship, Science, smiling Peace,
Thy gentlest influence own,
And love thy favourite name !

COWPER.

WILLIAM COWPER (1731–1800), after a brief spell as Clerk of the Journals to the House of Lords, became the victim of religious melancholy, and retired to a quiet life first at Huntingdon, then at Olney. His first volume of poetry appeared in 1782, and much of what followed was written to divert himself from his affliction of mind. His melancholy shows in many of his lyrics, but that he had a strong vein of humour is shown by his ballad *John Gilpin* and by many a line in *The Task.* The latter poem is a long one touching upon many subjects as different as sofas and poetic inspiration, but through it all are his quiet, loving descriptions of country life around the Ouse. He had a deep love for Nature and a noble patriotism.

THE POPLAR FIELD.

The poplars are felled; farewell to the shade,
And the whispering sound of the cool colonnade !
The winds play no longer and sing in the leaves,
Nor Ouse on his bosom their image receives.

Twelve years have elapsed since I first took a view
Of my favourite field, and the bank where they grew;
And now in the grass behold they are laid,
And the tree is my seat that once lent me a shade !

The blackbird has fled to another retreat,
Where the hazels afford him a screen from the heat,
And the scene where his melody charmed me before
Resounds with his sweet-flowing ditty no more.

My fugitive years are all hasting away,
And I must ere long lie as lowly as they,
With a turf on my breast, and a stone at my head,
Ere another such grove shall arise in its stead.

'Tis a sight to engage me, if anything can,
To muse on the perishing pleasures of man;
Though his life be a dream, his enjoyments, I see,
Have a being less durable even than he.

TO MARY UNWIN.

Mary ! I want a lyre with other strings,
Such aid from heaven as some have feign'd they drew
An eloquence scarce given to mortals, new
And undebased by praise of meaner things,

That ere through age or woe I shed my wings
I may record thy worth with honour due,
In verse as musical as thou art true,
And that immortalises whom it sings:—

But thou hast little need.   There is a Book
By seraphs writ with beams of heavenly light,
On which the eyes of God not rarely look,

A chronicle of actions just and bright—
There all thy deeds, my faithful Mary, shine;
And since thou own'st that praise, I spare thee mine.

TO THE SAME (1793).

The twentieth year is well-nigh past
Since first our sky was overcast;
Ah would that this might be the last !
    My Mary !

Thy spirits have a fainter flow,
I see thee daily weaker grow—
'Twas my distress that brought thee low,
    My Mary !

Thy needles, once a shining store,
For my sake restless heretofore,
Now rust disused, and shine no more,
    My Mary !

For though thou gladly wouldst fulfil
The same kind office for me still,
Thy sight now seconds not thy will,
    My Mary !

But well thou play'dst the housewife's part,
And all thy threads with magic art
Have wound themselves about this heart,
    My Mary !

Thy indistinct expressions seem
Like language utter'd in a dream;
Yet me they charm, whate'er the theme,
    My Mary !

Thy silver locks, once auburn bright,
Are still more lovely in my sight
Than golden beams of orient light,
    My Mary !

For could I view nor them nor thee,
What sight worth seeing could I see ?
The sun would rise in vain for me,
    My Mary !

Partakers of thy sad decline,
Thy hands their little force resign;
Yet, gently press'd, press gently mine,
    My Mary !

Such feebleness of limbs thou prov'st
That now at every step thou mov'st
Upheld by two; yet still thou lov'st,
    My Mary !

And still to love, though press'd with ill,
In wintry age to feel no chill,
With me is to be lovely still,
    My Mary !

But ah ! by constant heed I know
How oft the sadness that I show
Transforms thy smiles to looks of woe,
    My Mary !

And should my future lot be cast
With much resemblance of the past,
Thy worn-out heart will break at last—
    My Mary !

EPITAPH ON A HARE.

Here lies, whom hound did ne'er pursue,
    Nor swifter greyhound follow,
Whose foot ne'er tainted morning dew,
    Nor ear heard huntsman's halloo !

Old Tiney, surliest of his kind,
    Who, nursed with tender care,
And to domestic bounds confined,
    Was still a wild Jack-hare.

Though duly from my hand he took
  His pittance every night,
He did it with a jealous look,
  And, when he could, would bite.

His diet was of wheaten bread,
  And milk, and oats, and straw;
Thistles, or lettuces instead,
  With sand to scour his maw.

On twigs of hawthorn he regaled,
  On pippins' russet peel;
And when his juicy salads fail'd
  Sliced carrot pleased him well.

A Turkey carpet was his lawn,
  Whereon he loved to bound,
To skip and gambol like a fawn,
  And swing his rump around.

His frisking was at evening hours,
  For then he lost his fear,
But most before approaching showers,
  Or when a storm drew near.

Eight years and five round-rolling moons
  He thus saw steal away,
Dozing out all his idle noons,
  And every night at play.

I kept him for his humour's sake,
  For he would oft beguile
My heart of thoughts that made it ache,
  And force me to a smile.

But now, beneath this walnut shade,
    He finds his long last home,
And waits, in snug concealment laid,
    Till gentler Puss shall come.

He, still more aged, feels the shocks
    From which no care can save,
And, partner once of Tiney's box,
    Must soon partake his grave.

WHICH ONLY POETS KNOW.

There is a pleasure in poetic pains
Which only poets know.   The shifts and turns,
The expedients and inventions multiform
To which the mind resorts, in chase of terms
Though apt, yet coy, and difficult to win—
To arrest the fleeting images that fill
The mirror of the mind, and hold them fast,
And force them sit, till he has pencilled off
A faithful likeness of the forms he views;
Then to dispose his copies with such art
That each may find its most propitious light,
And shine by situation, hardly less
Than by the labour and the skill it cost,
Are occupations of the poet's mind,
So pleasing, and that steal away the thought
With such address, from themes of sad import,
That lost in his own musings, happy man !
He feels the anxieties of life, denied
Their wonted entertainment, all retire.
Such joys has he that sings.
                    (*The Task*, Book II.)

THE LEGS WITHOUT THE MAN.

From every herb and every spiry blade
Stretches a length of shadow o'er the field.
Mine, spindling into longitude immense,
In spite of gravity and sage remark
That I myself am but a fleeting shade,
Provokes me to a smile.   With eye askance
I view the muscular proportioned limb
Transformed to a lean shank. The shapeless pair,
As they designed to mock me, at my side
Take step for step, and as I near approach
The cottage, walk along the plastered wall.
Preposterous sight ! the legs without the man.

(*The Task*, Book V.)

BLAKE.

WILLIAM BLAKE (1757–1827), artist and poet, was above all a visionary. In childhood he saw God look in at his window, in manhood he saw trees full of angels, and he took down some of his later "prophetic" writings from the "dictation" of spirits. As a lyrist he is of no particular age, but his clear mystical songs are especially unexpected in the late eighteenth century. His longer works are generally far below his lyrics in beauty and artistry.

INTRODUCTION TO SONGS OF INNOCENCE.

Piping down the valleys wild,
    Piping songs of pleasant glee,
On a cloud I saw a child,
    And he laughing said to me:

" Pipe a song about a Lamb ! "
  So I piped with merry cheer.
" Piper, pipe that song again; "
  So I piped: he wept to hear.

" Drop thy pipe, thy happy pipe;
  Sing thy songs of happy cheer ! "
So I sung the same again,
  While he wept with joy to hear.

" Piper, sit thee down and write
  In a book, that all may read."
So he vanished from my sight;
  And I plucked a hollow reed,

And I made a rural pen,
  And I stained the water clear,
And I wrote my happy songs
  Every child may joy to hear.

THE LAMB.

  Little Lamb, who made thee ?
  Dost thou know who made thee ?
Gave thee life, and bid thee feed,
By the stream and o'er the mead;
Gave thee clothing of delight,
Softest clothing, woolly, bright;
Gave thee such a tender voice,
Making all the vales rejoice ?
  Little Lamb, who made thee ?
  Dost thou know who made thee ?

  Little Lamb, I'll tell thee,
  Little Lamb, I'll tell thee:
He is callèd by thy name,

For He calls Himself a Lamb.
He is meek, and He is mild;
He became a little child.
I a child, and thou a lamb,
We are callèd by His name.
  Little Lamb, God bless thee !
  Little Lamb, God bless thee !

THE TIGER.

Tiger ! Tiger ! burning bright
In the forests of the night,
What immortal hand or eye
Could frame thy fearful symmetry ?

In what distant deeps or skies
Burnt the fire of thine eyes ?
On what wings dare he aspire ?
What the hand dare seize the fire ?

And what shoulder, and what art,
Could twist the sinews of thy heart ?
And when thy heart began to beat,
What dread hand ? and what dread feet ?

What the hammer ? what the chain ?
In what furnace was thy brain ?
What the anvil ? what dread grasp
Dare its deadly terrors clasp ?

When the stars threw down their spears,
And water'd heaven with their tears,
Did he smile his work to see ?
Did he who made the Lamb make thee ?

Tiger ! Tiger ! burning bright
In the forests of the night,
What immortal hand or eye
Dare frame thy fearful symmetry ?

THE CHIMNEY SWEEPER.

When my mother died I was very young,
And my father sold me while yet my tongue
Could scarcely cry "'weep ! 'weep ! 'weep ! 'weep ! "
So your chimneys I sweep, and in soot I sleep.

There's little Tom Dacre, who cried when his head,
That curl'd like a lamb's back, was shav'd : so I said
" Hush, Tom ! never mind it, for when your head's bare
You know that the soot cannot spoil your white hair."

And so he was quiet, and that very night,
As Tom was a-sleeping, he had such a sight !—
That thousands of sweepers, Dick, Joe, Ned, and Jack,
Were all of them lock'd up in coffins of black.

And by came an Angel who had a bright key,
And he open'd the coffins and set them all free ;
Then down a green plain leaping, laughing, they run,
And wash in a river, and shine in the sun.

Then naked and white, all their bags left behind,
They rise upon clouds and sport in the wind ;
And the Angel told Tom, if he'd be a good boy,
He'd have God for his father, and never want joy.

And so Tom awoke ; and we rose in the dark,
And got with our bags and our brushes to work.
Tho' the morning was cold, Tom was happy and warm ;
So if all do their duty they need not fear harm.

HOLY THURSDAY.

'Twas on a Holy Thursday, their innocent faces clean,
The children walking two and two, in red and blue and
green,
Grey-headed beadles walk'd before, with wands as white
as snow,
Till in the high dome of Paul's they like Thames' waters
flow.

O what a multitude they seem'd, these flowers of London
town !
Seated in companies they sit with radiance all their own.
The hum of multitudes was there, but multitudes of lambs,
Thousands of little boys and girls raising their innocent
hands.

Now like a mighty wind they raise to Heaven the voice of
song,
Or like harmonious thunderings the seats of Heaven among.
Beneath them sit the agèd men, wise guardians of the poor;
Then cherish pity, lest you drive an angel from your door.

THE SCHOOLBOY.

I love to rise in a summer morn
When the birds sing on every tree;
The distant huntsman winds his horn,
And the skylark sings with me.
O ! what sweet company.

But to go to school in a summer morn
O ! it drives all joy away;
Under a cruel eye outworn,
The little ones spend the day
In sighing and dismay.

Ah ! then at times I drooping sit,
And spend many an anxious hour,
Nor in my book can I take delight,
Nor sit in learning's bower,
Worn thro' with the dreary shower.

How can the bird that is born for joy
Sit in a cage and sing ?
How can a child, when fears annoy,
But droop his tender wing,
And forget his youthful spring ?

O ! father and mother, if buds are nipp'd
And blossoms blown away,
And if the tender plants are stripp'd
Of their joy in the springing day,
By sorrow and care's dismay,

How shall the summer arise in joy,
Or the summer fruits appear ?
Or how shall we gather what griefs destroy,
Or bless the mellowing year,
When the blasts of winter appear ?

THE LAMENT OF THEL.

The daughters of the Seraphim led round their sunny
    flocks—
All but the youngest: she in paleness sought the secret
    air,
To fade away like morning beauty from her mortal day:
Down by the river of Adona her soft voice is heard,
And thus her gentle lamentation falls like morning dew:—

" O life of this our spring ! why fades the lotus of the water ?
Why fade these children of the spring, born but to smile
    and fall ?
Ah ! Thel is like a wat'ry bow, and like a parting cloud;
Like a reflection in a glass; like shadows in the water;
Like dreams of infants, like a smile upon an infant's face;
Like the dove's voice; like transient day; like music in
    the air.
Ah ! gentle may I lay me down, and gentle rest my head,
And gentle sleep the sleep of death, and gentle hear the
    voice
Of Him that walketh in the garden in the evening time."
                          (*The book of Thel.*)

From AUGURIES OF INNOCENCE.

To see a World in a grain of sand,
And a Heaven in a wild flower,
Hold Infinity in the palm of your hand,
And Eternity in an hour.

A robin readbreast in a cage
Puts all Heaven in a rage.
A dove-house fill'd with doves and pigeons
Shudders Hell thro' all its regions.
A dog starv'd at his master's gate
Predicts the ruin of the State.
A horse misus'd upon the road
Calls to Heaven for human blood.
Each outcry of the hunted hare
A fibre from the brain does tear.
A skylark wounded in the wing,
A cherubim does cease to sing. . . .
He who shall hurt the little wren
Shall never be belov'd by men. . . .

NEVER SEEK TO TELL THY LOVE.

Never seek to tell thy love,
Love that never told can be;
For the gentle wind does move
Silently, invisibly.

I told my love, I told my love,
I told her all my heart;
Trembling, cold, in ghastly fears,
Ah! she doth depart.

Soon as she was gone from me,
A traveller came by,
Silently, invisibly:
He took her with a sigh.

A NEW JERUSALEM.

And did those feet in ancient time
  Walk upon England's mountains green?
And was the holy Lamb of God
  On England's pleasant pastures seen?

And did the Countenance Divine
  Shine forth upon our clouded hills?
And was Jerusalem builded here
  Among these dark Satanic Mills?

Bring me my bow of burning gold!
  Bring me my arrows of desire!
Bring me my spear! O clouds, unfold!
  Bring me my chariot of fire!

I will not cease from mental fight,
  Nor shall my sword sleep in my hand,
Till we have built Jerusalem
  In England's green and pleasant land.

BURNS.

ROBERT BURNS (1759-1796), son of a small farmer near Ayr, had a hard life, much of it from boyhood being spent in farm-work. His solace was wine, love, and poetry, and wine and love inspire many of his songs; but his struggle also found expression in his satires, and in his republicanism founded on the conviction that "a man's a man for a' that." Hilarity, passion, pathos, humour, love of animals, scorn of hypocrisy—these are some of his many veins. Well acquainted with the traditional songs of the Scottish Lowlands he owed the suggestion of many of his poems to these popular tunes. Notable among his longer poems are *Tam O' Shanter*, *Hallowe'en*, and *The Cottar's Saturday Night*.

MY JEAN.

Of a' the airts the wind can blaw
   I dearly like the West,
For there the bonnie lassie lives,
   The lassie I lo'e best:
There wild woods grow, and rivers row,
   And mony a hill between;
But day and night my fancy's flight
   Is ever wi' my Jean.

I see her in the dewy flowers,
   I see her sweet and fair;
I hear her in the tunefu' birds,
   I hear her charm the air:
There's not a bonnie flower that springs
   By fountain, shaw, or green,
There's not a bonnie bird that sings
   But minds me o' my Jean.

MY BONNIE MARY.

Go fetch to me a pint o' wine,
   An' fill it in a silver tassie,

That I may drink, before I go,
  A service to my bonnie lassie.
The boat rocks at the pier o' Leith,
  Fu' loud the wind blaws frae the ferry,
The ship rides by the Berwick-law,
  And I maun leave my bonnie Mary.

The trumpets sound, the banners fly,
  The glittering spears are rankèd ready;
The shouts o' war are heard afar,
  The battle closes thick and bloody;
But it's no the roar o' sea or shore
  Wad make me langer wish to tarry;
Nor shout o' war that's heard afar—
  It's leaving thee, my bonnie Mary !

A RED, RED ROSE.

O my Luve's like a red, red rose
  That's newly sprung in June:
O my Luve's like the melodie
  That's sweetly play'd in tune.

As fair art thou, my bonnie lass,
  So deep in luve am I:
And I will luve thee still, my dear,
  Till a' the seas gang dry:

Till a' the seas gang dry, my dear,
  And the rocks melt wi' the sun;
I will luve thee still, my dear,
  While the sands o' life shall run.

And fare thee weel, my only Luve !
  And fare the weel awhile.
And I will come again, my Luve,
  Tho' it were ten thousand mile.

BONNIE LESLEY.

O saw ye bonnie Lesley,
   As she gaed o'er the border?
She's gane, like Alexander,
   To spread her conquests farther.

To see her is to love her,
   And love but her for ever;
For nature made her what she is,
   And ne'er made sic anither!

Thou art a queen, fair Lesley,
   Thy subjects we, before thee;
Thou art divine, fair Lesley,
   The hearts o' men adore thee.

The deil he could na scaith thee,
   Or aught that wad belang thee;
He'd look into thy bonnie face,
   And say " I canna wrang thee!"

The Powers aboon will tent thee,
   Misfortune sha' na steer thee;
Thou'rt like themselves sae lovely
   That ill they'll ne'er let near thee.

Return again, fair Lesley,
   Return to Caledonie!
That we may brag we hae a lass
   There's nane again sae bonnie.

DUNCAN GRAY.

Duncan Gray cam here to woo,
  Ha, ha, the wooing o't;
On blythe Yule night we were fou,
  Ha, ha, the wooing o't:
Maggie coost her head fu' high,
Looked asklent and unco skeigh,
Gart poor Duncan stand abeigh;
  Ha, ha, the wooing o't !

Duncan fleech'd, and Duncan pray'd;
Meg was deaf as Ailsa Craig;
Duncan sighed baith out and in,
Grat his een baith bleer't and blin',
Spak o' lowpin ower a linn !

Time and chance are but a tide,
Slighted love is sair to bide;
Shall I, like a fool, quoth he,
For a haughty hizzie dee ?
She may gae to—France for me !

How it comes let doctors tell,
Meg grew sick—as he grew heal;
Something in her bosom wrings,
For relief a sigh she brings;
And O, her een, they spak sic things.

Duncan was a lad o' grace;
Maggie's was a piteous case;
Duncan couldna be her death,
Swelling pity smoor'd his wrath;
Now they're crouse and canty baith:
  Ha, ha, the wooing o't !

TO A FIELD-MOUSE.

Wee, sleekit, cow'rin, tim'rous beastie,
O what a panic's in thy breastie !
Thou need na start awa sae hasty,
Wi' bickering brattle !
I wad be laith to rin and chase thee
Wi' murd'ring pattle !

I'm truly sorry man's dominion
Has broken nature's social union,
An' justifies that ill opinion
Which makes thee startle
At me, thy poor earth-born companion,
An' fellow-mortal !

I doubt na, whyles, but thou may thieve;
What then ? poor beastie, thou maun live!
A daimen icker in a thrave
'S a sma' request:
I'll get a blessin' wi' the lave,
And never miss't !

Thy wee bit housie, too, in ruin !
Its silly wa's the win's are strewin':
And naething, now, to big a new ane,
O' foggage green !
And bleak December's winds ensuin'
Baith snell an' keen !

Thou saw the fields laid bare and waste
An' weary winter comin' fast,
An' cozie here, beneath the blast,
Thou thought to dwell,
Till, crash ! the cruel coulter past
Out thro' thy cell.

That wee bit heap o' leaves an' stibble
Has cost thee mony a weary nibble !
Now thou's turn'd out, for a' thy trouble,
But house or hald,
To thole the winter's sleety dribble
An' cranreuch cauld !

But, Mousie, thou art no thy lane
In proving foresight may be vain:
The best laid schemes o' mice an' men
Gang aft a-gley,
An' lea'e us nought but grief an' pain,
For promised joy.

Still thou art blest, compared wi' me !
The present only toucheth thee:
But, och ! I backward cast my e'e
On prospects drear !
An' forward, tho' I canna see,
I guess and fear !

TO A MOUNTAIN DAISY.

Wee, modest, crimson-tippèd flower,
Thou's met me in an evil hour;
For I maun crush amang the stoure
Thy slender stem:
To spare thee now is past my power,
Thou bonnie gem.

Alas ! it's no thy neebor sweet,
The bonnie lark, companion meet !
Bending thee 'mang the dewy weet
Wi' speckled breast,
When upward-springing, blithe, to greet
The purpling east.

Cauld blew the bitter-biting north
Upon thy early humble birth;
Yet cheerfully thou glinted forth
   Amid the storm;
Scarce reared above the parent-earth
   Thy tender form.

The flaunting flowers our gardens yield,
High sheltering woods and wa's maun shield,
But thou, beneath the random bield
   O' clod, or stane,
Adorns the histie stubble-field,
   Unseen, alane.

There, in thy scanty mantle clad,
Thy snawie bosom sunward spread,
Thou lifts thy unassuming head
   In humble guise;
But now the share uptears thy bed,
   And low thou lies !

       (Abridged.)

YE BANKS AND BRAES O' BONNIE DOON.

Ye banks and braes o' bonnie Doon,
 How can ye bloom sae fair ?
How can ye chant, ye little birds,
 And I sae fu' o' care ?

Thou'll break my heart, thou bonnie bird
 That sings upon the bough;
Thou minds me o' the happy days
 When my fause Luve was true.

Thou'll break my heart, thou bonnie bird
　　That sings beside thy mate;
For sae I sat, and sae I sang,
　　And wist na o' my fate.

Aft hae I roved by bonnie Doon
　　To see the woodbine twine,
And ilka bird sang o' its love;
　　And sae did I o' mine.

Wi' lightsome heart I pu'd a rose,
　　Frae off its thorny tree;
And my fause luver staw the rose,
　　But left the thorn wi' me.

JOHN ANDERSON, MY JO.

John Anderson my jo, John,
　　When we were first acquent,
Your locks were like the raven,
　　Your bonnie brow was brent;
But now your brow is bald, John,
　　Your locks are like the snow;
But blessings on your frosty pow,
　　John Anderson my jo.

John Anderson my jo, John,
　　We clamb the hill thegither;
And mony a cantie day, John,
　　We've had wi' ane anither:
Now we maun totter down, John,
　　And hand in hand we'll go,
And sleep thegither at the foot,
　　John Anderson my jo.

HOGG.

JAMES HOGG (1770-1835) is perhaps better known as the Ettrick Shepherd. With Scott, John Wilson (" Christopher North "), Jeffreys, and others, he was one of those who made Edinburgh a great literary centre in the twenties of last century. Wilson made him one of the characters in his spate of discussion and merriment entitled *Noctes Ambrosianae*.

A BOY'S SONG.

Where the pools are bright and deep,
Where the grey trout lies asleep,
Up the river and over the lea,
That's the way for Billy and me.

Where the blackbird sings the latest,
Where the hawthorn blooms the sweetest,
Where the nestlings chirp and flee,
That's the way for Billy and me.

Where the mowers mow the cleanest,
Where the hay lies thick and greenest,
There to track the homeward bee,
That's the way for Billy and me.

Where the hazel bank is steepest,
Where the shadow falls the deepest,
Where the clustering nuts fall free,
That's the way for Billy and me.

Why the boys should drive away
Little sweet maidens from the play,
Or love to banter and fight so well,
That's the thing I never could tell.

But this I know, I love to play
Through the meadow, among the hay;
Up the water and over the lea,
That's the way for Billy and me.

WORDSWORTH.

WILLIAM WORDSWORTH (1770–1850) spent his boyhood in the Lake District, went to St. John's College, Cambridge, and then travelled in France. At first he was an ardent supporter of the Revolution then in progress, but after a while its excesses disillusioned him, and he was left sick at heart. Nature and the friendship of Coleridge made him whole again, and he became the poetic interpreter of Nature—in Matthew Arnold's phrase, " the priest to us all of the wonder and bloom of the world." *Lyrical Ballads* (1798) first showed his real power, and for some ten years after that date he continued to write with full inspiration. Until his death he was never silent, but he less often reached the heights. At first unpopular, his poetry came into its own about 1825, and in 1843 he was appointed Poet Laureate. *The Prelude* is his poetic autobiography.

THE DAFFODILS.

I wandered lonely as a cloud
That floats on high o'er vales and hills,
When all at once I saw a crowd,
A host of golden daffodils,
Beside the lake, beneath the trees
Fluttering and dancing in the breeze.

Continuous as the stars that shine
And twinkle on the milky way,
They stretched in never-ending line

Along the margin of a bay:
Ten thousand saw I at a glance
Tossing their heads in sprightly dance.

The waves beside them danced, but they
Out-did the sparkling waves in glee:—
A Poet could not but be gay
In such a jocund company!
I gazed—and gazed—but little thought
What wealth the show to me had brought;

For oft, when on my couch I lie
In vacant or in pensive mood,
They flash upon that inward eye
Which is the bliss of solitude,
And then my heart with pleasure fills,
And dances with the daffodils.

LINES

*Composed a few miles above Tintern Abbey, on Revisiting
the banks of the Wye during a Tour, July* 13, 1798.

Five years have passed; five summers, with the length
Of five long winters! and again I hear
These waters, rolling from their mountain-springs
With a sweet inland murmur.—Once again
Do I behold these steep and lofty cliffs,
That on a wild secluded scene impress
Thoughts of more deep seclusion; and connect
The landscape with the quiet of the sky.
The day is come when I again repose
Here, under this dark sycamore, and view
These plots of cottage-ground, these orchard-tufts,
Which at this season, with their unripe fruits,
Are clad in one green hue, and lose themselves

Among the woods and copses, nor disturb
The wild green landscape.   Once again I see
These hedgerows, hardly hedgerows, little lines
Of sportive wood run wild: these pastoral farms,
Green to the very door; and wreaths of smoke
Sent up, in silence, from among the trees !
With some uncertain notice, as might seem
Of vagrant dwellers in the houseless woods,
Or of some Hermit's cave, where by his fire
The Hermit sits alone.

                        These beauteous forms,
Through a long absence, have not been to me
As is a landscape to a blind man's eye:
But oft, in lonely rooms, and 'mid the din
Of towns and cities, I have owed to them,
In hours of weariness, sensations sweet,
Felt in the blood, and felt along the heart;
And passing even into my purer mind,
With tranquil restoration:—feelings too
Of unremembered pleasure: such, perhaps,
As have no slight or trivial influence
On that best portion of a good man's life,
His little, nameless, unremembered acts
Of kindness and of love.   Nor less, I trust,
To them I may have owed another gift,
Of aspect more sublime; that blessed mood,
In which the burthen of the mystery,
In which the heavy and the weary weight
Of all this unintelligible world,
Is lightened:—that serene and blessed mood,
In which the affections gently lead us on,—
Until, the breath of this corporeal frame
And even the motion of our human blood
Almost suspended, we are laid asleep
In body, and become a living soul:
While with an eye made quiet by the **power**

Of harmony, and the deep power of joy,
We see into the life of things.
                              If this
Be but a vain belief, yet, oh ! how oft—
In darkness, and amid the many shapes
Of joyless daylight; when the fretful stir
Unprofitable, and the fever of the world,
Have hung upon the beatings of my heart—
How oft, in spirit, have I turned to thee,
O sylvan Wye ! thou wanderer thro' the woods,
How often has my spirit turned to thee !

    And now, with gleams of half-extinguished thought,
With many recognitions dim and faint,
And somewhat of a sad perplexity,
The picture of the mind revives again:
While here I stand, not only with the sense
Of present pleasure, but with pleasing thoughts
That in this moment there is life and food
For future years.   And so I dare to hope,
Though changed, no doubt, from what I was when first
I came among these hills; when like a roe
I bounded o'er the mountains, by the sides
Of the deep rivers, and the lonely streams,
Wherever nature led: more like a man
Flying from something that he dreads than one
Who sought the thing he loved.   For nature then
(The coarser pleasures of my boyish days,
And their glad animal movements all gone by)
To me was all in all.—I cannot paint
What then I was.   The sounding cataract
Haunted me like a passion: the tall rock,
The mountain, and the deep and gloomy wood,
Their colours and their forms, were then to me
An appetite; a feeling and a love,
That had no need of a remoter charm,

By thought supplied, nor any interest
Unborrowed from the eye.—That time is past,
And all its aching joys are now no more,
And all its dizzy raptures. Not for this
Faint I, nor mourn nor murmur; other gifts
Have followed; for such loss, I would believe,
Abundant recompense. For I have learned
To look on nature, not as in the hour
Of thoughtless youth; but hearing oftentimes
The still, sad music of humanity,
Nor harsh nor grating, though of ample power
To chasten and subdue. And I have felt
A presence that disturbs me with the joy
Of elevated thoughts: a sense sublime
Of something far more deeply interfused,
Whose dwelling is the light of setting suns,
And the round ocean and the living air,
And the blue sky, and in the mind of man:
A motion and a spirit, that impels
All thinking things, all objects of all thought,
And rolls through all things. Therefore am I still
A lover of the meadows and the woods,
And mountains; and of all that we behold
From this green earth; of all the mighty world
Of eye and ear, both what they half create,
And what perceive; well pleased to recognise
In nature and the language of the sense
The anchor of my purest thoughts, the nurse,
The guide, the guardian of my heart, and soul
Of all my moral being.
              Nor perchance
If I were not thus taught, should I the more
Suffer my genial spirits to decay:
For thou art with me, here, upon the banks
Of this fair river; thou, my dearest Friend,
My dear, dear Friend; and in thy voice I catch

The language of my former heart, and read
My former pleasures in the shooting lights
Of thy wild eyes.   Oh ! yet a little while
May I behold in thee what I was once,
My dear, dear Sister ! and this prayer I make,
Knowing that Nature never did betray
The heart that loved her; 'tis her privilege,
Through all the years of this our life, to lead
From joy to joy: for she can so inform
The mind that is within us, so impress
With quietness and beauty, and so feed
With lofty thoughts, that neither evil tongues,
Rash judgments, nor the sneers of selfish men,
Nor greetings where no kindness is, nor all
The dreary intercourse of daily life,
Shall e'er prevail against us, or disturb
Our cheerful faith, that all which we behold
Is full of blessings.   Therefore let the moon
Shine on thee in thy solitary walk;
And let the misty mountain winds be free
To blow against thee: and, in after years,
When these wild ecstasies shall be matured
Into a sober pleasure, when thy mind
Shall be a mansion for all lovely forms,
Thy memory be as a dwelling-place
For all sweet sounds and harmonies; oh ! then,
If solitude, or fear, or pain, or grief,
Should be thy portion, with what healing thoughts
Of tender joy wilt thou remember me,
And these my exhortations !   Nor perchance—
If I should be where I no more can hear
Thy voice, nor catch from thy wild eyes these gleams
Of past existence—wilt thou then forget
That on the banks of this delightful stream
We stood together; and that I, so long
A worshipper of Nature, hither came

Unwearied in that service: rather say
With warmer love, oh! with far deeper zeal
Of holier love. Nor wilt thou then forget,
That after many wanderings, many years
Of absence, these steep woods and lofty cliffs,
And this green pastoral landscape, were to me
More dear, both for themselves and for thy sake!

THE EDUCATION OF NATURE.

Three years she grew in sun and shower,
Then Nature said, " A lovelier flower
On earth was never sown;
This Child I to myself will take;
She shall be mine, and I will make
A Lady of my own.

" Myself will to my darling be
Both law and impulse: and with me
The Girl, in rock and plain,
In earth and heaven, in glade and bower,
Shall feel an overseeing power
To kindle or restrain.

" She shall be sportive as the fawn
That wild with glee across the lawn
Or up the mountain springs;
And hers shall be the breathing balm,
And hers the silence and the calm
Of mute insensate things.

" The floating clouds their state shall lend
To her; for her the willow bend;
Nor shall she fail to see
Even in the motions of the Storm
Grace that shall mould the Maiden's form
By silent sympathy.

" The stars of midnight shall be dear
To her; and she shall lean her ear
In many a secret place
Where rivulets dance their wayward round,
And beauty born of murmuring sound
Shall pass into her face.

" And vital feelings of delight
Shall rear her form to stately height,
Her virgin bosom swell;
Such thoughts to Lucy I will give
While she and I together live
Here in this happy dell."

Thus Nature spake—The work was done—
How soon my Lucy's race was run !
She died, and left to me
This heath, this calm, and quiet scene;
The memory of what has been,
And never more will be.

IF LUCY SHOULD BE DEAD.

Strange fits of passion have I known:
And I will dare to tell,
But in the Lover's ear alone,
What once to me befell.

When she I loved looked every day
Fresh as a rose in June,
I to her cottage bent my way,
Beneath an evening-moon.

Upon the moon I fixed my eye,
All over the wide lea;

With quickening pace my horse drew nigh
Those paths so dear to me.

And now we reached the orchard-plot;
And, as we climbed the hill,
The sinking moon to Lucy's cot
Came near, and nearer still.

In one of those sweet dreams I slept,
Kind Nature's gentlest boon !
And all the while my eyes I kept
On the descending moon.

My horse moved on; hoof after hoof
He raised, and never stopped:
When down behind the cottage roof,
At once, the bright moon dropped.

What fond and wayward thoughts will slide
Into a Lover's head !
" O mercy ! " to myself I cried,
" If Lucy should be dead ! "

WHEN LUCY CEASED TO BE.

She dwelt among the untrodden ways
    Beside the springs of Dove;
A maid whom there were none to praise,
    And very few to love:

A violet by a mossy stone
    Half-hidden from the eye !
—Fair as a star, when only one
    Is shining in the sky.

She lived unknown, and few could know
    When Lucy ceased to be;
But she is in her grave, and, O !
    The difference to me !

I TRAVELLED AMONG UNKNOWN MEN.

I travelled among unknown men
    In lands beyond the sea;
Nor, England ! did I know till then
    What love I bore to thee.

'Tis past, that melancholy dream !
    Nor will I quit thy shore
A second time, for still I seem
    To love thee more and more.

Among thy mountains did I feel
    The joy of my desire;
And she I cherished turn'd her wheel
    Beside an English fire.

Thy mornings showed, thy nights concealed
    The bowers where Lucy played;
And thine too is the last green field
    That Lucy's eyes surveyed.

THE SOLITARY REAPER.

Behold her, single in the field,
Yon solitary Highland Lass !
Reaping and singing by herself;
Stop here or gently pass !

Alone she cuts and binds the grain,
And sings a melancholy strain;
O listen! for the vale profound
Is overflowing with the sound.

No nightingale did ever chaunt
More welcome notes to weary bands
Of travellers in some shady haunt,
Among Arabian sands:
A voice so thrilling ne'er was heard
In spring-time from the Cuckoo-bird,
Breaking the silence of the seas
Among the farthest Hebrides.

Will no one tell me what she sings?
Perhaps the plaintive numbers flow
For old, unhappy, far-off things,
And battles long ago:
Or is it some more humble lay,
Familiar matter of to-day?
Some natural sorrow, loss, or pain,
That has been, and may be again?

Whate'er the theme, the Maiden sang
As if her song could have no ending;
I saw her singing at her work,
And o'er the sickle bending;—
I listened, motionless and still;
And, as I mounted up the hill,
The music in my heart I bore,
Long after it was heard no more.

INTIMATIONS OF IMMORTALITY

FROM RECOLLECTIONS OF EARLY CHILDHOOD.

There was a time when meadow, grove, and stream,
The earth, and every common sight,
            To me did seem
            Apparelled in celestial light,
The glory and the freshness of a dream.
It is not now as it hath been of yore;—
            Turn wheresoe'er I may,
            By night or day,
The things which I have seen I now can see no more.

            The Rainbow comes and goes,
            And lovely is the Rose,
            The Moon doth with delight
Look round her when the heavens are bare,
            Waters on a starry night
            Are beautiful and fair;
        The sunshine is a glorious birth;
        But yet I know, where'er I go,
That there hath past away a glory from the earth.

Now, while the birds thus sing a joyous song,
        And while the young lambs bound
        As to the tabor's sound,
To me alone there came a thought of grief:
A timely utterance gave that thought relief,
        And I again am strong:
The cataracts blow their trumpets from the steep;
No more shall grief of mine the season wrong;
I hear the Echoes through the mountains throng,
The Winds come to me from the fields of sleep,
        And all the earth is gay;
            Land and sea
        Give themselves up to jollity,
            And with the heart of May

Doth every Beast keep holiday;—
Thou Child of Joy
Shout round me, let me hear thy shouts, thou happy
Shepherd-boy !

Ye blessèd Creatures, I have heard the call
Ye to each other make; I see
The heavens laugh with you in your jubilee;
My heart is at your festival,
My head hath its coronal,
The fulness of your bliss, I feel—I feel it all.
Oh evil day ! if I were sullen
While Earth herself is adorning,
This sweet May-morning,
And the children are culling
On every side,
In a thousand valleys far and wide,
Fresh flowers; while the sun shines warm,
And the Babe leaps up on his Mother's arm:—
I hear, I hear, with joy I hear !
—But there's a Tree, of many, one,
A single Field which I have looked upon,
Both of them speak of something that is gone:
The Pansy at my feet
Doth the same tale repeat:
Whither is fled the visionary gleam ?
Where is it now, the glory and the dream ?

Our birth is but a sleep and a forgetting:
The Soul that rises with us, our life's Star,
Hath had elsewhere its setting,
And cometh from afar:
Not in entire forgetfulness,
And not in utter nakedness,
But trailing clouds of glory do we come
From God, who is our home:

Heaven lies about us in our infancy !
Shades of the prison-house begin to close
   Upon the growing Boy,
But He beholds the light, and whence it flows,
   He sees it in his joy;
The Youth, who daily farther from the east
   Must travel, still is Nature's Priest,
   And by the vision splendid
   Is on his way attended;
At length the Man perceives it die away,
And fade into the light of common day.

Earth fills her lap with pleasures of her own;
Yearnings she hath in her own natural kind,
And, even with something of a Mother's mind,
   And no unworthy aim,
   The homely Nurse doth all she can
To make her Foster-child, her Inmate Man,
   Forget the glories he hath known,
And that imperial palace whence he came.

Behold the Child among his new-born blisses,
A six years' Darling of a pigmy size !
See, where 'mid work of his own hand he lies,
Fretted by sallies of his mother's kisses,
With light upon him from his father's eyes !
See, at his feet, some little plan or chart,
Some fragment from his dream of human life,
Shaped by himself with newly-learnèd art;
   A wedding or a festival,
   A mourning or a funeral;
   And this hath now his heart,
   And unto this he frames his song:
   Then will he fit his tongue
To dialogues of business, love, or strife;
   But it will not be long
   Ere this be thrown aside,

And with new joy and pride
The little Actor cons another part;
Filling from time to time his " humorous stage "
With all the Persons, down to palsied Age,
That Life brings with her in her equipage;
　　　As if his whole vocation
　　　Were endless imitation.

Thou, whose exterior semblance doth belie
　　　Thy Soul's immensity;
Thou best Philosopher, who yet dost keep
Thy heritage, thou Eye among the blind,
That, deaf and silent, read'st the eternal deep,
Haunted for ever by the eternal mind—
　　　Mighty Prophet! Seer blest!
　　　On whom those truths do rest,
Which we are toiling all our lives to find,
In darkness lost, the darkness of the grave;
Thou, over whom thy Immortality
Broods like the Day, a Master o'er a slave,
A Presence which is not to be put by;
Thou little Child, yet glorious in the might
Of heaven-born freedom on thy being's height,
Why with such earnest pains dost thou provoke
The years to bring the inevitable yoke,
Thus blindly with thy blessedness at strife?
Full soon thy Soul shall have her earthly freight,
And custom lie upon thee with a weight,
Heavy as frost, and deep almost as life!

　　　O joy! that in our embers
　　　Is something that doth live,
　　　That nature yet remembers
　　　What was so fugitive!
The thought of our past years in me doth breed
Perpetual benediction: not indeed
For that which is most worthy to be blest;

Delight and liberty, the simple creed
Of childhood, whether busy or at rest,
With new fledged hope still fluttering in his breast:—
      Not for these I raise
      The song of thanks and praise;
    But for those obstinate questionings
    Of sense and outward things,
    Fallings from us, vanishings;
    Blank misgivings of a Creature
Moving about in worlds not realised,
High instincts before which our mortal Nature
Did tremble like a guilty thing surprised:
      But for those first affections,
      Those shadowy recollections,
    Which, be they what they may,
Are yet the fountain-light of all our day,
Are yet a master-light of all our seeing;
    Uphold us, cherish, and have power to make
Our noisy years seem moments in the being
Of the eternal Silence: truths that wake,
      To perish never;
Which neither listlessness, nor mad endeavour,
      Nor Man nor Boy,
Nor all that is at enmity with joy,
Can utterly abolish or destroy!
    Hence in a season of calm weather
      Though inland far we be,
Our Souls have sight of that immortal sea
      Which brought us hither,
     Can in a moment travel thither,
And see the Children sport upon the shore,
And hear the mighty waters rolling evermore.

Then sing, ye Birds, sing, sing a joyous song!
      And let the young Lambs bound
      As to the tabor's sound!

We in thought will join your throng,
  Ye that pipe and ye that play,
  Ye that through your hearts to-day
  Feel the gladness of the May !
What though the radiance which was once so bright
Be now for ever taken from my sight,
  Though nothing can bring back the hour
Of splendour in the grass, of glory in the flower;
  We will grieve not, rather find
  Strength in what remains behind;
  In the primal sympathy
  Which having been must ever be;
  In the soothing thoughts that spring
  Out of human suffering;
  In the faith that looks through death,
In years that bring the philosophic mind.

And O, ye Fountains, Meadows, Hills and Groves,
Forebode not any severing of our loves !
Yet in my heart of hearts I feel your might;
I only have relinquished one delight
To live beneath your more habitual sway.
I love the Brooks which down their channels fret,
Even more than when I tripped lightly as they;
The innocent brightness of a new-born Day
  Is lovely yet;
The Clouds that gather round the setting sun
Do take a sober colouring from an eye
That hath kept watch o'er man's mortality;
Another race hath been, and other palms are won.
Thanks to the human heart by which we live,
Thanks to its tenderness, its joys, and fears,
To me the meanest flower that blows can give
Thoughts that do often lie too deep for tears.

WESTMINSTER BRIDGE, SEPTEMBER 3RD, 1802.

Earth has not any thing to show more fair:
Dull would he be of soul who could pass by
A sight so touching in its majesty:
This City now doth, like a garment, wear
The beauty of the morning; silent, bare,
Ships, towers, domes, theatres, and temples lie
Open unto the fields, and to the sky;
All bright and glittering in the smokeless air.
Never did sun more beautifully steep
In his first splendour, valley, rock, or hill;
Ne'er saw I, never felt, a calm so deep!
The river glideth at his own sweet will:
Dear God! the very houses seem asleep;
And all that mighty heart is lying still!

KING'S COLLEGE CHAPEL, CAMBRIDGE.

Tax not the royal Saint with vain expense,
With ill-matched aims the Architect who planned—
Albeit labouring for a scanty band
Of white-robed Scholars only—this immense
And glorious Work of fine intelligence!
Give all thou canst; high Heaven rejects the lore
Of nicely-calculated less or more;
So deemed the man who fashioned for the sense
These lofty pillars, spread that branching roof
Self-poised, and scooped into ten thousand cells,
Where light and shade repose, where music dwells
Lingering—and wandering on as loth to die;
Like thoughts whose very sweetness yieldeth proof
That they were born for immortality.

BRITISH FREEDOM.

It is not to be thought of that the Flood
Of British freedom, which, to the open sea

Of the world's praise, from dark antiquity
Hath flowed, " with pomp of waters, unwithstood,"
Roused though it be full often to a mood
Which spurns the check of salutary bands,
That this most famous Stream in bogs and sands
Should perish; and to evil and to good
Be lost for ever.   In our halls is hung
Armoury of the invincible Knights of old:
We must be free or die, who speak the tongue
That Shakespeare spake; the faith and morals hold
Which Milton held.—In everything we are sprung
Of Earth's first blood, have titles manifold.

RATHER A PAGAN.

The world is too much with us; late and soon,
Getting and spending, we lay waste our powers:
Little we see in Nature that is ours;
We have given our hearts away, a sordid boon.
This Sea that bares her bosom to the moon;
The winds that will be howling at all hours,
And are up-gathered now like sleeping flowers;
For this, for everything, we are out of tune;
It moves us not.—Great God ! I'd rather be
A Pagan suckled in a creed outworn;
So might I, standing on this pleasant lea,
Have glimpses that would make me less forlorn;
Have sight of Proteus rising from the sea;
Or hear old Triton blow his wreathèd horn.

AFTER-THOUGHT TO DUDDON SONNETS

I thought of Thee, my partner and my guide,
As being past away.—Vain sympathies !
For, backward, Duddon ! as I cast my eyes,
I see what was, and is, and will abide;
Still glides the Stream, and shall for ever glide;

The Form remains, the Function never dies;
While we, the brave, the mighty, and the wise,
We Men, who in our morn of youth defied
The elements, must vanish;—be it so !
Enough, if something from our hands have power
To live, and act, and serve the future hour;
And if, as toward the silent tomb we go,
Through love, through hope, and faith's transcendent
    dower,
We feel that we are greater than we know.

SCOTT.

SIR WALTER SCOTT (1770–1832) was called to the
Scotch bar, and became Sheriff of Selkirk in 1799 and
one of the Principal Clerks to the Court of Session in
1812. These posts left him leisure for the pursuit
of his antiquarian and literary tastes. At first he
rescued much old poetry in his *Minstrelsy of the Scottish
Border*; then beginning in 1805 with *The Lay of the
Last Minstrel* came his galloping, picturesque narrative
poems whose amazing popularity gave way only to the
more passionate and highly-coloured poems of Byron.
In 1814 with *Waverley* and the novels which, for
fifteen years, followed he conquered a fresh field. He
created with the rapidity and ease of a literary giant,
and was hailed as " the Wizard of the North."

COUNTY GUY.

Ah ! County Guy, the hour is nigh,
    The sun has left the lea,
The orange flower perfumes the bower,
    The breeze is on the sea.
The lark, his lay who thrill'd all day,
    Sits hush'd his partner nigh;
Breeze, bird, and flower, confess the hour,
    But where is County Guy ?

The village maid steals through the shade,
　　Her shepherd's suit to hear;
To beauty shy, by lattice high,
　　Sings high-born Cavalier.
The Star of Love, all stars above,
　　Now reigns o'er earth and sky;
And high and low the influence know—
　　But where is County Guy!

BONNIE DUNDEE.

To the Lords of Convention 'twas Claver'se who spoke,
" Ere the King's crown shall fall there are crowns to be
　　broke;
So let each Cavalier who loves honour and me,
Come follow the bonnet of Bonny Dundee.
　　Come fill up my cup, come fill up my can,
　　Come saddle your horses, and call up your men;
　　Come open the West Port, and let me gang free,
　　And it's room for the bonnets of Bonny Dundee ! "

Dundee he is mounted, he rides up the street,
The bells are rung backward, the drums they are beat;
But the Provost, douce man, said, " Just e'en let him be,
The Gude Town is weel quit of that Deil of Dundee."
　　Come fill up my cup, etc.

As he rode down the sanctified bends of the Bow,
Ilk carline was flyting and shaking her pow;
But the young plants of grace they look'd couthie and slee,
Thinking, " Luck to thy bonnet, thou Bonny Dundee ! "
　　Come fill up my cup, etc.

With sour-featured Whigs the Grassmarket was cramm'd
As if half the West had set tryst to be hang'd;

There was spite in each look, there was fear in each e'e,
As they watch'd for the bonnets of Bonny Dundee.
   .   Come fill up my cup, etc.

These cowls of Kilmarnock had spits and had spears,
And lang-hafted gullies to kill Cavaliers;
But they shrunk to close-heads, and the causeway was free,
At the toss of the bonnet of Bonny Dundee.
     Come fill up my cup, etc.

He spurr'd to the foot of the proud Castle rock,
And with the gay Gordon he gallantly spoke;
" Let Mons Meg and her marrows speak twa words or three,
For the love of the bonnet of Bonny Dundee."
     Come fill up my cup, etc.

The Gordon demands of him which way he goes—
" Where'er shall direct me the shade of Montrose !
Your Grace in short space shall hear tidings of me,
Or that low lies the bonnet of Bonny Dundee.
     Come fill up my cup, etc.

" There are hills beyond Pentland, and lands beyond Forth,
If there's lords in the Lowlands, there's chiefs in the North;
There are wild Duniewassals, three thousand times three,
Will cry *hoigh* ! for the bonnet of Bonny Dundee.
     Come fill up my cup, etc.

" There's brass on the target of barken'd bull-hide;
There's steel in the scabbard that dangles beside;
The brass shall be burnish'd, the steel shall flash free,
At a toss of the bonnet of Bonny Dundee.
     Come fill up my cup, etc.

" Away to the hills, to the caves, to the rocks—
Ere I own an usurper, I'll couch with the fox;

And tremble, false Whigs, in the midst of your glee,
You have not seen the last of my bonnet and me ! "
　　Come fill up my cup, etc.

He waved his proud hand, and the trumpets were blown,
The kettle-drums clash'd, and the horsemen rode on,
Till on Ravelston's cliffs and on Clermiston's lee,
Died away the wild war-notes of Bonny Dundee.
　　Come fill up my cup, come fill up my can,
　　Come saddle the horses and call up the men,
　　Come open your gates, and let me gae free,
　　For it's up with the bonnets of Bonny Dundee !

THE SUN UPON THE WEIRDLAW HILL.

　　The sun upon the Weirdlaw Hill,
　　　　In Ettrick's vale, is sinking sweet;
　　The westland wind is hush and still,
　　　　The lake lies sleeping at my feet.
　　Yet not the landscape to mine eye
　　　　Bears those bright hues that once it bore;
　　Though evening, with her richest dye,
　　　　Flames o'er the hill of Ettrick's shore.

　　With listless look along the plain,
　　　　I see Tweed's silver current glide,
　　And coldly mark the holy fane
　　　　Of Melrose rise in ruin'd pride.
　　The quiet lake, the balmy air,
　　　　The hill, the stream, the tower, the tree,—
　　Are they still such as once they were ?
　　　　Or is the dreary change in me ?

　　Alas, the warp'd and broken board,
　　　　How can it bear the painter's dye !

The harp of strain'd and tuneless chord,
　How to the minstrel's skill reply !
To aching eyes each landscape lowers,
　To feverish pulse each gale blows chill ;
And Araby's or Eden's bowers
　Were barren as this moorland hill.

CORONACH.

He is gone on the mountain,
　He is lost to the forest,
Like a summer-dried fountain,
　When our need was the sorest.
The font reappearing
　From the raindrops shall borrow,
But to us comes no cheering,
　To Duncan no morrow !

The hand of the reaper
　Takes the ears that are hoary,
But the voice of the weeper
　Wails manhood in glory.
The autumn winds rushing
　Waft the leaves that are searest,
But our flower was in flushing
　When blighting was nearest.

Fleet foot on the correi,
　Sage counsel in cumber,
Red hand in the foray,
　How sound is thy slumber !
Like the dew on the mountain,
　Like the foam on the river,
Like the bubble on the fountain,
　Thou art gone ; and for ever !

PROUD MAISIE.

Proud Maisie is in the wood,
    Walking so early;
Sweet Robin sits on the bush,
    Singing so rarely.

" Tell me, thou bonny bird
    When shall I marry me ? "—
" When six braw gentlemen
    Kirkward shall carry ye."

" Who makes the bridal bed,
    Birdie, say truly ? "—
" The grey-headed sexton
    That delves the grave duly.

" The glow-worm o'er grave and stone
    Shall light thee steady;
The owl from the steeple sing,
    ' Welcome, proud lady.' "

COLERIDGE.

SAMUEL TAYLOR COLERIDGE (1772-1834) was educated
at Christ's Hospital and at Jesus College, Cambridge.
At Christ's Hospital he had as schoolfellow and friend
Charles Lamb, who wrote of their schooldays in his
essay " Christ's Hospital Five and Thirty Years Ago."
In 1795 Coleridge began his friendship with Wordsworth, and in 1798 contributed *The Ancient Mariner* and
three other poems to *Lyrical Ballads*.   His best poetry
was all written by 1802; soon he had become a slave
to opium.   He was a great talker, and at Highgate
in his later years he was an oracle to whom many
interested in poetry and philosophy flocked.

From FROST AT MIDNIGHT.

                . . . I was reared
In the great city, pent 'mid cloisters dim,
And saw naught lovely but the sky and stars.
But *thou*, my babe ! shalt wander like a breeze
By lakes and sandy shores, beneath the crags
Of ancient mountain, and beneath the clouds,
Which image in their bulk both lakes and shores
And mountain crags: so shalt thou see and hear
The lovely shapes and sounds intelligible
Of that eternal language, which thy God
Utters, who from eternity doth teach
Himself in all, and all things in himself.
Great universal Teacher !   He shall mould
Thy Spirit, and by giving make it ask.

Therefore all seasons shall be sweet to thee,
Whether the summer clothe the general earth
With greenness, or the redbreast sit and sing
Betwixt the tufts of snow on the bare branch
Of mossy apple-tree, while the nigh thatch
Smokes in the sun-thaw; whether the eve-drops fall
Heard only in the trances of the blast,
Or if the secret ministry of frost
Shall hang them up in silent icicles,
Quietly shining to the quiet moon.

KUBLA KHAN.

In Xanadu did Kubla Khan
A stately pleasure-dome decree:
Where Alph, the sacred river, ran
Through caverns measureless to man
        Down to a sunless sea.

So twice five miles of fertile ground
With walls and towers were girdled round:
And here were gardens bright with sinuous rills
Where blossomed many an incense-bearing tree;
And here were forests ancient as the hills,
Enfolding sunny spots of greenery.

But oh! that deep romantic chasm which slanted
Down the green hill athwart a cedarn cover!
A savage place! as holy and enchanted
As e'er beneath a waning moon was haunted
By woman wailing for her demon-lover!
And from this chasm, with ceaseless turmoil seething,
As if this earth in fast thick pants were breathing,
A mighty fountain momently was forced:
Amid whose swift half-intermitted burst
Huge fragments vaulted like rebounding hail,
Or chaffy grain beneath the thresher's flail:
And 'mid these dancing rocks at once and ever
It flung up momently the sacred river.
Five miles meandering with a mazy motion
Through wood and dale the sacred river ran,
Then reached the caverns measureless to man,
And sank in tumult to a lifeless ocean:
And 'mid this tumult Kubla heard from far
Ancestral voices prophesying war!

The shadow of the dome of pleasure
Floated midway on the waves;
Where was heard the mingled measure
From the fountain and the caves.
It was a miracle of rare device,
A sunny pleasure-dome with caves of ice!
A damsel with a dulcimer

In a vision once I saw:
It was an Abyssinian maid,
And on her dulcimer she played,
Singing of Mount Abora.
Could I revive within me
Her symphony and song,
To such a deep delight 'twould win me,
That with music loud and long,
I would build that dome in air,
That sunny dome ! those caves of ice !
And all who heard should see them there,
And all should cry, Beware ! Beware !
His flashing eyes, his floating hair !
Weave a circle round him thrice,
And close your eyes with holy dread,
For he on honey dew hath fed,
And drunk the milk of Paradise.

From CHRISTABEL.

'Tis the middle of night by the castle clock,
And the owls have awakened the crowing cock;
Tu-whit !—Tu-whoo !
And hark, again ! the crowing cock,
How drowsily it crew.

Sir Leoline, the Baron rich,
Hath a toothless mastiff, which
From her kennel beneath the rock
Maketh answer to the clock,
Four for the quarters, and twelve for the hour;
Ever and ay, by shine and shower,
Sixteen short howls, not over loud;
Some say, she sees my lady's shroud.

Is the night chilly and dark?
The night is chilly, but not dark.
The thin grey cloud is spread on high,
It covers but not hides the sky.
The moon is behind, and at the full;
And yet she looks both small and dull.
The night is chill, the cloud is grey:
'Tis a month before the month of May,
And the Spring comes slowly up this way.

The lovely lady, Christabel,
Whom her father loves so well,
What makes her in the wood so late,
A furlong from the castle gate?
She had dreams all yesternight
Of her own bethrothèd knight;
And she in the midnight wood will pray
For the weal of her lover that's far away.

She stole along, she nothing spoke,
The sighs she heaved were soft and low,
And naught was green upon the oak,
But moss and rarest mistletoe:
She kneels beneath the huge oak tree,
And in silence prayeth she.

The lady sprang up suddenly,
The lovely lady, Christabel!
It moaned as near, as near can be,
But what it is, she cannot tell.—
On the other side it seems to be,
Of the huge, broad-breasted, old oak tree.

The night is chill; the forest bare;
Is it the wind that moaneth bleak?
There is not wind enough in the air

To move away the ringlet curl
From the lovely lady's cheek—
There is not wind enough to twirl
The one red leaf, the last of its clan,
That dances as often as dance it can,
Hanging so light, and hanging so high,
On the topmost twig that looks up at the sky.
Hush, beating heart of Christabel !
Jesu, Maria, shield her well !
She folded her arms beneath her cloak,
And stole to the other side of the oak.
What sees she there ?

There she sees a damsel bright,
Drest in a silken robe of white,
That shadowy in the moonlight shone :
The neck that made that white robe wan,
Her stately neck, and arms were bare ;
Her blue-veined feet unsandal'd were,
And wildly glittered here and there
The gems entangled in her hair.
I guess, 'twas frightful there to see
A lady so richly clad as she—
Beautiful exceedingly ! . . . .

CAMPBELL.

THOMAS CAMPBELL (1777–1844) won poetic fame when only twenty-one with *The Pleasures of Hope.* These melodious couplets of faintly romantic description, and of reflection of but moderate depth and capable expression, claimed attention because around 1799 there was little else in poetry to do so. Later, in the wake of Scott, Campbell tried his hand at narrative poetry such as *Gertrude of Wyoming* (1809). But his poetry that still lives consists of a few lyrics, and notably his stirring patriotic and war songs.

BATTLE OF THE BALTIC.

Of Nelson and the North
Sing the glorious day's renown,
When to battle fierce came forth
All the might of Denmark's crown,
And her arms along the deep proudly shone;
By each gun the lighted brand
In a bold determined hand,
And the Prince of all the land
Led them on.

Like leviathans afloat
Lay their bulwarks on the brine;
While the sign of battle flew
On the lofty British line:
It was ten of April morn by the chime:
As they drifted on their path
There was silence deep as death;
And the boldest held his breath
For a time.

But the might of England flush'd
To anticipate the scene;
And her van the fleeter rush'd
O'er the deadly space between.
" Hearts of oak ! " our captains cried, when each
        gun
From its adamantine lips
Spread a death-shade round the ships,
Like the hurricane eclipse
Of the sun.

Again ! again ! again !
And the havoc did not slack,
Till a feeble cheer the Dane

To our cheering sent us back;—
Their shots along the deep slowly boom:—
Then ceased—and all is wail,
As they strike the shatter'd sail;
Or in conflagration pale
Light the gloom.

Out spoke the victor then
As he hail'd them o'er the wave,
" Ye are brothers ! ye are men !
And we conquer but to save:—
So peace instead of death let us bring:
But yield, proud foe, thy fleet
With the crews, at England's feet,
And make submission meet
To our King."

Then Denmark bless'd our chief
That he gave her wounds repose;
And the sounds of joy and grief
From her people wildly rose,
As death withdrew his shades from the day:
While the sun look'd smiling bright
O'er a wide and woeful sight,
Where the fires of funeral light
Died away.

Now joy, old England, raise !
For the tidings of thy might,
By the festal cities' blaze,
Whilst the wine-cup shines in light;
And yet amidst that joy and uproar,
Let us think of them that sleep
Full many a fathom deep
By thy wild and stormy steep,
Elsinore !

Brave hearts! to Britain's pride
Once so faithful and so true,
On the deck of fame that died,
With the gallant good Riou:
Soft sigh the winds of Heaven o'er their grave!
While the billow mournful rolls
And the mermaid's song condoles,
Singing glory to the souls
Of the brave!

LORD ULLIN'S DAUGHTER.

A Chieftain to the Highlands bound
Cries "Boatman, do not tarry!
And I'll give thee a silver pound
To row us o'er the ferry!"

"Now, who be ye, would cross Lochgyle
This dark and stormy water?"
"O I'm the chief of Ulva's isle,
And this, Lord Ullin's daughter.

"And fast before her father's men
Three days we've fled together,
For should he find us in the glen,
My blood would stain the heather.

"His horsemen hard behind us ride—
Should they our steps discover,
Then who will cheer my bonny bride
When they have slain her lover?"

Out spoke the hardy Highland wight,
"I'll go, my chief, I'm ready:
It is not for your silver bright,
But for your winsome lady:

" And by my word ! the bonny bird
In danger shall not tarry;
So though the waves are raging white,
I'll row you o'er the ferry."

By this the storm grew loud apace,
The water-wraith was shrieking;
And in the scowl of heaven each face
Grew dark as they were speaking.

But still as wilder blew the wind,
And as the night grew drearer,
Adown the glen rode arméd men,
Their trampling sounded nearer.

" O haste thee, haste ! " the lady cries,
" Though tempests round us gather;
I'll meet the raging of the skies,
But not an angry father ! "

The boat has left a stormy land,
A stormy sea before her,—
When, O ! too strong for human hand
The tempest gather'd o'er her.

And still they row'd amidst the roar
Of waters fast prevailing:
Lord Ullin reach'd that fatal shore,—
His wrath was changed to wailing.

For, sore dismay'd, through storm and shade
His child he did discover:—
One lovely hand she stretch'd for aid,
And one was round her lover.

" Come back ! come back ! " he cried in grief,
" Across this stormy water:
And I'll forgive your Highland chief:—
My daughter !—O my daughter ! "

'Twas vain: the loud waves lash'd the shore,
Return or aid preventing:
The waters wild went o'er his child,
And he was left lamenting.

LORD BYRON.

GEORGE GORDON, LORD BYRON (1788–1824) came of
a wild family on his father's side, and his mother was
a woman of capricious and violent temper—thus he
inherited more than a usual share of headstrong
passion. His first considerable poem was the satire
English Bards and Scotch Reviewers (1809); then, after
Childe Harold (1812), came his vivid, melodramatic
narrative poems like *The Giaour*. In 1816 the scandal of
his unhappy marriage drove him from society and
from England. Shocked into deeper thinking he
became a finer poet, and in *Don Juan* (1818–23), a
medley of love, satire, and reflection, he found his
fullest expression. From his earliest years he showed
considerable mastery over the lyric form, though not
one of our greatest lyrists.

SHE WALKS IN BEAUTY.

She walks in beauty, like the night
    Of cloudless climes and starry skies;
And all that's best of dark and bright
    Meet in her aspect and her eyes:
Thus mellow'd to that tender light
    Which heaven to gaudy day denies.

One shade the more, one ray the less,
  Had half impair'd the nameless grace
Which waves in every raven tress,
  Or softly lightens o'er her face;
Where thoughts serenely sweet express
  How pure, how dear their dwelling-place.

And on that cheek, and o'er that brow,
  So soft, so calm, yet eloquent,
The smiles that win, the tints that glow,
  But tell of days in goodness spent,
A mind at peace with all below,
  A heart whose love is innocent.

NO MORE A ROVING.

So, we'll go no more a roving
  So late into the night,
Though the heart be still as loving,
  And the moon be still as bright.

For the sword outwears its sheath,
  And the soul wears out the breast,
And the heart must pause to breathe,
  And love itself have rest.

Though the night was made for loving,
  And the day returns too soon,
Yet we'll go no more a roving
  By the light of the moon.

LAKE LEMAN—A NOCTURNE.

Clear, placid Leman! thy contrasted lake,
With the wild world I dwelt in, is a thing

Which warns me, with its stillness, to forsake
Earth's troubled waters for a purer spring. . . .

It is the hush of night, and all between
Thy margin and the mountains, dusk, yet clear,
Mellow'd and mingling, yet distinctly seen,
Save darken'd Jura, whose capt heights appear
Precipitously steep; and drawing near,
There breathes a living fragrance from the shore,
Of flowers yet fresh with childhood; on the ear
Drops the light drip of the suspended oar,
Or chirps the grasshopper one good-night carol more ;

He is an evening reveller, who makes
His life an infancy, and sings his fill;
At intervals, some bird from out the brakes
Starts into voice a moment, then is still.
There seems a floating whisper on the hill,
But that is fancy, for the starlight dews
All silently their tears of love instil,
Weeping themselves away, till they infuse
Deep into nature's breast the spirit of her hues. . . .

All heaven and earth are still—though not in sleep,
But breathless, as we grow when feeling most;
And silent, as we stand in thoughts too deep:—
All heaven and earth are still: From the high host
Of stars to the lull'd lake and mountain-coast,
All is concenter'd in a life intense,
Where not a beam, nor air, nor leaf is lost,
But hath a part of being, and a sense
Of that which is of all Creator and defence.

Then stirs the feeling infinite, so felt
In solitude when we are *least* alone . . .

                              (*Childe Harold*, Canto III.)

CHILLON.

Eternal Spirit of the chainless Mind !
Brightest in dungeons, Liberty ! thou art,
For there thy habitation is the heart—
The heart which love of thee alone can bind;
And when thy sons to fetters are consign'd—
To fetters, and the damp vault's dayless gloom,
Their country conquers with their martyrdom,
And Freedom's fame finds wings on every wind.
Chillon ! thy prison is a holy place,
And thy sad floor an altar—for 'twas trod,
Until his very steps have left a trace
Worn, as if thy cold pavement were a sod,
By Bonnivard ! May none those marks efface !
For they appeal from tyranny to God.

THE DESTRUCTION OF SENNACHERIB.

The Assyrian came down like the wolf on the fold,
And his cohorts were gleaming in purple and gold;
And the sheen of their spears was like stars on the sea,
When the blue wave rolls nightly on deep Galilee.

Like the leaves of the forest when Summer is green,
That host with their banners at sunset were seen:
Like the leaves of the forest when Autumn hath blown,
That host on the morrow lay wither'd and strown.

For the Angel of Death spread his wings on the blast,
And breathed in the face of the foe as he pass'd;
And the eyes of the sleepers wax'd deadly and chill,
And their hearts but once heaved, and forever grew still !

And there lay the steed with his nostril all wide,
But through it there roll'd not the breath of his pride;

And the foam of his gasping lay white on the turf,
And cold as the spray of the rock-beating surf.

And there lay the rider distorted and pale,
With the dew on his brow, and the rust on his mail;
And the tents were all silent, the banners alone,
The lances unlifted, the trumpet unblown.

And the widows of Ashur are loud in their wail,
And the idols are broke in the temple of Baal !
And the might of the Gentile, unsmote by the sword,
Hath melted like snow in the glance of the Lord !

'T IS SWEET.

'T is sweet to hear
At midnight on the blue and moonlit deep
The song and oar of Adria's gondolier,
By distance mellow'd, o'er the waters sweep;
'T is sweet to listen as the night-winds creep
From leaf to leaf; 't is sweet to view on high
The rainbow, based on ocean, span the sky.

'T is sweet to hear the watch-dog's honest bark
Bay deep-mouth'd welcome as we draw near home;
'T is sweet to know there is an eye will mark
Our coming, and look brighter when we come;
'T is sweet to be awaken'd by the lark,
Or lull'd by falling waters; sweet the hum
Of bees, the voice of girls, the song of birds,
The lisp of children, and their earliest words.

Sweet is the vintage, when the showering grapes
In Bacchanal profusion reel to earth,
Purple and gushing; sweet are our escapes
From civic revelry to rural mirth;

Sweet to the miser are his glittering heaps,
Sweet to the father is his first-born's birth,
Sweet is revenge—especially to women,
Pillage to soldiers, prize-money to seamen. . . .

'T is sweet to win, no matter how, one's laurels,
By blood or ink; 't is sweet to put an end
To strife; 't is sometimes sweet to have our quarrels,
Particularly with a tiresome friend:
Sweet is old wine in bottles, ale in barrels;
Dear is the helpless creature we defend
Against the world; and dear the schoolboy spot
We ne'er forget, though there we are forgot.

But sweeter still than this, than these, than all,
Is first and passionate love—it stands alone. . . .

(Don Juan, Canto I.)

AVE MARIA.

The feast was over, the slaves gone,
The dwarfs and dancing girls had all retired;
The Arab lore and poet's song were done,
And every sound of revelry expired;
The lady and her lover, left alone,
The rosy flood of twilight's sky admired;—
Ave Maria! o'er the earth and sea,
That heavenliest hour of Heaven is worthiest thee!

Ave Maria! blessed be the hour!
The time, the clime, the spot, where I so oft
Have felt that moment in its fullest power
Sink o'er the earth so beautiful and soft,
While swung the deep bell in the distant tower,
Or the faint dying day-hymn stole aloft,
And not a breath crept through the rosy air,
And yet the forest leaves seem'd stirr'd with prayer.

Ave Maria ! 't is the hour of prayer !
Ave Maria ! 't is the hour of love !
Ave Maria ! may our spirits dare
Look up to thine and to thy Son's above !
Ave Maria ! oh that face so fair !
Those downcast eyes beneath the Almighty dove—
What though 't is but a pictured image strike,
That painting is no idol—'t is too like.

(*Don Juan*, Canto III.)

SHELLEY.

PERCY BYSSHE SHELLEY (1792–1822), son of a Sussex
baronet, was a young man of revolutionary enthusiasm,
and for his atheism, avowed in a pamphlet, he was
sent down from Oxford. Love of Liberty was his
ruling passion, and nearly all his longer poems such as
The Revolt of Islam, and the lyric drama *Prometheus
Unbound*, were the expression of his idealism. His
finest work was in the lyric, although his longer poems,
and notably *Adonais*, his elegy on Keats, contain
magnificent passages. Drowned while sailing in the
Gulf of Spezzia, he died while still seemingly in the
steady development of his genius.

TO ——.

Music, when soft voices die,
Vibrates in the memory—
Odours, when sweet violets sicken,
Live within the sense they quicken.

Rose leaves, when the rose is dead,
Are heaped for the belovèd's bed;
And so thy thoughts, when thou art gone,
Love itself shall slumber on.

MORNING GLORY.

                    I arose, and for a space
The scene of woods and waters seemed to keep,

Though it was now broad day, a gentle trace
Of light diviner than the common sun
Sheds on the common earth, and all the place

Was filled with magic sounds woven into one
Oblivious melody, confusing sense
Amid the gliding waves and shadows dun;

And, as I looked, the bright omnipresence
Of morning through the orient cavern flowed,
And the sun's image radiantly intense

Burned on the waters of the well that glowed
Like gold, and threaded all the forest's maze
With winding paths of emerald fire; there stood

Amid the sun, as he amid the blaze
Of his own glory, on the vibrating
Floor of the fountain, paved with flashing rays,

A Shape all light, which with one hand did fling
Dew on the earth, as if she were the dawn,
And the invisible rain did ever sing

A silver music on the mossy lawn. . . .

                              (*The Triumph of Life.*)

AWAY, AWAY!

Away! the moor is dark beneath the moon,
    Rapid clouds have drunk the last pale beam of even:
Away! the gathering winds will call the darkness soon,
    And profoundest midnight shroud the serene lights of
        Heaven.

Pause not ! the time is past ! Every voice cries, Away !
 Tempt not with one last tear thy friend's ungentle
  mood:
Thy lover's eye, so glazed and cold, dares not entreat
  thy stay;
 Duty and dereliction guide thee back to solitude.

Away, away ! to thy sad and silent home;
 Pour bitter tears on its desolated hearth;
Watch the dim shades as like ghosts they go and come,
 And complicate strange webs of melancholy mirth.

The leaves of wasted autumn woods shall float around
  thine head:
 The blooms of dewy spring shall gleam beneath thy
  feet:
But thy soul or this world must fade in the frost that
  binds the dead,
 Ere midnight's frown and morning's smile, ere thou
  and peace may meet.

The clouds of midnight possess their own repose,
 For the weary winds are silent, or the moon is in the
  deep;
Some respite to its turbulence unresting ocean knows;
 Whatever moves, or toils, or grieves, hath its appointed
  sleep.

Thou in the grave shalt rest—yet till the phantoms flee
 Which that house and heath and garden made dear to
  thee erewhile,
Thy remembrance, and repentance, and deep musings
 are not free
 From the music of two voices and the light of one
  sweet smile.

ODE TO THE WEST WIND.

I.

O wild West Wind, thou breath of Autumn's being,
Thou, from whose unseen presence the leaves dead
Are driven, like ghosts from an enchanter fleeing,

Yellow, and black, and pale, and hectic red,
Pestilence-stricken multitudes: O thou,
Who chariotest to their dark wintry bed

The wingèd seeds, where they lie cold and low,
Each like a corpse within its grave, until
Thine azure sister of the Spring shall blow

Her clarion o'er the dreaming earth, and fill
(Driving sweet buds like flocks to feed in air)
With living hues and odours plain and hill:

Wild Spirit, which art moving everywhere;
Destroyer and preserver; hear, oh, hear!

II.

Thou on whose stream, 'mid the steep sky's commotion,
Loose clouds like earth's decaying leaves are shed,
Shook from the tangled boughs of Heaven and Ocean,

Angels of rain and lightning: there are spread
On the blue surface of thine aery surge,
Like the bright hair uplifted from the head

Of some fierce Maenad, even from the dim verge
Of the horizon to the zenith's height,
The locks of the approaching storm.   Thou dirge

Of the dying year, to which this closing night
Will be the dome of a vast sepulchre,
Vaulted with all thy congregated might

Of vapours, from whose solid atmosphere
Black rain, and fire, and hail will burst: oh, hear!

III.

Thou who didst waken from his summer dreams
The blue Mediterranean, where he lay,
Lulled by the coil of his crystalline streams,

Beside a pumice isle in Baiae's bay,
And saw in sleep old palaces and towers
Quivering within the wave's intenser day,

All overgrown with azure moss and flowers
So sweet, the sense faints picturing them.   Thou
For whose path the Atlantic's level powers

Cleave themselves into chasms, while far below
The sea-blooms and the oozy woods which wear
The sapless foliage of the ocean, know

Thy voice, and suddenly grow gray with fear,
And tremble and despoil themselves: oh, hear !

IV.

If I were a dead leaf thou mightest bear;
If I were a swift cloud to fly with thee;
A wave to pant beneath thy power, and share

The impulse of thy strength, only less free
Than thou, O uncontrollable ! If even
I were as in my boyhood, and could be

The comrade of thy wanderings over Heaven,
As then, when to outstrip thy skiey speed
Scarce seemed a vision; I would ne'er have striven

As thus with thee in prayer in my sore need.
Oh, lift me as a wave, a leaf, a cloud !
I fall upon the thorns of life ! I bleed !

A heavy weight of hours has chained and bowed
One too like thee: tameless, and swift, and proud.

V.

Make me thy lyre, even as the forest is:
What if my leaves are falling like its own!
The tumult of thy mighty harmonies

Will take from both a deep, autumnal tone,
Sweet though in sadness.   Be thou, Spirit fierce,
My spirit! Be thou me, impetuous one!

Drive my dead thoughts over the universe
Like withered leaves to quicken a new birth!
And, by the incantation of this verse,

Scatter, as from an unextinguished hearth
Ashes and sparks, my words among mankind!
Be through my lips to unawakened earth

The trumpet of a prophecy! O, Wind,
If Winter comes, can Spring be far behind?

TO ——.

One word is too often profaned
    For me to profane it,
One feeling too falsely disdained
    For thee to disdain it;
One hope is too like despair
    For prudence to smother,
And pity from thee more dear
    Than that from another.

I can give not what men call love,
    But wilt thou accept not
The worship the heart lifts above
    And the heavens reject not—
The desire of the moth for the star,
    Of the night for the morrow,

The devotion to something afar
    From the sphere of our sorrow ?

A LAMENT.

O world ! O life ! O time !
On whose last steps I climb,
    Trembling at that where I had stood before;
When will return the glory of your prime ?
    No more—Oh, never more !

Out of the day and night
A joy has taken flight;
    Fresh spring, and summer, and winter hoar,
Move my faint heart with grief, but with delight
    No more—Oh, never more !

Song from PROMETHEUS UNBOUND.

Life of Life ! thy lips enkindle
  With their love the breath between them;
And thy smiles before they dwindle
  Make the cold air fire; then screen them
In those looks, where whoso gazes
Faints, entangled in their mazes.

Child of Light ! thy limbs are burning
  Through the vest which seems to hide them:
As the radiant lines of morning
  Through the clouds ere they divide them;
And this atmosphere divinest
Shrouds thee wheresoe'er thou shinest.

Fair are others; none beholds thee,
  But thy voice sounds low and tender,

Like the fairest, for it folds thee
   From the sight, that liquid splendour,
And all feel, yet see thee never,
As I feel now, lost for ever !

Lamp of Earth ! where'er thou movest
Its dim shapes are clad with brightness,
And the souls of whom thou lovest
   Walk upon the winds with lightness,
Till they fail, as I am failing,
Dizzy, lost, yet unbewailing !

TO A SKYLARK.

Hail to thee, blithe spirit !
   Bird thou never wert,
That from heaven, or near it,
   Pourest thy full heart
In profuse strains of unpremeditated art.

Higher still and higher,
   From the earth thou springest
Like a cloud of fire;
   The blue deep thou wingest,
And singing still dost soar, and soaring ever singest.

In the golden lightning
   Of the sunken sun,
O'er which clouds are brightening,
   Thou dost float and run,
Like an unbodied joy whose race is just begun

The pale purple even
   Melts around thy flight;
Like a star of heaven,
   In the broad daylight
Thou art unseen, but yet I hear thy shrill delight,

Keen as are the arrows
    Of that silver sphere,
Whose intense lamp narrows
    In the white dawn clear
Until we hardly see—we feel that it is there.

All the earth and air
    With thy voice is loud,
As, when night is bare,
    From one lonely cloud
The moon rains out her beams, and heaven is overflowed.

What thou art we know not;
    What is most like thee?
From rainbow clouds there flow not
    Drops so bright to see
As from thy presence showers a rain of melody.

Like a poet hidden
    In the light of thought,
Singing hymns unbidden,
    Till the world is wrought
To sympathy with hopes and fears it heeded not:

Like a high-born maiden
    In a palace tower,
Soothing her love-laden
    Soul in secret hour
With music sweet as love, which overflows her bower:

Like a glow-worm golden
    In a dell of dew,
Scattering unbeholden
    Its aërial hue
Among the flowers and grass which screen it from the
    view:

Like a rose embowered
    In its own green leaves,
By warm winds deflowered,
    Till the scent it gives
Makes faint with too much sweet these heavy-wingèd
    thieves:

Sound of vernal showers
    On the twinkling grass,
Rain-awakened flowers,
    All that ever was
Joyous, and clear, and fresh, thy music doth surpass:

Teach us, sprite or bird,
    What sweet thoughts are thine:
I have never heard
    Praise of love or wine
That panted forth a flood of rapture so divine.

Chorus hymeneal,
    Or triumphal chant,
Matched with thine would be all
    But an empty vaunt,
A thing wherein we feel there is some hidden want.

What objects are the fountains
    Of thy happy strain?
What fields, or waves, or mountains?
    What shapes of sky or plain?
What love of thine own kind? what ignorance of pain?

With thy clear keen joyance
    Languor cannot be:
Shadow of annoyance
    Never came near thee:
Thou lovest—but ne'er knew love's sad satiety.

Waking or asleep,
 Thou of death must deem
Things more true and deep
 Than we mortals dream,
Or how could thy notes flow in such a crystal stream?

We look before and after,
 And pine for what is not:
Our sincerest laughter
 With some pain is fraught:
Our sweetest songs are those that tell of saddest thought.

Yet if we could scorn
 Hate, and pride, and fear;
If we were things born
 Not to shed a tear,
I know not how thy joy we ever should come near.

Better than all measures
 Of delightful sound,
Better than all treasures
 That in books are found,
Thy skill to poet were, thou scorner of the ground!

Teach me half the gladness
 That thy brain must know,
Such harmonious madness
 From my lips would flow,
The world should listen then, as I am listening now.

From ADONAIS.

Peace, peace! he is not dead, he doth not sleep—
He hath awakened from the dream of life—
'Tis we, who lost in stormy visions, keep
With phantoms an unprofitable strife,

And in mad trance, strike with our spirit's knife
Invulnerable nothings.—*We* decay
Like corpses in a charnel; fear and grief
Convulse us and consume us day by day,
And cold hopes swarm like worms within our living clay.

He has outsoared the shadow of our night;
Envy and calumny and hate and pain,
And that unrest which men miscall delight,
Can touch him not and torture not again;
From the contagion of the world's slow stain
He is secure, and now can never mourn
A heart grown cold, a head grown gray in vain;
Nor, when the spirit's self has ceased to burn,
With sparkless ashes load an unlamented urn.

He lives, he wakes—'tis Death is dead, not he;
Mourn not for Adonais.—Thou young Dawn,
Turn all thy dew to splendour, for from thee
The spirit thou lamentest is not gone;
Ye caverns and ye forests, cease to moan!
Cease, ye faint flowers and fountains, and thou Air,
Which like a mourning veil thy scarf hadst thrown
O'er the abandoned Earth, now leave it bare
Even to the joyous stars which smile on its despair.

He is made one with Nature: there is heard
His voice in all her music, from the moan
Of thunder, to the song of night's sweet bird;
He is a presence to be felt and known
In darkness and in light, from herb and stone,
Spreading itself where'er that Power may move
Which has withdrawn his being to its own;
Which wields the world with never-wearied love,
Sustains it from beneath, and kindles it above.

He is a portion of the loveliness
Which once he made more lovely: he doth bear
His part, while the one Spirit's plastic stress
Sweeps through the dull dense world, compelling there
All new successions to the forms they wear;
Torturing th' unwilling dross that checks its flight
To its own likeness, as each mass may bear;
And bursting in its beauty and its might
From trees and beasts and men into the Heaven's light.

The splendours of the firmament of time
May be eclipsed, but are extinguished not;
Like stars to their appointed height they climb,
And death is a low mist which cannot blot
The brightness it may veil.   When lofty thought
Lifts a young heart above its mortal lair,
And love and life contend in it, for what
Shall be its earthly doom, the dead live there
And move like winds of light on dark and stormy air.

The inheritors of unfulfilled renown
Rose from their thrones, built beyond mortal thought,
Far in the Unapparent.   Chatterton
Rose pale,—his solemn agony had not
Yet faded from him; Sidney, as he fought
And as he fell and as he lived and loved
Sublimely mild, a spirit without spot,
Arose; and Lucan, by his death approved:
Oblivion as they rose shrank like a thing reproved.

And many more, whose names on Earth are dark,
But whose transmitted effluence cannot die
So long as fire outlives the parent spark,
Rose, robed in dazzling immortality.
" Thou art become as one of us," they cry,

" It was for thee yon kingless sphere has long
  Swung blind in unascended majesty,
  Silent alone amid an Heaven of Song.
Assume thy wingèd throne, thou Vesper of our throng !"

KEATS.

JOHN KEATS (1795–1821), London born and bred, was apprenticed to a surgeon and walked the hospitals, but having no love for this profession soon gave himself up to poetry. " The Genius of Poetry," he wrote, " must work out its own salvation in a man," and as we pass from his early descriptive poetry of rich and sensuous detail like " I stood tip-toe upon a little hill " to his great unfinished *Hyperion* we see how it was working out in Keats. Among his greatest works are his Odes, but his narratives like *The Eve of St. Agnes* reach the first class in their kind, while *Endymion* is a tangled thicket of beauty. Keats died of consumption.

LIFE.

Life is but a day;
A fragile dewdrop on its perilous way
From a tree's summit; a poor Indian's sleep
While his boat hastens to the monstrous steep
Of Montmorenci. Why so sad a moan ?
Life is the rose's hope while yet unblown;
The reading of an ever-changing tale;
The light uplifting of a maiden's veil;
A pigeon tumbling in clear summer air;
A laughing schoolboy, without grief or care,
Riding the springy branches of an elm.

(*Sleep and Poetry.*)

PEERLESS POESY.

                    A drainless shower
Of light is poesy; 'tis the supreme of power;
'Tis might half slumbering on its own right arm:
The very archings of her eyelids charm
A thousand willing agents to obey,
And still she governs with the mildest sway:
But strength alone, though of the muses born,
Is like a fallen angel: trees uptorn,
Darkness, and worms, and shrouds, and sepulchres
Delight it; for it feeds upon the burrs
And thorns of life; forgetting the great end
Of poesy, that it should be a friend
To soothe the cares, and lift the thoughts of man.

ON FIRST LOOKING INTO CHAPMAN'S HOMER.

Much have I travell'd in the realms of gold
And many goodly states and kingdoms seen;
Round many western islands have I been
Which bards in fealty to Apollo hold.
Oft of one wide expanse had I been told
That deep-brow'd Homer ruled as his demesne:
Yet did I never breathe its pure serene
Till I heard Chapman speak out loud and bold:
Then felt I like some watcher of the skies
When a new planet swims into his ken;
Or like stout Cortez when with eagle eyes
He stared at the Pacific—and all his men
Look'd at each other with a wild surmise—
Silent, upon a peak in Darien.

MADELINE ON ST. AGNES' EVE.

Out went the taper as she hurried in;
Its little smoke, in pallid moonshine, died:

She closed the door, she panted, all akin
To spirits of the air, and visions wide:
No utter'd syllable, or woe betide!
But to her heart, her heart was voluble,
Paining with eloquence her balmy side;
As though a tongueless nightingale should swell
Her throat in vain, and die, heart-stifled, in her dell.

A casement high and triple-arch'd there was,
All garlanded with carven imageries,
Of fruits and flowers, and bunches of knot-grass,
And diamonded with panes of quaint device,
Innumerable of stains and splendid dyes,
As are the tiger-moth's deep-damask'd wings;
And in the midst, 'mong thousand heraldries,
And twilight saints, and dim emblazonings,
A shielded scutcheon blush'd with blood of queens
    and kings.

Full on this casement shone the wintry moon,
And threw warm gules on Madeline's fair breast,
As down she knelt for Heaven's grace and boon;
Rose-bloom fell on her hands, together prest,
And on her silver cross soft amethyst,
And on her hair a glory, like a saint:
She seem'd a splendid angel, newly drest,
Save wings, for heaven:—Porphyro grew faint:
She knelt, so pure a thing, so free from mortal taint.

LA BELLE DAME SANS MERCI.

"O what can ail thee, knight-at-arms,
    Alone and palely loitering?
The sedge is withered from the lake,
    And no birds sing.

"O what can ail thee, knight-at-arms,
 So haggard and so woe-begone?
The squirrel's granary is full,
 And the harvest's done.

"I see a lily on thy brow,
 With anguish moist and fever-dew;
And on thy cheek a fading rose
 Fast withereth too."

"I met a lady in the meads,
 Full beautiful—a faery's child;
Her hair was long, her foot was light,
 And her eyes were wild.

"I made a garland for her head,
 And bracelets too, and fragrant zone;
She looked at me as she did love,
 And made sweet moan.

"I set her on my pacing steed,
 And nothing else saw all day long;
For sideways would she bend, and sing
 A faery's song.

"She found me roots of relish sweet,
 And honey wild, and manna dew;
And sure in language strange she said,
 'I love thee true.'

"She took me to her elfin grot,
 And there she wept and sighed full sore,
And there I shut her wild wild eyes—
 With kisses four.

"And there she lullèd me asleep,
    And there I dreamed, ah! woe betide!
The latest dream I ever dream'd,
    On the cold hill's side.

"I saw pale kings and princes too,
    Pale warriors, death-pale were they all;
Who cried, 'La Belle Dame sans Merci
    Hath thee in thrall!'

"I saw their starved lips in the gloam,
    With horrid warning gapèd wide;
And I awoke, and found me here
    On the cold hill's side.

"And this is why I sojourn here,
    Alone and palely loitering,
Though the sedge is withered from the lake,
    And no birds sing."

TO A NIGHTINGALE.

In the spring of 1819 a nightingale built her nest next Mr. Bevan's
house. Keats took great pleasure in her song, and one morning took his
chair from the breakfast-table to the grass plot under a plum tree, where
he remained between two and three hours. He then reached the house
with some scraps of paper in his hand, which he soon put together in the
form of this Ode.

My heart aches, and a drowsy numbness pains
    My sense, as though of hemlock I had drunk,
Or emptied some dull opiate to the drains
    One minute past, and Lethe-wards had sunk:
'Tis not through envy of thy happy lot,
    But being too happy in thy happiness,—
        That thou, light-wingèd Dryad of the trees,
            In some melodious plot
Of beechen green, and shadows numberless,
    Singest of summer in full-throated ease.

O for a draught of vintage, that hath been
  Cool'd a long age in the deep-delvèd earth,
Tasting of Flora and the country-green,
  Dance, and Provençal song, and sun-burnt mirth !
O for a beaker full of the warm South,
  Full of the true, the blushful Hippocrene,
    With beaded bubbles winking at the brim,
      And purple-stainèd mouth;
  That I might drink, and leave the world unseen,
    And with thee fade away into the forest dim:

Fade far away, dissolve, and quite forget
  What thou among the leaves hast never known,
The weariness, the fever, and the fret
  Here, where men sit and hear each other groan;
Where palsy shakes a few, sad, last grey hairs,
  Where youth grows pale, and spectre-thin, and dies;
    Where but to think is to be full of sorrow
      And leaden-eyed despairs;
  Where beauty cannot keep her lustrous eyes,
    Or new Love pine at them beyond to-morrow.

Away ! away ! for I will fly to thee,
  Not charioted by Bacchus and his pards,
But on the viewless wings of Poesy,
  Though the dull brain perplexes and retards:
Already with thee ! tender is the night,
  And haply the Queen-Moon is on her throne,
    Cluster'd around by all her starry Fays;
      But here there is no light,
  Save what from heaven is with the breezes blown
    Through verdurous glooms and winding mossy ways.

I cannot see what flowers are at my feet,
  Nor what soft incense hangs upon the boughs,

But, in embalmèd darkness, guess each sweet
　　Wherewith the seasonable month endows
The grass, the thicket, and the fruit-tree wild;
　　White hawthorn, and the pastoral eglantine;
　　　　Fast-fading violets cover'd up in leaves;
　　　　　　And mid-May's eldest child,
　　The coming musk-rose, full of dewy wine,
　　　　The murmurous haunt of flies on summer eves.

Darkling I listen; and for many a time
　　I have been half in love with easeful Death,
Call'd him soft names in many a musèd rhyme,
　　To take into the air my quiet breath;
Now more than ever seems it rich to die,
　　To cease upon the midnight with no pain,
　　　　While thou art pouring forth thy soul abroad
　　　　　　In such an ecstasy !
　　Still wouldst thou sing, and I have ears in vain—
　　　　To thy high requiem become a sod.

Thou wast not born for death, immortal Bird !
　　No hungry generations tread thee down;
The voice I hear this passing night was heard
　　In ancient days by emperor and clown:
Perhaps the self-same song that found a path
　　Through the sad heart of Ruth, when sick for home,
　　　　She stood in tears amid the alien corn;
　　　　　　The same that oft-times hath
　　Charm'd magic casements, opening on the foam
　　　　Of perilous seas, in faery lands forlorn.

Forlorn ! the very word is like a bell
　　To toll me back from thee to my sole self.
Adieu ! the fancy cannot cheat so well
　　As she is famed to do, deceiving elf.

Adieu ! adieu ! thy plaintive anthem fades
　　Past the near meadows, over the still stream,
Up the hill-side; and now 'tis buried deep
　　In the next valley-glades:
Was it a vision, or a waking dream ?
Fled is that music:—do I wake or sleep ?

ON A GRECIAN URN.

Thou still unravish'd bride of quietness !
　　Thou foster-child of Silence and slow Time,
Sylvan historian, who canst thus express
　　A flowery tale more sweetly than our rhyme:
What leaf-fringed legend haunts about thy shape
　　Of deities or mortals, or of both,
　　　　In Tempe or the dales of Arcady ?
　　What men or gods are these ?   What maidens loath ?
What mad pursuit ?   What struggle to escape ?
　　　　What pipes and timbrels ?   What wild ecstasy ?

Heard melodies are sweet, but those unheard
　　Are sweeter; therefore, ye soft pipes, play on;
Not to the sensual ear, but, more endear'd,
　　Pipe to the spirit ditties of no tone:
Fair youth, beneath the trees, thou canst not leave
　　Thy song, nor ever can those trees be bare;
　　　　Bold Lover, never, never canst thou kiss,
Though winning near the goal—yet, do not grieve;
　　　　She cannot fade, though thou hast not thy bliss,
　　For ever wilt thou love, and she be fair !

Ah, happy, happy boughs ! that cannot shed
　　Your leaves, nor ever bid the Spring adieu;
And, happy melodist, unwearièd,
　　For ever piping songs for ever new;

More happy love ! more happy, happy love !
　For ever warm and still to be enjoy'd,
　　For ever panting and for ever young;
All breathing human passion far above,
　That leaves a heart high sorrowful and cloy'd,
　　A burning forehead, and a parching tongue.

Who are these coming to the sacrifice ?
　To what green altar, O mysterious priest,
Lead'st thou that heifer lowing at the skies,
　And all her silken flanks with garlands drest ?
What little town by river or sea-shore,
　Or mountain-built with peaceful citadel,
　　Is emptied of its folk, this pious morn ?
And, little town, thy streets for evermore
　Will silent be; and not a soul to tell
　　Why thou art desolate, can e'er return.

O Attic shape ! Fair attitude ! with brede
　Of marble men and maidens overwrought,
With forest branches and the trodden weed;
　Thou, silent form ! dost tease us out of thought
As doth eternity: Cold Pastoral !
When old age shall this generation waste,
　Thou shalt remain, in midst of other woe
Than ours, a friend to man, to whom thou say'st,
" Beauty is truth, truth beauty,"—that is all
　Ye know on earth, and all ye need to know.

AUTUMN.

Season of mists and mellow fruitfulness !
　Close bosom-friend of the maturing sun;
Conspiring with him how to load and bless
　With fruit the vines that round the thatch-eaves run;

To bend with apples the moss'd cottage trees,
　And fill all fruit with ripeness to the core;
　　To swell the gourd, and plump the hazel shells
　With a sweet kernel; to set budding more,
And still more, later flowers for the bees,
Until they think warm days will never cease,
　　For Summer has o'er-brimm'd their clammy cells.

Who hath not seen thee oft amid thy store?
　Sometimes whoever seeks abroad may find
Thee sitting careless on a granary floor,
　Thy hair soft-lifted by the winnowing wind;
Or on a half-reap'd furrow sound asleep,
　Drowsed with the fumes of poppies while thy hook
　　Spares the next swath and all its twinèd flowers;
And sometime like a gleaner thou dost keep
　Steady thy laden head across a brook;
　Or by a cider-press, with patient look,
　　Thou watchest the last oozings, hours by hours.

Where are the songs of Spring? Ay, where are they?
　Think not of them, thou hast thy music too,
　　While barred clouds bloom the soft-dying day,
And touch the stubble-plains with rosy hue;
　Then in a wailful choir, the small gnats mourn
　Among the river sallows, borne aloft
　　Or sinking as the light wind lives or dies;
And full-grown lambs loud bleat from hilly bourn;
　Hedge-crickets sing, and now with treble soft
　The redbreast whistles from a garden-croft,
　　And gathering swallows twitter in the skies.

HYMN TO PAN.

" O thou, whose mighty palace roof doth hang
From jagged trunks, and overshadoweth
Eternal whispers, glooms, the birth, life, death
Of unseen flowers in heavy peacefulness;
Who lovest to see the hamadryads dress
Their ruffled locks where meeting hazels darken;
And through whole solemn hours dost sit, and hearken
The dreamy melody of bedded reeds—
In desolate places, where dank moisture breeds
The pipy hemlock to strange overgrowth,
Bethinking thee, how melancholy loth
Thou wast to lose fair Syrinx—do thou now,
By thy love's milky brow !
By all the trembling mazes that she ran,
Hear us, Great Pan !

" O thou, for whose soul-soothing quiet, turtles
Passion their voices cooingly 'mong myrtles,
What time thou wanderest at eventide
Through sunny meadows, that outskirt the side
Of thine enmossèd realms : O thou, to whom
Broad-leavèd fig-trees even now foredoom
Their ripen'd fruitage; yellow-girted bees
Their golden honeycombs; our village leas
Their fairest-blossom'd beans and poppied corn;
The chuckling linnet its five young unborn,
To sing for thee; low-creeping strawberries
Their summer coolness; pent-up butterflies
Their freckled wings; yea, the fresh-budding year
All its completions—be quickly near,
By every wind that nods the mountain pine,
O forester divine !

" Thou, to whom every faun and satyr flies
For willing service; whether to surprise

The squatted hare while in half-sleeping fit;
Or upward ragged precipices flit
To save poor lambkins from the eagle's maw;
Or by mysterious enticement draw
Bewilder'd shepherds to their path again;
Or to tread breathless round the frothy main,
And gather up all fancifullest shells
For thee to tumble into Naiads' cells,
And, being hidden, laugh at their out-peeping;
Or to delight thee with fantastic leaping,
The while they pelt each other on the crown
With silvery oak-apples, and fir-cones brown—
By all the echoes that about thee ring,
Hear us, O satyr king !

"O Hearkener to the loud-clapping shears,
While ever and anon to his shorn peers
A ram goes bleating: winder of the horn,
When snouted wild-boars routing tender corn
Anger our huntsman: Breather round our farms,
To keep off mildews, and all weather harms:
Strange ministrant of undescribèd sounds,
That come a-swooning over hollow grounds,
And wither drearily on barren moors:
Dread opener of the mysterious doors
Leading to universal knowledge—see,
Great son of Dryope,
The many that are come to pay their vows
With leaves about their brows !

"Be still the unimaginable lodge
For solitary thinkings; such as dodge
Conception to the very bourne of Heaven,
Then leave the naked brain: be still the leaven
That spreading in this dull and clodded earth,
Gives it a touch ethereal—a new birth:
Be still a symbol of immensity;

A firmament reflected in a sea;
An element filling the space between;
An unknown—but no more: we humbly screen
With uplift hands our foreheads, lowly bending,
And giving out a shout most heaven-rending,
Conjure thee to receive our humble Paean,
Upon thy Mount Lycean ! "

(Endymion, Book I.)

LAST SONNET.

Bright star ! would I were steadfast as thou art—
   Not in lone splendour hung aloft the night,
And watching, with eternal lids apart,
   Like Nature's patient, sleepless Eremite,
The moving waters at their priest-like task
   Of pure ablution round earth's human shores,
Or gazing on the new soft-fallen mask
   Of snow upon the mountains and the moors—
No—yet still steadfast, still unchangeable,
   Pillow'd upon my fair love's ripening breast,
To feel for ever its soft fall and swell,
   Awake for ever in a sweet unrest,
Still, still to hear her tender-taken breath,
   And so live ever—or else swoon to death.

LORD TENNYSON.

ALFRED, LORD TENNYSON (1809–1892) succeeded
Wordsworth as Laureate in 1850, and until his death
he was regarded as the great poet of his age. He began
as a lyrical poet with volumes published in 1830 and
1833, whose reception was not very favourable. It
was *Poems in Two Volumes* (1842), containing much of
the earlier work revised and perfected, that proclaimed
him the undeniable successor to the great poets of the
Romantic Revival. His poetry was constantly in

touch with contemporary problems—*The Princess* (1847) dealt with the education of women, *In Memoriam,* the elegy on his friend Arthur Hallam, considered religion in relation to science. The *Idylls of the King* (1859–85) is a noble series of episodes. Tennyson wrote to the very end of his life, and *Crossing the Bar* was the fitting herald of his own departure. As a lyrist he is perhaps at his highest, but in all his varied work he is one of our few supreme artists.

THE SPLENDOUR FALLS.

The splendour falls on castle walls
    And snowy summits old in story:
The long light shakes across the lakes,
    And the wild cataract leaps in glory.
Blow, bugle, blow, set the wild echoes flying,
Blow, bugle; answer, echoes, dying, dying, dying.

O hark, O hear! how thin and clear,
    And thinner, clearer, farther going!
O sweet and far from cliff and scar
    The horns of Elfland faintly blowing!
Blow, let us hear the purple glens replying:
Blow, bugle; answer, echoes, dying, dying, dying.

O love, they die in yon rich sky,
    They faint on hill or field or river:
Our echoes roll from soul to soul,
    And grow for ever and for ever.
Blow, bugle, blow, set the wild echoes flying,
And answer, echoes, answer, dying, dying, dying.

TEARS, IDLE TEARS.

Tears, idle tears, I know not what they mean,
Tears from the depth of some divine despair

Rise in the heart, and gather to the eyes,
In looking on the happy Autumn-fields,
And thinking of the days that are no more.

Fresh as the first beam glittering on a sail,
That brings our friends up from the underworld,
Sad as the last which reddens over one
That sinks with all we love below the verge;
So sad, so fresh, the days that are no more.

Ah, sad and strange as in dark summer dawns
The earliest pipe of half-awakened birds
To dying ears, when unto dying eyes
The casement slowly grows a glimmering square;
So sad, so strange, the days that are no more.

Dear as remembered kisses after death,
And sweet as those by hopeless fancy feigned
On lips that are for others; deep as love,
Deep as first love, and wild with all regret;
O Death in Life, the days that are no more.

"BREAK, BREAK, BREAK."

Break, break, break,
  On thy cold gray stones, O Sea!
And I would that my tongue could utter
  The thoughts that arise in me.

O well for the fisherman's boy,
  That he shouts with his sister at play!
O well for the sailor lad,
  That he sings in his boat on the bay!

And the stately ships go on
  To their haven under the hill;

But O for the touch of a vanish'd hand,
   And the sound of a voice that is still !

Break, break, break,
   At the foot of thy crags, O Sea !
But the tender grace of a day that is dead
   Will never come back to me.

" SWEET AND LOW."

Sweet and low, sweet and low,
   Wind of the western sea,
Low, low, breathe and blow,
   Wind of the western sea !
Over the rolling waters go,
Come from the dropping moon, and blow,
   Blow him again to me;
While my little one, while my pretty one, sleeps.

Sleep and rest, sleep and rest,
   Father will come to thee soon;
Rest, rest, on mother's breast,
   Father will come to thee soon;
Father will come to his babe in the nest,
Silver sails all out of the west
   Under the silver moon:
Sleep, my little one, sleep, my pretty one, sleep.

ST. AGNES' EVE.

Deep on the convent-roof the snows
   Are sparkling to the moon:
My breath to heaven like vapour goes:
   May my soul follow soon !
The shadows of the convent-towers
   Slant down the snowy sward,

Still creeping with the creeping hours
    That lead me to my Lord:
Make Thou my spirit pure and clear
    As are the frosty skies,
Or this first snowdrop of the year
    That in my bosom lies.

As these white robes are soil'd and dark,
    To yonder shining ground;
As this pale taper's earthly spark,
    To yonder argent round;
So shows my soul before the Lamb,
    My spirit before Thee;
So in mine earthly house I am,
    To that I hope to be.
Break up the heavens, O Lord! and far,
    Thro' all yon starlight keen,
Draw me, thy bride, a glittering star,
    In raiment white and clean.

He lifts me to the golden doors;
    The flashes come and go;
All heaven bursts her starry floors,
    And strows her lights below,
And deepens on and up! the gates
    Roll back, and far within
For me the Heavenly Bridegroom waits,
    To make me pure of sin.
The sabbaths of Eternity,
    One sabbath deep and wide—
A light upon the shining sea—
    The Bridegroom with his bride!

KING ARTHUR.

THE COMING.

Then from the castle gateway by the chasm
Descending thro' the dismal night—a night
In which the bounds of heaven and earth were lost—
Beheld, so high upon the dreary deeps
It seem'd in heaven, a ship, the shape thereof
A dragon wing'd, and all from stem to stern
Bright with a shining people on the decks,
And gone as soon as seen.   And then the two*
Dropt to the cove, and watch'd the great sea fall,
Wave after wave, each mightier than the last,
Till last, a ninth one, gathering half the deep
And full of voices, slowly rose and plunged
Roaring, and all the wave was in a flame:
And down the wave and in the flame was borne
A naked babe, and rode to Merlin's feet,
Who stoopt and caught the babe, and cried " The
    King !
Here is an heir for Uther ! "   And the fringe
Of that great breaker sweeping up the strand,
Lash'd at the wizard as he spake the word,
And all at once all round him rose in fire,
So that the child and he were clothed in fire.
And presently thereafter follow'd calm,
Free sky and stars. . . .

THE PASSING.

Slowly answer'd Arthur from the barge:
" The old order changeth, yielding place to new,
And God fulfils himself in many ways,
Lest one good custom should corrupt the world.

* Merlin and his servant Bleys.

Comfort thyself: what comfort is in me ?
I have lived my life, and that which I have done
May He within himself make pure ! but thou,
If thou shouldst never see my face again,
Pray for my soul.   More things are wrought by prayer
Than this world dreams of.   Wherefore, let thy voice
Rise like a fountain for me night and day.
For what are men better than sheep or goats
That nourish a blind life within the brain,
If, knowing God, they lift not hands of prayer
Both for themselves and those who call them friend ?
For so the whole round earth is every way
Bound by gold chains about the feet of God.
But now farewell.   I am going a long way. . . .
To the island-valley of Avilion;
Where falls not hail, or rain, or any snow,
Nor ever wind blows loudly; but it lies
Deep-meadow'd, happy, fair with orchard lawns
And bowery hollows crowned with summer sea,
Where I will heal me of my grievous wound."

So said he, and the barge with oar and sail
Moved from the brink, like some full-breasted swan
That, fluting a wild carol ere her death,
Ruffles her pure cold plume, and takes the flood
With swarthy webs. . . .

CHORIC SONG OF THE LOTOS-EATERS
I.

There is sweet music here that softer falls
Than petals from blown roses on the grass,
Or night-dews on still waters between walls
Of shadowy granite, in a gleaming pass;
Music that gentlier on the spirit lies,
Than tir'd eyelids upon tir'd eyes;

Music that brings sweet sleep down from the blissful
    skies.
Here are cool mosses deep,
And thro' the moss the ivies creep,
And in the stream the long-leaved flowers weep,
And from the craggy ledge the poppy hangs in sleep.

II.

Why are we weigh'd upon with heaviness,
And utterly consumed with sharp distress,
While all things else have rest from weariness ?
All things have rest: why should we toil alone,
We only toil, who are the first of things,
And make perpetual moan,
Still from one sorrow to another thrown:
Nor ever fold our wings,
And cease from wanderings,
Nor steep our brows in slumber's holy balm;
Nor harken what the inner spirit sings,
" There is no joy but calm ! "
Why should we only toil, the roof and crown of things

III.

  Lo ! in the middle of the wood,
The folded leaf is woo'd from out the bud
With winds upon the branch, and there
Grows green and broad, and takes no care,
Sun-steep'd at noon, and in the moon
Nightly dew-fed; and turning yellow
Falls, and floats adown the air.
Lo ! sweeten'd with the summer light,
The full-juiced apple, waxing over-mellow,
Drops in a silent autumn night.
All its allotted length of days,
The flower ripens in its place,

Ripens and fades, and falls, and hath no toil,
Fast-rooted in the fruitful soil.

IV.

Hateful is the dark-blue sky,
Vaulted o'er the dark-blue sea.
Death is the end of life; ah, why
Should life all labour be?
Let us alone.   Time driveth onward fast,
And in a little while our lips are dumb.
Let us alone.   What is it that will last?
All things are taken from us, and become
Portions and parcels of the dreadful Past.
Let us alone.   What pleasure can we have
To war with evil?   Is there any peace
In ever climbing up the climbing wave?
All things have rest, and ripen toward the grave
In silence; ripen, fall and cease:
Give us long rest or death, dark death, or dreamful ease.

V.

How sweet it were, hearing the downward stream,
With half-shut eyes ever to seem
Falling asleep in a half-dream!
To dream and dream, like yonder amber light,
Which will not leave the myrrh-bush on the height;
To hear each other's whisper'd speech;
Eating the Lotos day by day,
To watch the crisping ripples on the beach,
And tender curving lines of creamy spray;
To lend our hearts and spirits wholly
To the influence of mild-minded melancholy;
To muse and brood and live again in memory,
With those old faces of our infancy
Heap'd over with a mound of grass,
Two handfuls of white dust, shut in an urn of brass!

VI.

Dear is the memory of our wedded lives,
And dear the last embraces of our wives
And their warm tears: but all hath suffer'd change
For surely now our household hearths are cold:
Our sons inherit us: our looks are strange:
And we should come like ghosts to trouble joy.
Or else the island princes over-bold
Have eat our substance, and the minstrel sings
Before them of the ten years' war in Troy,
And our great deeds, as half-forgotten things.
Is there confusion in the little isle?
Let what is broken so remain.
The Gods are hard to reconcile:
'Tis hard to settle order once again.
There *is* confusion worse than death,
Trouble on trouble, pain on pain,
Long labour unto aged breath,
Sore task to hearts worn out by many wars
And eyes grown dim with gazing on the pilot-stars.

VII.

But, propt on beds of amaranth and moly,
How sweet (while warm airs lull us, blowing lowly)
With half-dropt eyelid still,
Beneath a heaven dark and holy,
To watch the long bright river drawing slowly
His waters from the purple hill—
To hear the dewy echoes calling
From cave to cave thro' the thick-twinèd vine—
To watch the emerald-colour'd water falling
Thro' many a wov'n acanthus-wreath divine!
Only to hear and see the far-off sparkling brine,
Only to hear were sweet, stretch'd out beneath the pine.

VIII.

The Lotos blooms below the barren peak:
The Lotos blows by every winding creek:
All day the wind breathes low with mellower tone:
Thro' every hollow cave and alley lone
Round and round the spicy downs the yellow Lotos-
    dust is blown.

We have had enough of action, and of motion we,
Roll'd to starboard, roll'd to larboard, when the surge
    was seething free,
Where the wallowing monster spouted his foam-
    fountains in the sea.

Let us swear an oath, and keep it with an equal mind,
In the hollow Lotos-land to live and lie reclined
On the hills like Gods together, careless of mankind.
For they lie beside their nectar, and the bolts are hurl'd
Far below them in the valleys, and the clouds are
    lightly curl'd
Round their golden houses, girdled with the gleaming
    world:
Where they smile in secret, looking over wasted lands,
Blight and famine, plague and earthquake, roaring
    deeps and fiery sands,
Clanging fights, and flaming towns, and sinking ships,
    and praying hands.
But they smile, they find a music centred in a doleful
    song
Steaming up, a lamentation and an ancient tale of
    wrong,
Like a tale of little meaning, tho' the words are strong;
Chanted from an ill-used race of men that cleave the
    soil,
Sow the seed, and reap the harvest with enduring toil,
Storing yearly little dues of wheat, and wine and oil;
Till they perish and they suffer—some, 'tis whisper'd
    —down in hell

Suffer endless anguish, others in Elysian valleys dwell,
Resting weary limbs at last on beds of asphodel.
Surely, surely, slumber is more sweet than toil, the
    shore
Than labour in the deep mid-ocean, wind and wave
    and oar;
Oh rest ye, brother mariners, we will not wander
    more.

THE HIGHER PANTHEISM.

The sun, the moon, the stars, the seas, the hills and the
    plains—
Are not these, O Soul, the Vision of Him who reigns?

Is not the Vision He? tho' He be not that which He
    seems?
Dreams are true while they last, and do we not live in
    dreams?

Earth, these solid stars, this weight of body and limb,
Are they not sign and symbol of thy division from Him?

Dark is the world to thee: thyself art the reason why;
For is He not all but that which has power to feel "I
    am I"?

Glory about thee, without thee; and thou fulfillest thy doom
Making Him broken gleams, and a stifled splendour and
    gloom.

Speak to Him thou for He hears, and Spirit with Spirit
    can meet—
Closer is He than breathing, and nearer than hands and feet.

God is law, say the wise; O Soul, and let us rejoice,
For if He thunder by law the thunder is yet His voice.

Law is God, say some: no God at all, says the fool;
For all we have power to see is a straight staff bent in a
    pool;

And the ear of man cannot hear, and the eye of man
    cannot see;
But if we could see and hear, this Vision—were it not He?

ULYSSES.

It little profits that an idle king,
By this still hearth, among these barren crags,
Match'd with an aged wife, I mete and dole
Unequal laws unto a savage race,
That hoard, and sleep, and feed, and know not me.
I cannot rest from travel: I will drink
Life to the lees: all times I have enjoy'd
Greatly, have suffer'd greatly, both with those
That loved me, and alone; on shore, and when
Thro' scudding drifts the rainy Hyades
Vext the dim sea: I am become a name;
For always roaming with a hungry heart
Much have I seen and known; cities of men
And manners, climates, councils, governments,
Myself not least, but honour'd of them all;
And drunk delight of battle with my peers,
Far on the ringing plains of windy Troy.
I am a part of all that I have met;
Yet all experience is an arch wherethro'
Gleams that untravell'd world, whose margin fades
For ever and for ever when I move.
How dull it is to pause, to make an end,
To rust unburnish'd, not to shine in use!
As tho' to breathe were life. Life piled on life
Were all too little, and of one to me
Little remains: but every hour is saved
From that eternal silence, something more,
A bringer of new things; and vile it were
For some three suns to store and hoard myself,
And this gray spirit yearning in desire

To follow knowledge, like a sinking star,
Beyond the utmost bound of human thought.
      This is my son, mine own Telemachus,
To whom I leave the sceptre and the isle—
Well-loved of me, discerning to fulfil
This labour, by slow prudence to make mild
A rugged people, and thro’ soft degrees
Subdue them to the useful and the good.
Most blameless is he, centred in the sphere
Of common duties, decent not to fail
In offices of tenderness, and pay
Meet adoration to my household gods,
When I am gone.   He works his work, I mine.
      There lies the port: the vessel puffs her sail:
There gloom the dark broad seas.   My mariners,
Souls that have toil’d, and wrought, and thought with
      me—
That ever with a frolic welcome took
The thunder and the sunshine, and opposed
Free hearts, free foreheads—you and I are old;
Old age hath yet his honour and his toil;
Death closes all: but something ere the end,
Some work of noble note, may yet be done,
Not unbecoming men that strove with Gods.
The lights begin to twinkle from the rocks:
The long day wanes: the slow moon climbs: the deep
Moans round with many voices.   Come, my friends,
’Tis not too late to seek a newer world.
Push off, and sitting well in order smite
The sounding furrows; for my purpose holds
To sail beyond the sunset, and the baths
Of all the western stars, until I die.
It may be that the gulfs will wash us down:
It may be we shall touch the Happy Isles,
And see the great Achilles, whom we knew.
Tho’ much is taken, much abides; and tho’

We are not now that strength which in old days
Moved earth and heaven; that which we are, we are;
One equal temper of heroic hearts,
Made weak by time and fate, but strong in will
To strive, to seek, to find, and not to yield.

From IN MEMORIAM.

Love is and was my Lord and King,
    And in his presence I attend
    To hear the tidings of my friend,
Which every hour his couriers bring.

Love is and was my King and Lord,
    And will be, tho' as yet I keep
    Within his court on earth, and sleep
Encompass'd by his faithful guard,

And hear at times a sentinel
    Who moves about from place to place,
    And whispers to the worlds of space,
In the deep night, that all is well.

BROWNING.

ROBERT BROWNING (1812–1889) devoted his life to
poetry, and the only event to break the even tenour
was his romantic elopement with his wife, Elizabeth
Barrett Browning the poetess, from the eccentric
oppression of her father. His first poems were *Pauline*
(1833) and *Paracelsus* (1835); then came *Strafford* and
some other dramas; *Dramatic Lyrics* (1842), *Dramatic
Romances and Lyrics* (1845), *Christmas Eve and Easter
Day* (1850), and *Men and Women* (1855) contain on the
whole his best work, though the enormous *Ring and the*

Book (1868–9) is undoubtedly his masterpiece. His later work became too much the mere expression of his philosophy, and in it the thinker far outdistances the artist. His unique strength lay in the dramatic monologue; his fault is deliberate indulgence in the grotesque and obscure.

Song from PIPPA PASSES.

The year's at the spring,
And day's at the morn;
Morning's at seven;
The hill-side's dew-pearled;
The lark's on the wing;
The snail's on the thorn;
God's in His heaven—
All's right with the world !

HOME-THOUGHTS FROM ABROAD.

Oh, to be in England
Now that April's there,
And whoever wakes in England
Sees, some morning, unaware,
That the lowest boughs and the brushwood sheaf
Round the elm-tree bole are in tiny leaf,
While the chaffinch sings on the orchard bough
In England—now !

And after April, when May follows,
And the whitethroat builds, and all the swallows !
Hark, where my blossomed pear-tree in the hedge
Leans to the field and scatters on the clover
Blossoms and dewdrops—at the bent spray's edge—
That's the wise thrush; he sings each song twice over,
Lest you should think he never could recapture
The first fine careless rapture !

And though the fields look rough with hoary dew,
All will be gay when noontide wakes anew
The buttercups, the little children's dower
—Far brighter than this gaudy melon-flower !

HOME-THOUGHTS FROM THE SEA.

Nobly, nobly Cape Saint Vincent to the North-West died
    away;
Sunset ran, one glorious blood-red, reeking into Cadiz Bay;
Bluish mid the burning water, full in face Trafalgar lay;
In the dimmest North-East distance, dawned Gibraltar
    grand and gray;
" Here and here did England help me: how can I help
    England ? "—say,
Whoso turns as I, this evening, turn to God to praise and
    pray,
While Jove's planet rises yonder, silent over Africa.

HOW THEY BROUGHT THE GOOD NEWS FROM GHENT TO AIX.

I.

I sprang to the stirrup, and Joris, and he;
I galloped, Dirck galloped, we galloped all three;
" Good speed ! " cried the watch, as the gate-bolts
    undrew;
" Speed ! " echoed the wall to us galloping through;
Behind shut the postern, the lights sank to rest,
And into the midnight we galloped abreast.

II.

Not a word to each other; we kept the great pace
Neck by neck, stride by stride, never changing our place;
I turned in my saddle and made its girths tight,

Then shortened each stirrup, and set the pique right,
Rebuckled the cheek-strap, chained slacker the bit,
Nor galloped less steadily Roland a whit.

III.

'Twas moonset at starting; but while we drew near
Lokeren, the cocks crew and twilight dawned clear;
At Boom, a great yellow star came out to see;
At Düffeld, 'twas morning as plain as could be;
And from Mecheln church-steeple we heard the half-
    chime,
So Joris broke silence with, " Yet there is time ! "

IV.

At Aerschot, up leaped of a sudden the sun,
And against him the cattle stood black every one,
To stare thro' the mist at us galloping past,
And I saw my stout galloper Roland at last,
With resolute shoulders, each butting away
The haze, as some bluff river headland its spray.

V.

And his low head and crest, just one sharp ear bent back
For my voice, and the other pricked out on his track;
And one eye's black intelligence,—ever that glance
O'er its white edge at me, his own master, askance !
And the thick heavy spume-flakes which aye and anon
His fierce lips shook upwards in galloping on.

VI.

By Hasselt, Dirck groaned; and cried Joris, " Stay spur !
Your Roos galloped bravely the fault's not in her,
We'll remember at Aix "—for one heard the quick
    wheeze
Of her chest, saw the stretched neck and staggering knees,

And sunk tail, and horrible heave of the flank,
As down on her haunches she shuddered and sank.

VII.

So we were left galloping, Joris and I,
Past Looz and past Tongres, no cloud in the sky;
The broad sun above laughed a pitiless laugh,
'Neath our feet broke the brittle bright stubble like chaff;
Till over by Dalhem a dome-spire sprang white,
And " Gallop," gasped Joris, " for Aix is in sight ! "

VIII.

" How they'll greet us ! "—and all in a moment his roan
Rolled neck and croup over, lay dead as a stone;
And there was my Roland to bear the whole weight
Of the news which alone could save Aix from her fate,
With his nostrils like pits full of blood to the brim,
And with circles of red for his eye-sockets' rim.

IX.

Then I cast loose my buffcoat, each holster let fall,
Shook off both my jack-boots, let go belt and all,
Stood up in the stirrup, leaned, patted his ear,
Called my Roland his pet-name, my horse without peer;
Clapped my hands, laughed and sang, any noise, bad or
    good,
Till at length into Aix Roland galloped and stood.

X.

And all I remember is, friends flocking round
As I sat with his head 'twixt my knees on the ground;
And no voice but was praising this Roland of mine,
As I poured down his throat our last measure of wine,
Which (the burgesses voted by common consent)
Was no more than his due who brought good news from
    Ghent.

THE LAST RIDE TOGETHER.

I.

I said—Then, Dearest, since 'tis so,
Since now at length my fate I know,
Since nothing all my love avails,
Since all, my life seemed meant for, fails,
    Since this was written and needs must be—
My whole heart rises up to bless
Your name in pride and thankfulness !
Take back the hope you gave,—I claim
Only a memory of the same,
—And this beside, if you will not blame,
    Your leave for one more last ride with me.

II.

My mistress bent that brow of hers;
Those deep dark eyes, where pride demurs
When pity would be softening through,
Fixed me a breathing-while or two
    With life or death in the balance: right !
The blood replenished me again;
My last thought was at least not vain;
I and my mistress, side by side
Shall be together, breathe and ride,
So one day more am I deified—
    Who knows but the world may end to-night.

III.

Hush ! if you saw some western cloud
All billowy-bosomed, over-bowed
By many benedictions—sun's,
And moon's and evening-star's at once—
    And so, you, looking and loving best,
Conscious grew, your passion drew
Cloud, sunset, moonrise, star-shine too,

Down on you, near and yet more near,
Till flesh must fade for heaven was here !—
Thus leant she and lingered—joy and fear !
  Thus lay she a moment on my breast.

IV.

Then we began to ride.   My soul
Smoothed itself out—a long—cramped scroll
Freshening and fluttering in the wind.
Past hopes already lay behind.
  What need to strive with a life awry ?
Had I said that, had I done this,
So might I gain, so might I miss.
Might she have loved me ? just as well
She might have hated,—who can tell ?
Where had I been now if the worst befell ?
  And here we are riding, she and I.

V.

Fail I alone, in words and deeds ?
Why, all men strive and who succeeds ?
We rode; it seemed my spirit flew,
Saw other regions, cities new,
  As the world rushed by on either side.
I thought,—All labour, yet no less
Bear up beneath their unsuccess.
Look at the end of work, contrast
The petty Done, the Undone vast,
This Present of theirs with the hopeful Past !
  I hoped she would love me: here we ride.

VI.

What hand and brain went ever paired ?
What heart alike conceived and dared ?
What act proved all its thought had been ?

What will but felt the fleshly screen?
    We ride and I see her bosom heave.
There's many a crown for who can reach.
Ten lines, a statesman's life in each!
The flag stuck on a heap of bones,
A soldier's doing! what atones?
They scratch his name on the Abbey-stones.
    My riding is better, by their leave.

VII.

What does it all mean, poet? well,
Your brains beat into rhythm—you tell
What we felt only; you expressed
You hold things beautiful the best,
    And pace them in rhyme so, side by side.
'Tis something, nay 'tis much—but then,
Have you yourself what's best for men?
Are you—poor, sick, old ere your time—
Nearer one whit your own sublime
Than we who never have turned a rhyme?
    Sing, riding's a joy! For me, I ride.

VIII.

And you, great sculptor—so, you gave
A score of years to Art, her slave,
And that's your Venus—whence we turn
To yonder girl that fords the burn!
    You acquiesce, and shall I repine?
What, man of music, you, grown grey
With notes and nothing else to say,
Is this your sole praise from a friend,
" Greatly his opera's strains intend,
But in music we know how fashions end!"
    I gave my youth—but we ride, in fine.

IX.

Who knows what's fit for us ? Had fate
Proposed bliss here should sublimate
My being; had I signed the bond—
Still one must lead some life beyond,
　—Have a bliss to die with, dim-descried.
This foot once planted in the goal,
This glory-garland round my soul.
Could I descry such ? Try and test !
I sink back shuddering from the quest—
Earth being so good, would Heaven seem best ?
　Now, Heaven and she are beyond this ride.

X.

And yet—she has not spoke so long !
What if Heaven be that, fair and strong
At life's best, with our eyes upturned,
Whither life's flower is first discerned,
　We, fixed so, ever should so abide ?
What if we still ride on, we two,
With life for ever old yet new,
Changed not in kind but in degree,
The instant made eternity,—
And Heaven just prove that I and she
　Ride, ride together, for ever ride ?

Song from PIPPA PASSES.

You'll love me yet !—and I can tarry
　Your love's protracted growing:
June reared that bunch of flowers you carry,
　From seeds of April's sowing.

I plant a heartfull now: some seed
   At least is sure to strike,
And yield—what you'll not pluck indeed,
   Not love, but, may be, like !

You'll look at least on love's remains,
   A grave's one violet:
Your look ?—that pays a thousand pains.
   What's death !—You'll love me yet !

A FACE.

If one could have that little head of hers
Painted upon a background of pale gold,
Such as the Tuscan's early art prefers !
No shade encroaching on the matchless mould
Of those two lips, which should be opening soft
In the pure profile; not as when she laughs,
For that spoils all: but rather as if aloft
Yon hyacinth, she loves so, leaned its staff's
Burthen of honey-coloured buds to kiss
And capture 'twixt the lips apart for this.
Then her lithe neck, three fingers might surround,
How it should waver on the pale gold ground
Up to the fruit-shaped, perfect chin it lifts !
I know, Correggio loves to mass, in rifts
Of heaven, his angel faces, orb on orb
Breaking its outline, burning shades absorb:
But these are only massed there, I should think,
Waiting to see some wonder momently
Grow out, stand full, fade slow against the sky
(That's the pale ground you'd see this sweet face by),
All heaven, meanwhile, condensed into one eye
Which fears to lose the wonder, should it wink.

EVELYN HOPE.

I.

Beautiful Evelyn Hope is dead !
  Sit and watch by her side an hour.
That is her book-shelf, this her bed;
  She plucked that piece of geranium-flower,
Beginning to die too, in the glass;
  Little has yet been changed, I think:
The shutters are shut, no light may pass
  Save two long rays thro' the hinge's chink.

II.

Sixteen years old when she died !
  Perhaps she had scarcely heard my name;
It was not her time to love; beside,
  Her life had many a hope and aim,
Duties enough and little cares,
  And now was quiet, now astir,
Till God's hand beckoned unawares,—
  And the sweet white brow is all of her.

III.

Is it too late then, Evelyn Hope ?
  What, your soul was pure and true,
The good stars met in your horoscope,
  Made you of spirit, fire and dew—
And, just because I was thrice as old
  And our paths in the world diverged so wide,
Each was nought to each, must I be told ?
  We were fellow mortals, nought beside ?

IV.

No, indeed ! for God above
  Is great to grant, as mighty to make,
And creates the love to reward the love:
  I claim you still, for my own love's sake !

Delayed it may be for more lives yet,
  Through worlds I shall traverse, not a few:
Much is to learn and much to forget
  Ere the time be come for taking you.

V.

But the time will come,—at last it will,
  When, Evelyn Hope, what meant, I shall say,
In the lower earth, in the years long still,
  That body and soul so pure and gay?
Why your hair was amber, I shall divine,
  And your mouth of your own geranium's red—
And what you would do with me, in fine,
  In the new life come in the old one's stead.

VI.

I have lived, I shall say, so much since then,
  Given up myself so many times,
Gained me the gains of various men,
  Ransacked the ages, spoiled the climes;
Yet one thing, one, in my soul's full scope,
  Either I missed or itself missed me:
And I want and find you, Evelyn Hope!
  What is the issue? let us see!

VII.

I loved you, Evelyn, all the while!
  My heart seemed full as it could hold—
There was place and to spare for the frank young smile
  And the red young mouth and the hair's young gold.
So, hush,—I will give you this leaf to keep—
  See, I shut it inside the sweet cold hand.
There, that is our secret! go to sleep;
  You will wake, and remember, and understand.

THE WILD JOYS OF LIVING.

Oh, our manhood's prime vigour ! no spirit feels waste,
Not a muscle is stopped in its playing, nor sinew unbraced.
Oh, the wild joys of living ! the leaping from rock up to
  rock—
The strong rending of boughs from the fir-tree,—the cool
  silver shock
Of the plunge in a pool's living water,—the hunt of the
  bear,
And the sultriness showing the lion is couched in his lair.
And the meal—the rich dates yellowed over with gold
  dust divine,
And the locust's-flesh steeped in the pitcher ! the full
  draught of wine,
And the sleep in the dried river-channel where bulrushes
  tell
That the water was wont to go warbling so softly and well.
How good is man's life, the mere living ! how fit to employ
All the heart and the soul and the senses, for ever in joy !

  (*Saul.*)

CHRIST ON CHRISTMAS EVE.

Suddenly
The rain and the wind ceased, and the sky
Received at once the full fruition
Of the moon's consummate apparition.
The black cloud-barricade was riven,
Ruined beneath her feet, and driven
Deep in the West; while, bare and breathless,
North and South and East lay ready
For a glorious Thing, that, dauntless, deathless,
Sprang across them, and stood steady.
'Twas a moon-rainbow, vast and perfect,
From heaven to heaven extending, perfect

As the mother-moon's self, full in face.
It rose, distinctly at the base
With its seven proper colours chorded,
Which still, in the rising, were compressed,
Until at last they coälesced,
And supreme the spectral creature lorded
In a triumph of whitest white,—
Above which intervened the night.
But above night too, like only the next,
The second of a wondrous sequence,
Reaching in rare and rarer frequence,
Till the heaven of heavens were circumflext,
Another rainbow rose, a mightier,
Fainter, flushier, and flightier,—
Rapture dying along its verge !
Oh, whose foot shall I see emerge,
Whose, from the straining topmost dark,
On to the keystone of that arc ?

This sight was shown me, there and then,—
Me, one out of a world of men,
Singled forth, as the chance might hap
To another, if in a thunderclap
Where I heard noise, and you saw flame,
Some one man knew God called his name.
For me, I think I said, " Appear !
Good were it to be ever here.
If Thou wilt, let me build to Thee
Service tabernacles Three,
Where, forever in Thy presence,
In ecstatic acquiescence,
Far alike from thriftless learning
And ignorance's undiscerning,
I may worship and remain ! "
Thus, at the show above me, gazing
With upturned eyes, I felt my brain

Glutted with the glory, blazing
Throughout its whole mass, over and under,
Until at length it burst asunder,
And out of it bodily there streamed
The too-much glory, as it seemed,
Passing from out me to the ground,
Then palely serpentining round
Into the dark with mazy error.

All at once I looked up with terror.
He was there.
He Himself with His human air.
(*Christmas-Eve and Easter-Day.*)

PROSPICE.

Fear death ?—to feel the fog in my throat,
    The mist in my face,
When the snows begin, and the blasts denote
    I am nearing the place,
The power of the night, the press of the storm,
    The post of the foe;
Where he stands, the Arch Fear in a visible form,
    Yet the strong man must go:
For the journey is done and the summit attained,
    And the barriers fall,
Though a battle's to fight ere the guerdon be gained,
    The reward of it all.
I was ever a fighter, so—one fight more,
    The best and the last !
I would hate that death bandaged my eyes, and forbore,
    And bade me creep past.
No ! let me taste the whole of it, fare like my peers
    The heroes of old,
Bear the brunt, in a minute pay glad life's arrears
    Of pain, darkness, and cold.

For sudden the worst turns the best to the brave,
　　The black minute's at end,
And the elements' rage, the fiend-voices that rave,
　　Shall dwindle, shall blend,
Shall change, shall become first a peace, then a joy,
　　Then a light, then thy breast,
O thou soul of my soul ! I shall clasp thee again,
　　And with God be the rest !

ARNOLD.

MATTHEW ARNOLD (1822–1888), son of Thomas Arnold, headmaster of Rugby, was an Inspector of Schools, and from 1857 to 1867 Professor of Poetry at Oxford.　His poetry is mainly lyrical and narrative, *Empedocles on Etna* standing high among his lyrical work, *Sohrab and Rustum* and *Balder Dead* among his narrative.　The decay of faith before the advance of science troubled him, and there is a strongly elegiac note in much of his poetry : *Thyrsis* is an elegy on his friend Arthur Hugh Clough the poet, and *Rugby Chapel* was inspired by the death of his father, while *The Scholar Gipsy, Dover Beach,* and other poems have an elegiac tone.　His prose literary criticism and theological writings were very influential—e.g. *Essays in Criticism,* and *God and the Bible.*

DOVER BEACH.

The sea is calm to-night.
The tide is full, the moon lies fair
Upon the straits;—on the French coast the light
Gleams and is gone; the cliffs of England stand,
Glimmering and vast, out in the tranquil bay.
Come to the window, sweet is the night-air !
Only, from the long line of spray
Where the sea meets the moon-blanch'd land,

Listen ! you hear the grating roar
Of pebbles which the waves draw back, and fling,
At their return, up the high strand,
Begin, and cease, and then again begin,
With tremulous cadence slow, and bring
The eternal note of sadness in.

Sophocles long ago
Heard it on the Aegean, and it brought
Into his mind the turbid ebb and flow
Of human misery; we
Find also in the sound a thought,
Hearing it by this distant northern sea.

The Sea of Faith
Was once, too, at the full, and round earth's shore
Lay like the folds of a bright girdle furl'd.
But now I only hear
Its melancholy, long, withdrawing roar,
Retreating, to the breath
Of the night-wind, down the vast edges drear
And naked shingles of the world.

Ah, love, let us be true
To one another ! for the world, which seems
To lie before us like a land of dreams,
So various, so beautiful, so new,
Hath really neither joy, nor love, nor light,
Nor certitude, nor peace, nor help for pain;
And we are here as on a darkling plain
Swept with confused alarms of struggle and flight,
Where ignorant armies clash by night.

THE SCHOLAR GIPSY.

Go, for they call you, Shepherd, from the hill;
  Go, Shepherd, and untie the wattled cotes:
    No longer leave thy wistful flock unfed,
  Nor let thy bawling fellows rack their throats,
    Nor the cropp'd grasses shoot another head.
        But when the fields are still,
    And the tired men and dogs all gone to rest,
      And only the white sheep are sometimes seen
      Cross and recross the strips of moon-blanch'd green;
  Come, Shepherd, and again renew the quest.

Here, where the reaper was at work of late—
  In this high field's dark corner, where he leaves
    His coat, his basket, and his earthen cruise,
  And in the sun all morning binds the sheaves,
    Then here, at noon, comes back his stores to use—
        Here will I sit and wait,
    While to my ear from uplands far away
      The bleating of the folded flocks is borne,
      With distant cries of reapers in the corn—
  All the live murmur of a summer's day.

Screen'd in this nook o'er the high, half-reap'd field,
  And here till sun-down, Shepherd, will I be.
    Through the thick corn the scarlet poppies peep,
  And round green roots and yellowing stalks I see
    Pale blue convolvulus in tendrils creep;
        And air-swept lindens yield
    Their scent, and rustle down their perfumed showers
      Of bloom on the bent grass where I am laid,
      And bower me from the August sun with shade ;
  And the eye travels down to Oxford's towers.

And near me on the grass lies Glanvil's book—
    Come, let me read the oft-read tale again,
      The story of that Oxford scholar poor
    Of pregnant parts and quick inventive brain,
      Who, tired of knocking at preferment's door,
          One summer morn forsook
    His friends, and went to learn the gipsy lore,
      And roam'd the world with that wild brotherhood,
      And came, as most men deem'd, to little good,
But came to Oxford and his friends no more.

But once, years after, in the country lanes,
    Two scholars whom at college erst he knew
      Met him, and of his way of life inquired.
    Whereat he answer'd, that the gipsy crew,
      His mates, had arts to rule as they desired
          The workings of men's brains;
    And they can bind them to what thoughts they will:
      " And I," he said, " the secret of their art,
      When fully learn'd, will to the world impart;
But it needs heaven-sent moments for this skill."

This said, he left them, and return'd no more,
    But rumours hung about the country-side
      That the lost Scholar long was seen to stray,
    Seen by rare glimpses, pensive and tongue-tied,
      In hat of antique shape, and cloak of grey,
          The same the gipsies wore.
Shepherds had met him on the Hurst in spring:
    At some lone alehouse in the Berkshire moors,
      On the warm ingle-bench, the smock-frock'd boors
Had found him seated at their entering.

But, mid their drink and clatter, he would fly;
    And I myself seem half to know thy looks,
      And put the shepherds, Wanderer, on thy trace;

And boys who in lone wheatfields scare the rooks
　　I ask if thou hast pass'd their quiet place;
　　　　Or in my boat I lie
Moor'd to the cool bank in the summer heats,
　　Mid wide grass meadows which the sunshine fills,
　　And watch the warm green-muffled Cumner hills,
And wonder if thou haunt'st their shy retreats.

For most, I know, thou lov'st retired ground.
　　Thee, at the ferry, Oxford riders blithe,
　　　　Returning home on summer nights, have met
Crossing the stripling Thames at Bablock-hithe,
　　Trailing in the cool stream thy fingers wet,
　　　　As the slow punt swings round:
And leaning backwards in a pensive dream,
　　And fostering in thy lap a heap of flowers
　　Pluck'd in shy fields and distant Wychwood bowers,
And thine eyes resting on the moonlit stream.

And then they land, and thou art seen no more.
　　Maidens who from the distant hamlets come
　　　　To dance around the Fyfield elm in May,
Oft through the darkening fields have seen thee roam,
　　Or cross a stile into the public way.
　　　　Oft thou hast given them store
Of flowers—the frail-leav'd, white anemone—
　　Dark bluebells drench'd with dews of summer eves—
　　And purple orchises with spotted leaves—
But none has words she can report of thee.

And, above Godstow Bridge, when hay-time's here
　　In June, and many a scythe in sunshine flames,
　　　　Men who through those wide fields of breezy grass
　　Where black-wing'd swallows haunt the glittering
　　　　Thames,

To bathe in the abandon'd lasher pass,
    Have often pass'd thee near
Sitting upon the river bank o'ergrown:
    Mark'd thy outlandish garb, thy figure spare,
    Thy dark vague eyes, and soft abstracted air;
But, when they came from bathing, thou wert gone.

At some lone homestead in the Cumner hills,
    Where at her open door the housewife darns,
    Thou hast been seen, or hanging on a gate
To watch the threshers in the mossy barns.
    Children, who early range these slopes and late
    For cresses from the rills,
Have known thee watching, all an April day,
    The springing pastures and the feeding kine;
    And mark'd thee, when the stars come out and shine,
Through the long dewy grass move slow away.

In Autumn, on the skirts of Bagley wood,
    Where most the gipsies by the turf-edged way
    Pitch their smoked tents, and every bush you see
With scarlet patches tagged and shreds of grey,
    Above the forest ground call'd Thessaly—
    The blackbird picking food
Sees thee, nor stops his meal, nor fears at all;
    So often has he known thee past him stray
    Rapt, twirling in thy hand a wither'd spray,
And waiting for the spark from Heaven to fall.

And once, in Winter, on the causeway chill
    Where home through flooded fields foot-travellers go,
    Have I not pass'd thee on the wooden bridge
Wrapt in thy cloak and battling with the snow,
    Thy face towards Hinksey and its wintry ridge?
    And thou hast climb'd the hill

And gain'd the white brow of the Cumner range,
　　Turn'd once to watch, while thick the snow-flakes
　　　　fall,
　　The line of festal light in Christ-Church hall—
Then sought thy straw in some sequester'd grange.

But what—I dream !　Two hundred years are flown
　Since first thy story ran through Oxford halls,
　　And the grave Glanvil did the tale inscribe
　That thou wert wander'd from the studious walls
　　To learn strange arts, and join a gipsy tribe.
　　　　And thou from earth art gone
　Long since, and in some quiet churchyard laid;
　　Some country nook, where o'er thy unknown grave
　　Tall grasses and white flowering nettles wave—
Under a dark red-fruited yew-tree's shade.

—No, no, thou hast not felt the lapse of hours.
　For what wears out the life of mortal men ?
　　'Tis that from change to change their being rolls:
　'Tis that repeated shocks, again, again,
　　Exhaust the energy of strongest souls,
　　　　And numb the elastic powers.
　Till having used our nerves with bliss and teen,
　　And tired upon a thousand schemes our wit,
　　To the just-pausing Genius we remit
Our worn-out life, and are—what we have been.

Thou hast not lived, why should'st thou perish, so ?
　Thou hadst *one* aim, *one* business, *one* desire:
　　Else wert thou long since number'd with the dead—
　Else hadst thou spent, like other men, thy fire.
　　The generations of thy peers are fled,
　　　　And we ourselves shall go;

But thou possessest an immortal lot,
    And we imagine thee exempt from age
    And living as thou liv'st on Glanvil's page,
Because thou hadst—what we, alas, have not!

For early didst thou leave the world, with powers
    Fresh, undiverted to the world without,
      Firm to their mark, not spent on other things;
    Free from the sick fatigue, the languid doubt,
      Which much to have tried, in much been baffled,
        brings.
        O Life unlike to ours!
Who fluctuate idly without term or scope,
    Of whom each strives, nor knows for what he strives,
    And each half lives a hundred different lives;
Who wait like thee, but not, like thee, in hope.

Thou waitest for the spark from Heaven: and we,
    Light half-believers of our casual creeds,
    Who never deeply felt, nor clearly will'd,
    Whose insight never has borne fruit in deeds,
      Whose vague resolves never have been fulfill'd;
        For whom each year we see
Breeds new beginnings, disappointments new;
    Who hesitate and falter life away,
    And lose to-morrow the ground won to-day—
Ah, do not we, Wanderer, await it too?

Yes, we await it, but it still delays,
    And then we suffer; and amongst us One,
      Who most has suffer'd, takes dejectedly
    His seat upon the intellectual throne;
      And all his store of sad experience he
        Lays bare of wretched days;

Tells us his misery's birth and growth and signs,
  And how the dying spark of hope was fed,
  And how the breast was soothed, and how the head,
And all his hourly varied anodynes.

This for our wisest! and we others pine,
  And wish the long unhappy dream would end,
    And waive all claim to bliss, and try to bear,
  With close-lipp'd patience for our only friend,
    Sad patience, too near neighbour to despair—
      But none has hope like thine!
  Thou through the fields and through the woods dost
      stray,
    Roaming the countryside, a truant boy,
    Nursing thy project in unclouded joy,
  And every doubt long blown by time away.

O born in days when wits were fresh and clear,
  And life ran gaily as the sparkling Thames;
    Before this strange disease of modern life,
  With its sick hurry, its divided aims,
    Its heads o'ertax'd, its palsied hearts, was rife—
      Fly hence, our contact fear!
  Still fly, plunge deeper in the bowering wood!
    Averse, as Dido did with gesture stern
    From her false friend's approach in Hades turn,
  Wave us away, and keep thy solitude!

Still nursing the unconquerable hope,
  Still clutching the inviolable shade,
    With a free, onward impulse brushing through,
  By night, the silver'd branches of the glade—
    Far on the forest-skirts, where none pursue,
      On some mild pastoral slope

Emerge, and resting on the moonlit pales
 Freshen thy flowers as in former years
 With dew, or listen with enchanted ears,
From the dark dingles, to the nightingales !

But fly our paths, our feverish contact fly !
 For strong the infection of our mental strife,
  Which, though it gives no bliss, yet spoils for rest;
 And we should win thee from thy own fair life,
  Like us distracted, and like us unblest.
  Soon, soon thy cheer would die,
Thy hopes grow timorous, and unfix'd thy powers,
 And thy clear aims be cross and shifting made;
 And then thy glad perennial youth would fade,
Fade and grow old at last, and die like ours.

Then fly our greetings, fly our speech and smiles !
 —As some grave Tyrian trader, from the sea,
  Descried at sunrise an emerging prow
Lifting the cool-hair'd creepers stealthily,
  The fringes of a southward-facing brow
   Among the Aegean isles;
 And saw the merry Grecian coaster come,
  Freighted with amber grapes, and Chian wine,
  Green bursting figs, and tunnies steep'd in brine—
 And knew the intruders on his ancient home,

The young light-hearted masters of the waves—
 And snatch'd his rudder, and shook out more sail,
  And day and night held on indignantly
O'er the blue Midland waters with the gale,
  Betwixt the Syrtes and soft Sicily,
   To where the Atlantic raves

Outside the western straits; and unbent sails
　　There, where down cloudy cliffs, through sheets of
　　　　foam,
　　Shy traffickers, the dark Iberians come;
And on the beach undid his corded bales.

MEREDITH.

GEORGE MEREDITH (1828–1909) began as a poet and journalist; after *The Ordeal of Richard Feverel* (1859) he showed himself one of the outstanding novelists of the age, *Beauchamp's Career* and *The Egoist* being two others of his best novels; all his life, however, he continued to write poetry. Both in his poems and in his novels Meredith used literature as the vehicle of his philosophy, and his style in both media was often perversely obscure. His finest poetry is lyrical—notably the beautiful *Love in the Valley*. *The Woods of Westermain* is a typical verse exposition of his philosophy; the sonnet sequence *Modern Love* shows the analyst of emotion as in the novels.

From LOVE IN THE VALLEY.

(STANZAS I., II., AND VI.).

Under yonder beech-tree single on the green-sward,
　　Couched with her arms behind her golden head,
Knees and tresses folded to slip and ripple idly,
　　Lies my young love sleeping in the shade.
Had I the heart to slide an arm beneath her,
　　Press her parting lips as her waist I gather slow,
Waking in amazement she could not but embrace me:
　　Then would she hold me and never let me go?

Shy as the squirrel and wayward as the swallow,
  Swift as the swallow along the river's light
Circleting the surface to meet his mirrored winglets,
  Fleeter she seems in her stay than in her flight.
Shy as the squirrel that leaps among the pine-tops,
  Wayward as the swallow overhead at set of sun,
She whom I love is hard to catch and conquer,
  Hard, but O the glory of the winning were she won!

Stepping down the hill with her fair companions,
  Arm in arm, all against the raying West,
Boldly she sings, to the merry tune she marches,
  Brave is her shape, and sweeter unpossess'd.
Sweeter, for she is what my heart first awaking
  Whisper'd the world was; morning light is she.
Love that so desires would fain keep her changeless;
  Fain would fling the net, and fain have her free. . .

THE ORCHARD AND THE HEATH.

I chanced upon an early walk to spy
A troop of children through an orchard gate:
  The boughs hung low, the grass was high;
  They had but to lift hands or wait
For fruits to fill them; fruits were all their sky.

They shouted, running on from tree to tree,
And played the game the wind plays, on and round.
  'Twas visible invisible glee
  Pursuing; and a fountain's sound
Of laughter spouted, pattering fresh on me.

I could have watched them till the daylight fled,
Their pretty bower made such a light of day.
  A small one tumbling sang, "Oh! head!"
  The rest to comfort her straightway
Seized on a branch and thumped down apples red.

The tiny creature flashing through green grass,
And laughing with her feet and eyes among
    Fresh apples, while a little lass
    Over as o'er breeze-ripples hung:
That sight I saw, and passed as aliens pass.

My footpath left the pleasant farms and lanes,
Soft cottage-smoke, straight cocks a-crow, gay flowers;
    Beyond the wheel-ruts of the wains,
    Across a heath I walked for hours,
And met its rival tenants, rays and rains.

Still in my view mile-distant firs appeared,
When, under a patched channel-bank enriched
    With foxglove whose late bells drooped seared,
    Behold, a family had pitched
Their camp, and labouring the low tent upreared.

Here, too, were many children, quick to scan
A new thing coming; swarthy cheeks, white teeth:
    In many-coloured rags they ran,
    Like iron runlets of the heath.
Dispersed lay broth-pot, sticks, and drinking-can.

Three girls, with shoulders like a boat at sea
Tipped sideways by the wave (their clothing slid
    From either ridge unequally),
    Lean, swift and voluble, bestrid
A starting-point, unfrocked to the bent knee.

They raced; their brothers yelled them on, and broke
In act to follow, but as one they snuffed
    Wood-fumes, and by the fire that spoke
    Of provender, its pale flame puffed,
And rolled athwart dwarf furzes grey-blue smoke.

Soon on the dark edge of a ruddier gleam,
The mother-pot perusing, all, stretched flat,
    Paused for its bubbling-up supreme:
    A dog upright in circle sat,
And oft his nose went with the flying steam.

I turned and looked on heaven awhile, where now
The moor-faced sunset broadened with red light;
    Threw high aloft a golden bough,
    And seemed the desert of the night
Far down with mellow orchards to endow.

LUCIFER IN STARLIGHT.

On a starred night Prince Lucifer uprose.
Tired of his dark dominion swung the fiend
Above the rolling ball in cloud part-screened,
Where sinners hugged their spectre of repose.
Poor prey to his hot fit of pride were those.
And now upon his western wing he leaned,
Now his huge bulk o'er Afric's sands careened,
Now the black planet shadowed Arctic snows.
Soaring through wider zones that pricked his scars
With memory of the old revolt from Awe,
He reached a middle height, and at the stars,
Which are the brain of heaven, he looked, and sank.
Around the ancient track marched, rank on rank,
The army of unalterable law.

JUGGLING JERRY.

I.

Pitch here the tent, while the old horse grazes:
    By the old hedge-side we'll halt a stage.
It's nigh my last above the daisies:
    My next leaf'll be man's blank page.

Yes, my old girl ! and it's no use crying:
    Juggler, constable, king, must bow.
One that outjuggles all's been spying
    Long to have me, and he has me now.

II.

We've travelled times to this old common:
    Often we've hung our pots in the gorse.
We've had a stirring life, old woman !
    You, and I, and the old grey horse.
Races, and fairs, and royal occasions,
    Found us coming to their call:
Now they'll miss us at our stations:
    There's a Juggler outjuggles all !

III.

Up goes the lark, as if all were jolly !
    Over the duck-pond the willow shakes.
Easy to think that grieving's folly,
    When the hand's firm as driven stakes !
Ay, when we're strong, and braced, and manful,
    Life's a sweet fiddle: but we're a batch
Born to become the Great Juggler's han'ful:
    Balls he shies up, and is safe to catch.

IV.

Here's were the lads of the village cricket:
    I was a lad not wide from here:
Couldn't I whip off the bail from the wicket ?
    Like an old world those days appear !
Donkey, sheep, geese, and thatched ale-house—
        I know them !
    They are old friends of my halts, and seem,
Somehow, as if kind thanks I owe them:
    Juggling don't hinder the heart's esteem.

V.

Juggling's no sin, for we must have victual:
    Nature allows us to bait for the fool.
Holding one's own makes us juggle no little;
    But, to increase it, hard juggling's the rule.
You that are sneering at my profession,
    Haven't you juggled a vast amount ?
There's the Prime Minister, in one Session,
    Juggles more games than my sins'll count.

VI.

I've murdered insects with mock thunder:
    Conscience, for that, in men don't quail.
I've made bread from the bump of wonder:
    That's my business, and there's my tale.
Fashion and rank all praised the professor:
    Ay ! and I've had my smile from the Queen:
Bravo, Jerry, she meant: God bless her !
    Ain't this a sermon on that scene ?

VII.

I've studied men from my topsy-turvy
    Close, and, I reckon, rather true.
Some are fine fellows: some, right scurvy:
    Most, a dash between the two.
But it's a woman, old girl, that makes me
    Think more kindly of the race:
And it's a woman, old girl, that shakes me
    When the Great Juggler I must face.

VIII.

We two were married, due and legal:
    Honest we've lived since we've been one.
Lord ! I could then jump like an eagle:
    You danced bright as a bit o' the sun.

Birds in a May-bush we were ! right merry !
  All night we kiss'd, we juggled all day.
Joy was the heart of Juggling Jerry !
  Now from his old girl he's juggled away.

IX.

It's past parsons to console us:
  No, nor no doctor fetch for me:
I can die without my bolus;
  Two of a trade, lass, never agree !
Parson and Doctor !—don't they love rarely,
  Fighting the devil in other men's fields !
Stand up yourself and match him fairly:
  Then see how the rascal yields !

X.

I, lass, have lived no gipsy, flaunting
  Finery while his poor helpmate grubs:
Coin I've stored, and you won't be wanting:
  You shan't beg from the troughs and tubs.
Nobly you've stuck to me, though in his kitchen
  Many a Marquis would hail you Cook !
Palaces you could have ruled and grown rich in,
  But your old Jerry you never forsook.

XI.

Hand up the chirper ! ripe ale winks in it;
  Let's have comfort and be at peace.
Once a stout draught made me light as a linnet.
  Cheer up ! the Lord must have his lease.
May be—for none see in that black hollow—
  It's just a place where we're held in pawn,
And, when the Great Juggler makes as to swallow,
  It's just the sword-trick—I ain't quite gone !

XII.

Yonder came smells of the gorse, so nutty,
   Gold-like and warm: it's the prime of May.
Better than mortar, brick and putty,
   Is God's house on a blowing day.
Lean me more up the mound; now I feel it:
   All the old heath-smells ! Ain't it strange ?
There's the world laughing, as if to conceal it,
   But He's by us, juggling the change.

XIII

I mind it well, by the sea-beach lying,
   Once—it's long gone—when two gulls we beheld,
Which, as the moon got up, were flying
   Down a big wave that sparked and swelled.
Crack, went a gun: one fell: the second
   Wheeled round him twice, and was off for new luck:
There in the dark her white wing beckon'd:—
   Drop me a kiss—I'm the bird dead-struck !

DANTE GABRIEL ROSSETTI.

DANTE GABRIEL ROSSETTI (1828–1882), the son of
an Italian patriot and refugee who had settled in
London, became eminent both as an artist and as a
poet.   He was one of the founders of the Pre-
Raphaelite Brotherhood.   In 1870 he published *Poems*,
most of which had been written before he reached the
age of twenty-five.   In this collection were *The Blessed
Damozel* and *The Portrait*.   In 1881 he published
Ballads and Poems.   Included in this volume was *The
House of Life*, a series of sonnets which contains
Rossetti's best work.

THE BLESSED DAMOZEL.

The blessèd damozel leaned out
   From the gold bar of Heaven;
Her eyes were deeper than the depths
   Of waters stilled at even;
She had three lilies in her hand,
   And the stars in her hair were seven.

Her robe, ungirt from clasp to hem,
   No wrought flowers did adorn,
But a white rose of Mary's gift
   For service meetly worn;
Her hair that lay along her back
   Was yellow like ripe corn.

Herseemed she scarce had been a day
   One of God's choristers;
The wonder was not yet quite gone
   From that still look of hers;
Albeit, to them she left, her day
   Had counted as ten years.

(To one, it is ten years of years.
   . . . Yet now, and in this place,
Surely she leaned o'er me—her hair
   Fell all about my face. . . .
Nothing: the autumn fall of leaves.
   The whole year sets apace).

It was the rampart of God's House
   That she was standing on;
By God built over the sheer depth
   The which is Space begun;
So high, that looking downward thence
   She scarce could see the sun.

It lies in Heaven, across the flood
    Of ether, as a bridge.
Beneath, the tides of day and night
    With flame and darkness ridge
The void, as low as where this earth
    Spins like a fretful midge.

Heard hardly, some of her new friends
    Amid their loving games
Spake evermore among themselves
    Their virginal chaste names;
And the souls mounting up to God
    Went by her like thin flames.

And still she bowed herself and stooped
    Out of the circling charm;
Until her bosom must have made
    The bar she leaned on warm,
And the lilies lay as if asleep
    Along her bended arm.

From the fixed place of Heaven she saw
    Time like a pulse shake fierce
Through all the worlds.   Her gaze still strove
    Within the gulf to pierce
Its path; and now she spoke as when
    The stars sang in their spheres.

The sun was gone now; the curled moon
    Was like a little feather
Fluttering far down the gulf; and now
    She spoke through the still weather.
Her voice was like the voice the stars
    Had when they sang together.

(Ah sweet! Even now, in that bird's song,
    Strove not her accents there,

Fain to be hearkened ?   When those bells
  Possessed the mid-day air,
Strove not her steps to reach my side
  Down all the echoing stair ?)

" I wish that he were come to me,
  For he will come," she said.
" Have I not prayed in Heaven ?—on earth,
  Lord, Lord, has he not pray'd ?
Are not two prayers a perfect strength ?
  And shall I feel afraid ?

" When round his head the aureole clings,
  And he is clothed in white,
I'll take his hand and go with him
  To the deep wells of Light;
We will step down, as to a stream,
  And bathe there in God's sight.

" We two will stand beside that shrine,
  Occult, withheld, untrod,
Whose lamps are stirred continually
  With prayer sent up to God;
And see our old prayers, granted, melt
  Each like a little cloud.

" We two will lie i' the shadow of
  That living mystic tree
Within whose secret growth the Dove
  Is sometimes felt to be,
While every leaf that His plumes touch
  Saith His Name audibly.

" And I myself will teach to him,
  I myself, lying so,

The songs I sing here; which his voice
    Shall pause in, hushed and slow,
And find some knowledge at each pause,
    Or some new thing to know."

(Alas ! we two, we two, thou say'st !
    Yea, one wast thou with me
That once of old.   But shall God lift
    To endless unity
The soul whose likeness with thy soul
    Was but its love for thee ?)

" We two," she said, " will seek the groves
    Where the lady Mary is,
With her five handmaidens, whose names
    Are five sweet symphonies,
Cecily, Gertrude, Magdalen,
    Margaret and Rosalys.

" Circlewise sit they, with bound locks
    And foreheads garlanded;
Into the fine cloth white like flame
    Weaving the golden thread,
To fashion the birth-robes for them
    Who are just born, being dead.

" He shall fear, haply, and be dumb:
    Then will I lay my cheek
To his, and tell about our love,
    Not once abashed or weak:
And the dear Mother will approve
    My pride, and let me speak.

" Herself shall bring us, hand in hand,
    To Him round whom all souls

Kneel, the clear-ranged unnumbered heads
    Bowed with their aureoles:
And angels meeting us shall sing
    To their citherns and citoles.

" There will I ask of Christ the Lord
    Thus much for him and me:—
Only to live as once on earth
    With Love,—only to be,
As then awhile, for ever now
    Together, I and he."

She gazed and listened and then said,
    Less sad of speech than mild,—
" All this is when he comes."   She ceased.
    The light thrilled towards her, fill'd
With angels in strong level flight.
    Her eyes prayed, and she smil'd.

(I saw her smile.)   But soon their path
    Was vague in distant spheres:
And then she cast her arms along
    The golden barriers,
And laid her face between her hands,
    And wept.   (I heard her tears.)

CHRISTINA ROSSETTI.

CHRISTINA ROSSETTI (1830–1894), was the sister of
Dante Rossetti.   After *Goblin Market* (1862) and *The
Prince's Progress* (1866), her work was chiefly
devotional.   She disputes with Elizabeth Browning
the rank of our greatest woman poet, and stands high
as a writer of sacred verse.   For colour and music,
deep human passion and bizarre fancy, *Goblin Market*
is likely to be immortal.

GOBLIN MARKET.

" Good folk," said Lizzie,
Mindful of Jeanie,
" Give me much and many ":
Held out her apron,
Tossed them her penny.
" Nay, take a seat with us,
Honour and eat with us,"
They answered grinning:
" Our feast is but beginning.
Night yet is early,
Warm and dew-pearly,
Wakeful and starry:
Such fruits as these
No man can carry;
Half their bloom would fly,
Half their dew would dry,
Half their flavour would pass by.
Sit down and feast with us,
Be welcome guest with us,
Cheer you and rest with us."—
" Thank you," said Lizzie: " but one waits
At home alone for me:
So without further parleying,
If you will not sell me any
Of your fruits though much and many,
Give me back my silver penny
I tossed you for a fee."—
They began to scratch their pates,
No longer wagging, purring,
But visibly demurring,
Grunting and snarling.
One called her proud,
Cross-grained, uncivil;
Their tones waxed loud,

Their looks were evil.
Lashing their tails
They trod and hustled her,
Elbowed and jostled her,
Clawed with their nails,
Barking, mewing, hissing, mocking,
Tore her gown and soiled her stocking,
Twitched her hair out by the roots,
Stamped upon her tender feet,
Held her hands and squeezed their fruits
Against her mouth to make her eat.

White and golden Lizzie stood,
Like a lily in a flood,—
Like a rock of blue-veined stone
Lashed by tides obstreperously,—
Like a beacon left alone
In a hoary roaring sea,
Sending up a golden fire,—
Like a fruit-crowned orange-tree
White with blossoms honey-sweet
Sore beset by wasp and bee,—
Like a royal virgin town
Topped with gilded dome and spire,
Close beleaguered by a fleet
Mad to tug her standard down.

One may lead a horse to water,
Twenty cannot make him drink.
Though the goblins cuffed and caught her,
Coaxed and fought her,
Bullied and besought her,
Scratched her, pinched her black as ink,
Kicked and knocked her,
Mauled and mocked her,
Lizzie uttered not a word;
Would not open lip from lip

Lest they should cram a mouthful in:
But laughed in heart to feel the drip
Of juice that syruped all her face,
And lodged in dimples of her chin,
And streaked her neck which quaked like curd.
At last the evil people,
Worn out by her resistance,
Flung back her penny, kicked their fruit
Along whichever road they took,
Not leaving root or stone or shoot;
Some writhed into the ground,
Some dived into the brook,
With ring and ripple,
Some scudded on the gale without a sound,
Some vanished in the distance.

In a smart, ache, tingle,
Lizzie went her way;
Knew not was it night or day;
Sprang up the bank, tore thro' the furze,
Threaded copse and dingle,
And heard her penny jingle
Bouncing in her purse,—
Its bounce was music to her ear.
She ran and ran
As if she feared some goblin man
Dogged her with gibe or curse
Or something worse;
But not one goblin skurried after,
Nor was she pricked by fear;
The kind heart made her windy-paced
That urged her home quite out of breath with haste
And inward laughter.

She cried, " Laura," up the garden,
" Did you miss me?
Come and kiss me.

Never mind my bruises,
Hug me, kiss me, suck my juices
Squeezed from goblin fruits for you,
Goblin pulp and goblin dew.
Eat me, drink me, love me;
Laura, make much of me:
For your sake I have braved the glen
And had to do with goblin merchant men."

UP-HILL.

Does the road wind up-hill all the way ?
    Yes, to the very end.
Will the day's journey take the whole long day ?
    From morn to night, my friend.

But is there for the night a resting place ?
    A roof for when the slow dark hours begin.
May not the darkness hide it from my face ?
    You cannot miss that inn.

Shall I meet other wayfarers at night ?
    Those who have gone before.
Then must I knock, or call when just in sight ?
    They will not keep you standing at that door.

Shall I find comfort, travel-sore and weak ?
    Of labour you shall find the sum.
Will there be beds for me and all who seek ?
    Yea, beds for all who come.

BROWN.

Thomas Edward Brown (1830–1897) was a clerical
schoolmaster, who was born in the Isle of Man, and
spent part of his life there.   He was a prolific writer of
lyrics, and he wrote a good deal of verse in the Manx
dialect.

MY GARDEN.

A Garden is a lovesome thing, God wot !
Rose plot,
Fringed pool,
Ferned grot—
The veriest school
Of peace; and yet the fool
Contends that God is not—
Not God ! in gardens ! when the eve is cool ?
Nay, but I have a sign;
'Tis very sure God walks in mine.

SWINBURNE.

ALGERNON CHARLES SWINBURNE (1837–1909) travelled much in France and Italy, and his verse reveals his
sympathy with all fighters for political liberty at home
and abroad.   His works include *Atalanta in Calydon*,
a Greek drama;   *Bothwell*, and other plays;   and the
lyrical series *Poems and Ballads* and *Songs before
Sunrise*.   He had a remarkable mastery of complex
verse music.

Chorus from ATALANTA IN CALYDON.

When the hounds of spring are on winter's traces,
    The mother of months in meadow or plain
Fills the shadows and windy places
    With lisp of leaves and ripple of rain;
And the brown bright nightingale amorous
Is half assuaged for Itylus,
For the Thracian ships and the foreign faces,
    The tongueless vigil, and all the pain.

Come with bows bent and with emptying of quivers,
   Maiden most perfect, lady of light,
With a noise of winds and many rivers,
   With a clamour of waters, and with might;
Bind on thy sandals, O thou most fleet,
Over the splendour and speed of thy feet;
For the faint east quickens, the wan west shivers,
   Round the feet of the day and the feet of the night.

Where shall we find her, how shall we sing to her,
   Fold our hands round her knees, and cling?
O that man's heart were as fire and could spring to her,
   Fire, or the strength of the streams that spring!
For the stars and the winds are unto her
As raiment, as songs of the harp-player;
For the risen stars and the fallen cling to her,
   And the southwest-wind and the west-wind sing.

For winter's rains and ruins are over,
   And all the season of snows and sins;
The days dividing lover and lover,
   The light that loses, the night that wins;
And time remembered is grief forgotten,
And frosts are slain and flowers begotten,
And in green underwood and cover
   Blossom by blossom the spring begins.

The full streams feed on flower of rushes,
   Ripe grasses trammel a travelling foot,
The faint fresh flame of the young year flushes
   From leaf to flower and flower to fruit;
And fruit and leaf are as gold and fire,
And the oat is heard above the lyre,
And the hoofèd heel of a satyr crushes
   The chestnut-husk at the chestnut-root.

And Pan by noon and Bacchus by night,
　Fleeter of foot than the fleet-foot kid,
Follows with dancing and fills with delight
　The Maenad and the Bassarid;
And soft as lips that laugh and hide
The laughing leaves of the trees divide,
And screen from seeing and leave in sight
　The god pursuing, the maiden hid.

The ivy falls with the Bacchanal's hair
　Over her eyebrows hiding her eyes;
The wild vine slipping down leaves bare
　Her bright breast shortening into sighs;
The wild vine slips with the weight of its leaves,
But the berried ivy catches and cleaves
To the limbs that glitter, the feet that scare
　The wolf that follows, the fawn that flies.

A FORSAKEN GARDEN.

In a coign of the cliff between lowland and highland,
　At the sea-down's edge between windward and lee,
Walled round with rocks as an inland island,
　The ghost of a garden fronts the sea.
A girdle of brushwood and thorn encloses
　The steep square slope of the blossomless bed
Where the weeds that grew green from the graves of its
　　roses
　　　　　Now lie dead.

The fields fall southward, abrupt and broken,
　To the low last edge of the long lone land.
If a step should sound or a word be spoken,
　Would a ghost not rise at the strange guest's hand?

So long have the grey bare walks lain guestless,
    Through branches and briars if a man make way,
He shall find no life but the sea-wind's, restless
            Night and day.

The dense hard passage is blind and stifled,
    That crawls by a track none turn to climb
To the strait waste place that the years have rifled
    Of all but the thorns that are touched not of time.
The thorns he spares when the rose is taken;
    The rocks are left when he wastes the plain.
The wind that wanders, the weeds wind-shaken,
            These remain.

Not a flower to be pressed of the foot that falls not;
    As the heart of a dead man the seed-plots are dry;
From the thicket of thorns whence the nightingale calls
        not,
    Could she call, there were never a rose to reply.
Over the meadows that blossom and wither
    Rings but the note of a sea-bird's song;
Only the sun and the rain come hither
            All year long.

The sun burns sere and the rain dishevels
    One gaunt bleak blossom of scentless breath.
Only the wind here hovers and revels
    In a round where life seems barren as death.
Here there was laughing of old, there was weeping,
    Haply, of lovers none ever will know,
Whose eyes went seaward a hundred sleeping
            Years ago.

Heart handfast in heart as they stood, " Look thither,"
    Did he whisper ? " look forth from the flowers to the
        sea;
For the foam-flowers endure when the rose-blossoms
    wither,
    And men that love lightly may die—but we ? "
And the same wind sang and the same waves whitened,
    And or ever the garden's last petals were shed,
In the lips that had whispered, the eyes that had
    lightened,
            Love was dead.

Or they loved their life through, and then went whither ?
    And were one to the end—but what end who knows ?
Love deep as the sea as a rose must wither,
    As the rose-red seaweed that mocks the rose.
Shall the dead take thought for the dead to love them ?
    What love was ever as deep as a grave ?
They are loveless now as the grass above them
           Or the wave.

All are at one now, roses and lovers,
    Not known of the cliffs and the fields and the sea.
Not a breath of the time that has been hovers
    In the air now soft with a summer to be.
Not a breath shall there sweeten the seasons hereafter
    Of the flowers or the lovers that laugh now or weep,
When as they that are free now of weeping and laughter,
           We shall sleep.

Here death may deal not again for ever:
    Here change may come not till all change end.

From the graves they have made they shall rise up never,
  Who have left nought living to ravage and rend.
Earth, stones, and thorns of the wild ground growing,
  While the sun and the rain live, these shall be:
Till a last wind's breath upon all these blowing
          Roll the sea.

Till the slow sea rise and the sheer cliff crumble,
  Till terrace and meadow the deep gulfs drink,
Till the strength of the waves of the high tides humble
  The fields that lessen, the rocks that shrink,
Here now in his triumph where all things falter,
  Stretched out on the spoils that his own hand spread,
As a god self-slain on his own strange altar,
          Death lies dead.

BLUNT.

WILFRED SCAWEN BLUNT (1840-1922) has much
verse to his name, but little of real distinction. He had
a gift for witty satire.

ST. VALENTINE'S DAY.

To-Day, all day, I rode upon the down,
With hounds and horsemen, a brave company.
On this side in its glory lay the sea,
On that the Sussex weald, a sea of brown.
The wind was light, and brightly the sun shone,
And still we galloped on from gorse to gorse.
And once, when checked, a thrush sang, and my horse
Pricked his quick ears as to a sound unknown.
  I knew the Spring was come.   I knew it even
Better than all by this, that through my chase
In bush and stone and hill and sea and heaven

I seemed to see and follow still your face.
Your face my quarry was.   For it I rode,
My horse a thing of wings, myself a god.

HARDY.

THOMAS HARDY (1840–1928) wrote his great novels between 1871 and 1896. His poems mostly belong to the subsequent years. His greatest poetic work is his epic-drama of the Napoleonic Wars, *The Dynasts* (1904–8). The deep sombre philosophy which pervades the novels penetrates the poems too, giving them a bitter strength, but his lyric muse, though often musical, is not seldom inclined to an unlyrical harshness.

THE DARKLING THRUSH.

I leant upon a coppice gate
　　When Frost was spectre-gray,
And Winter's dregs made desolate
　　The weakening eye of day.
The tangled bine-stems scored the sky
　　Like strings of broken lyres,
And all mankind that haunted nigh
　　Had sought their household fires.

The land's sharp features seemed to be
　　The Century's corpse outleant,
His crypt the cloudy canopy,
　　The wind his death-lament;
The ancient pulse of germ and birth
　　Was shrunken hard and dry,
And every spirit upon earth
　　Seemed fervourless as I.

At once a voice outburst among
    The bleak twigs overhead
In a full-hearted evensong
    Of joy illimited;
An aged thrush, frail, gaunt, and small,
    In blast-beruffled plume,
Had chosen thus to fling his soul
    Upon the growing gloom.

So little cause for carolings
    Of such ecstatic sound
Was written on terrestrial things
    Afar or nigh around,
That I could think there trembled through
    His happy good-night air
Some blessèd hope, whereof he knew
    And I was unaware.

SHELLEY'S SKYLARK.

The neighbourhood of Leghorn: March 1887.

Somewhere afield here something lies
In Earth's oblivious eyeless trust
That moved a poet to prophecies—
A pinch of unseen, unguarded dust:

The dust of the lark that Shelley heard,
And made immortal through times to be;—
Though it only lived like another bird,
And knew not its immortality:

Lived its meek life; then, one day, fell—
A little ball of feather and bone;
And how it perished, when piped farewell,
And where it wastes, are alike unknown.

Maybe it rests in the loam I view,
Maybe it throbs in a myrtle's green,
Maybe it sleeps in the coming hue
Of a grape on the slope of yon inland scene.

Go find it, faeries, go and find,
That tiny pinch of priceless dust,
And bring a casket silver-lined,
And framed of gold that gems encrust;

And we will lay it safe therein,
And consecrate it to endless time;
For it inspired a bard to win
Ecstatic heights in thought and rhyme.

Song from THE QUEEN OF CORNWALL.

Let's meet again to-night, my Fair,
  Let's meet unseen of all;
The day-god labours to his lair,
  And then the evenfall !

O living lute, O lily rose,
  O form of fantasie,
When torches waste and warders doze
  Steal to the stars will we !

While nodding knights carouse at meat,
  And Shepherds shamble home,
We'll cleave in close embracements—sweet
  As honey in the comb !

Till crawls the dawn from Condol's crown,
  And over Neitan's Kieve,
As grimly ghosts we conjure down
  And hopes still weave and weave !

THE OXEN.

Christmas Eve, and twelve of the clock.
    " Now they are all on their knees,"
An elder said as we sat in a flock
    By the embers in hearthside ease.

We pictured the meek mild creatures where
    They dwelt in their strawy pen,
Nor did it occur to one of us there
    To doubt they were kneeling then.

So fair a fancy few would weave
    In these years !   Yet, I feel,
If some one said on Christmas Eve,
    " Come; see the oxen kneel,

" In the lonely barton by yonder coomb
    Our childhood used to know,"
I should go with him in the gloom,
    Hoping it might be so.

IN TIME OF " THE BREAKING OF NATIONS."

I.

Only a man harrowing clods
    In a slow silent walk
With an old horse that stumbles and nods
    Half asleep as they stalk.

II.

Only thin smoke without flame
    From the heaps of couch-grass:
Yet this will go onward the same
    Though Dynasties pass.

III.

Yonder a maid and her wight
    Come whispering by:
War's annals will cloud into night
    Ere their story die.

"MEN WHO MARCH AWAY."

(SONG OF THE SOLDIERS.)

What of the faith and fire within us
    Men who march away
    Ere the barn-cocks say
    Night is growing gray,
Leaving all that here can win us;
What of the faith and fire within us
    Men who march away?

Is it a purblind prank, O think you,
    Friend with the musing eye,
    Who watch us stepping by
    With doubt and dolorous sigh?
Can much pondering so hoodwink you!
Is it a purblind prank, O think you,
    Friend with the musing eye?

Nay. We well see what we are doing,
    Though some may not see—
    Dalliers as they be—
    England's need are we;
Her distress would leave us rueing:
Nay. We well see what we are doing,
    Though some may not see!

In our heart of hearts believing
    Victory crowns the just,

And that braggarts must
Surely bite the dust,
Press we to the field ungrieving,
In our heart of hearts believing
Victory crowns the just.

Hence the faith and fire within us
Men who march away
Ere the barn-cocks say
Night is growing gray,
Leaving all that here can win us;
Hence the faith and fire within us
Men who march away.

September 5th, 1914.

BRIDGES.

ROBERT BRIDGES (1844–1930) was appointed Poet Laureate in succession to Alfred Austin. He was a poet of exquisite workmanship and one of our greatest masters of prosody, constantly experimenting in metrical forms. His greatest poem is *The Testament of Beauty* (1929), but his body of fine lyric work is considerable.

SPRING GOETH ALL IN WHITE.

Spring goeth all in white,
Crowned with milk-white may:
In fleecy flocks of light
O'er heaven the white clouds stray:

White butterflies in the air;
White daisies prank the ground:
The cherry and hoary pear
Scatter their snow around.

A PASSER-BY.

Whither, O splendid ship, thy white sails crowding,
  Leaning across the bosom of the urgent West,
That fearest nor sea rising, nor sky clouding,
  Whither away, fair rover, and what thy quest ?
  Ah ! soon, when Winter has all our vales opprest,
When skies are cold and misty, and hail is hurling,
  Wilt thóu glíde on the blue Pacific, or rest
In a summer haven asleep, thy white sails furling.

I there before thee, in the country that well thou knowest,
  Already arrived am inhaling the odorous air :
I watch thee enter unerringly where thou goest,
  And anchor queen of the strange shipping there,
  Thy sails for awnings spread, thy masts bare ;
Nor is aught from the foaming reef to the snow-capped,
    grandest
  Peak, that is over the feathery palms more fair
Than thou, so upright, so stately, and still thou standest.

And yet, O splendid ship, unhailed and nameless,
  I know not if, aiming a fancy, I rightly divine
That thou hast a purpose joyful, a courage blameless,
  Thy port assured in a happier land than mine.
  But for all I have given thee, beauty enough is thine,
As thou, aslant with trim tackle and shrouding,
  From the proud nostril curve of a prow's line
In the offing scatterest foam, thy white sails crowding.

LONDON SNOW.

When men were all asleep the snow came flying,
In large white flakes falling on the city brown,
Stealthily and perpetually settling and loosely lying,
  Hushing the latest traffic of the drowsy town ;

Deadening, muffling, stifling its murmurs failing;
Lazily and incessantly floating down and down:
   Silently sifting and veiling road, roof and railing;
Hiding difference, making unevenness even,
Into angles and crevices softly drifting and sailing.
   All night it fell, and when full inches seven
It lay in the depth of its uncompacted lightness,
The clouds blew off from a high and frosty heaven;
   And all woke earlier for the unaccustomed brightness
Of the winter dawning, the strange unheavenly glare:
The eye marvelled—marvelled at the dazzling whiteness;
   The ear hearkened to the stillness of the solemn air;
No sound of wheel rumbling nor of foot falling,
And the busy morning cries came thin and spare.
   Then boys I heard, as they went to school, calling,
They gathered up the crystal manna to freeze
Their tongues with tasting, their hands with snowballing;
   Or rioted in a drift, plunging up to the knees;
Or peering up from under the white-mossed wonder,
" O look at the trees ! " they cried, " O look at the trees ! "
   With lessened load a few carts creak and blunder,
Following along the white deserted way,
A country company long dispersed asunder:
   When now already the sun, in pale display
Standing by Paul's high dome, spread forth below
His sparkling beams, and awoke the stir of the day.
   For now doors open, and war is waged with the snow;
And trains of sombre men, past tale of number,
Tread long brown paths, as toward their toil they go:
   But even for them awhile no cares encumber
Their minds diverted; the daily word is unspoken,
The daily thoughts of labour and sorrow slumber
At the sight of the beauty that greets them, for the charm
     they have broken.

ON A DEAD CHILD.

Perfect little body, without fault or stain on thee,
   With promise of strength and manhood full and fair !
        Though cold and stark and bare,
The bloom and the charm of life doth awhile remain
      on thee.

Thy mother's treasure wert thou;—alas ! no longer
   To visit her heart with wondrous joy; to be
        Thy father's pride;—ah, he
Must gather his faith together, and his strength make
      stronger.

To me, as I move thee now in the last duty,
   Dost thou with a turn or gesture anon respond;
        Startling my fancy fond
With a chance attitude of the head, a freak of beauty.

Thy hand clasps, as 'twas wont, my finger, and holds it:
   But the grasp is the clasp of Death, heartbreaking and
      stiff;
        Yet feels to my hand as if
'Twas still thy will, thy pleasure and trust that enfolds it.

So I lay thee there, thy sunken eyelids closing,—
   Go, lie thou there in thy coffin, thy last little bed !—
        Propping thy wise, sad head,
Thy firm, pale hands across thy chest disposing.

So quiet ! doth the change content thee ?—Death,
        whither hath he taken thee ?
   To a world, do I think, that rights the disaster of this ?
        The vision of which I miss,
Who weep for the body, and wish but to warm thee and
      awaken thee ?

Ah ! little at best can all our hopes avail us
 To lift this sorrow, or cheer us, when in the dark,
  Unwilling, alone we embark,
And the things we have seen and have known and have
  heard of, fail us.

STEVENSON.

ROBERT LOUIS STEVENSON (1850–1894), son of the
famous lighthouse builder, went to Edinburgh University and was called to the Bar, but soon turned to
letters, producing novels, essays, and poems. After
a gallant struggle with poverty and ill-health, he died
at Vailima in the South Seas.

His vivid, romantic work, his exquisite prose style,
and the charm of his personal character had a tonic
influence upon late Victorian literature.

I WILL MAKE YOU BROOCHES.

I will make you brooches and toys for your delight
Of bird-song at morning and star-shine at night.
I will make a palace fit for you and me
Of green days in forests and blue days at sea.

I will make my kitchen, and you shall keep your room,
Where white flows the river and bright blows the broom.
And you shall wash your linen and keep your body white
In rainfall at morning and dewfall at night.

And this shall be for music when no one else is near,
The fine song for singing, the rare song to hear !
That only I remember, that only you admire,
 Of the broad road that stretches and the roadside fire.
                              (*The Roadside Fire.*)

CHRISTMAS AT SEA.

The sheets were frozen hard, and they cut the naked hand;
The decks were like a slide, where a seaman scarce could
    stand;
The wind was a nor'wester, blowing squally off the sea;
And cliffs and spouting breakers were the only things a-lee.

They heard the surf a-roaring before the break of day;
But 'twas only with the peep of light we saw how ill we lay.
We tumbled every hand on deck instanter, with a shout,
And we gave her the maintops'l, and stood by to go about.

All day we tacked and tacked between the South Head and
    the North,
All day we hauled the frozen sheets, and got no further
    forth;
All day as cold as charity, in bitter pain and dread,
For very life and nature we tacked from head to head.

We gave the South a wider berth, for there the tide-race
    roared;
But every tack we made we brought the North Head close
    aboard:
So's we saw the cliffs and houses, and the breakers running
    high,
And the coastguard in his garden, with his glass against
    his eye.

The frost was on the village roofs as white as ocean foam;
The good red fires were burning bright in every 'longshore
    home;
The windows sparkled clear, and the chimneys volleyed out;
And I vow we sniffed the victuals as the vessel went about.

The bells upon the church were rung with a mighty jovial
cheer,
For it's just that I should tell you how (of all days in the
year)
This day of our adversity was blessèd Christmas morn,
And the house above the coastguard's was the house where
I was born.

O well I saw the pleasant room, the pleasant faces there,
My mother's silver spectacles, my father's silver hair;
And well I saw the firelight, like a flight of homely elves,
Go dancing round the china-plates that stand upon the
shelves.

And well I knew the talk they had, the talk that was of me,
Of the shadow on the household and the son that went to
sea;
And O the wicked fool I seemed, in every kind of way,
To be here and hauling frozen ropes on blessèd Christmas
Day.

They lit the high sea-light, and the dark began to fall.
" All hands to loose topgallant sails," I heard the captain
call,
" By the Lord, she'll never stand it." our first mate,
Jackson, cried.
. . . " It's the one way or the other, Mr. Jackson, " he
replied.

She staggered to her bearings, but the sails were new and
good,
And the ship smelt up to windward just as though she
understood.
As the winter's day was ending, in the entry of the night,
We cleared the weary headland, and passed below the light.

And they heaved a mighty breath, every soul on board
    but me,
As they saw her nose again pointing handsome out to sea;
But all I could think of, in the darkness and the cold,
Was just that I was leaving home and my folks were
    growing old.

TO S. R. CROCKETT.

Blows the wind to-day, and the sun and the rain are flying,
    Blows the wind on the moors to-day and now,
Where about the graves of the martyrs the whaups are
    crying,
    My heart remembers how!

Grey recumbent tombs of the dead in desert places,
    Standing stones on the vacant wine-red moor,
Hills of sheep, and the homes of the silent vanished races,
    And winds, austere and pure:

Be it granted me to behold you again in dying,
    Hills of home! and to hear again the call;
Hear about the graves of the martyrs the peewees crying,
    And hear no more at all.

REQUIEM.

Under the wide and starry sky,
    Dig the grave and let me lie.
Glad did I live and gladly die,
    And I laid me down with a will.

This be the verse you grave for me:
    Here he lies where he longed to be;
Home is the sailor, home from sea,
    And the hunter home from the hill.

MEYNELL.

ALICE MEYNELL (1847–1922) was a friend of Francis Thompson; her husband did much to bring Thompson into notice. Like Thompson she had a strain of mysticism, but more evenly serene than his. She had a special aptitude for the Sonnet form, as in *Renouncement*.

CHIMES.

Brief, on a flying night,
   From the shaken tower
A flock of bells take flight,
   And go with the hour.

Like birds from the cote to the gales,
   Abrupt—O hark !
A fleet of bells set sails,
   And go to the dark.

Sudden the cold airs swing.
   Alone, aloud,
A verse of bells takes wing
   And flies with the cloud.

RENOUNCEMENT.

I must not think of thee; and, tired yet strong,
   I shun the thought that lurks in all delight—
   The thought of thee—and in the blue Heaven's height,
And in the sweetest passage of a song.

O just beyond the fairest thoughts that throng
   This breast, the thought of thee waits, hidden yet
      bright;
   But it must never, never come in sight;
I must stop short of thee the whole day long.

But when sleep comes to close each difficult day,
  When night gives pause to the long watch I keep,
    And all my bonds I needs must loose apart,

Must doff my will as raiment laid away,—
  With the first dream that comes with the first sleep
    I run, I run, I am gathered to thy heart.

TO A DAISY.

Slight as thou art, thou art enough to hide
  Like all created things, secrets from me,
  And stand a barrier to eternity.
And I, how can I praise thee well and wide

From where I dwell—upon the hither side?
  Thou little veil for so great a mystery,
  When shall I penetrate all things and thee,
And then look back?   For this I must abide,

Till thou shalt grow and fold and be unfurled
Literally between me and the world.
  Then I shall drink from in beneath a spring,

And from a poet's side shall read his book.
O daisy mine, what will it be to look
  From God's side even of such a simple thing?

THE SHEPHERDESS.

She walks—the lady of my delight—
  A shepherdess of sheep.
Her flocks are thoughts.   She keeps them white;
  She guards them from the steep;
She feeds them on the fragrant height,
  And folds them in for sleep.

She roams maternal hills and bright,
    Dark valleys safe and deep.
Into that tender breast of night
    The chastest stars may peep.
She walks—the lady of my delight—
    A shepherdess of sheep.

She holds her little thoughts in sight,
    Though gay they run and leap.
She is so circumspect and right;
    She has her soul to keep.
She walks—the lady of my delight—
    A shepherdess of sheep.

DAVIDSON.

JOHN DAVIDSON (1857–1909) was a Scotch school-master who, in 1889, settled in London, where he produced a novel, some volumes of poetry, and several plays. His poems are *Fleet Street Eclogues* (1893, 1896), *Ballads and Songs* (1894), and *New Ballads* (1897).

IN ROMNEY MARSH.

As I went down to Dymchurch Wall,
    I heard the South sing o'er the land;
I saw the yellow sunlight fall
    On knolls where Norman churches stand.

And ringing shrilly, taut and lithe,
    Within the wind a core of sound,
The wire from Romney town to Hythe
    Alone its airy journey wound.

A veil of purple vapour flowed
    And trailed its fringe along the Straits;
The upper air like sapphire glowed;
    And roses filled Heaven's central gates.

Masts in the offing wagged their tops;
    The swinging waves pealed on the shore;
The saffron beach, all diamond drops
    And beads of surge, prolonged the roar.

As I came up from Dymchurch Wall,
    I saw above the Downs' low crest
The crimson brands of sunset fall,
    Flicker and fade from out the west.

Night sank: like flakes of silver fire
    The stars in one great shower came down;
Shrill blew the wind; and shrill the wire
    Rang out from Hythe to Romney town.

The darkly shining salt sea drops
    Streamed as the waves clashed on the shore;
The beach, with all its organ stops
    Pealing again, prolonged the roar.

A RUNNABLE STAG.

When the pods went pop on the broom, green broom,
    And apples began to be golden-skinn'd,
We harbour'd a stag in the Priory coomb,
    And we feather'd his trail up-wind, up-wind,
    We feather'd his trail up-wind—
        A stag of warrant, a stag, a stag,
        A runnable stag, a kingly crop,
        Brow, bay and tray and three on top,
        A stag, a runnable stag.

Then the huntsman's horn rang yap, yap, yap,
  And " Forwards " we heard the harbourer shout;
But 'twas only a brocket that broke a gap
  In the beechen underwood, driven out,
    From the underwood antler'd out
      By warrant and might of the stag, the stag,
      The runnable stag, whose lordly mind
      Was bent on sleep, though beam'd and tined
      He stood, a runnable stag.

So we tufted the covert till afternoon
  With Tinkerman's Pup and Bell-of-the-North;
And hunters were sulky and hounds out of tune
  Before we tufted the right stag forth,
    Before we tufted him forth,
      The stag of warrant, the wily stag,
      The runnable stag with his kingly crop,
      Brow, bay and tray and three on top,
      The royal and runnable stag.

It was Bell-of-the-North and Tinkerman's Pup
  That stuck to the scent till the copse was drawn.
" Tally ho ! Tally ho ! " and the hunt was up,
  The tufters whipp'd, and the pack laid on,
    The resolute pack laid on,
      And the stag of warrant away at last,
      The runnable stag, the same, the same,
      His hoofs on fire, his horns like flame,
      A stag, a runnable stag.

" Let your gelding be: if you check or chide
  He stumbles at once and you're out of the hunt;
For three hundred gentlemen, able to ride,
  On hunters accustom'd to bear the brunt,
    Accustom'd to bear the brunt,

Are after the runnable stag, the stag,
The runnable stag with his kingly crop,
Brow, bay, and tray and three on top,
The right, the runnable stag."

By perilous paths in coomb and dell,
  The heather, the rocks, and the river-bed,
The pace grew hot, for the scent lay well,
  And a runnable stag goes right ahead,
  The quarry went right ahead—
    Ahead, ahead, and fast and far;
    His antler'd crest, his cloven hoof,
    Brow, bay and tray and three aloof,
    The stag, the runnable stag.

For a matter of twenty miles and more
  By the densest hedge and the highest wall,
Through herds of bullocks he baffled the lore
  Of harbourer, huntsman, hounds, and all,
  Of harbourer, hounds and all—
    The stag of warrant, the wily stag,
    For twenty miles, and five and five,
    He ran, and he never was caught alive,
    This stag, this runnable stag.

When he turn'd at bay in the leafy gloom,
  In the emerald gloom where the brook ran deep,
He heard in the distance the rollers boom,
  And he saw in a vision of peaceful sleep
  In a wonderful vision of sleep,
    A stag of warrant, a stag, a stag,
    A runnable stag in a jewell'd bed,
    Under the sheltering ocean dead,
    A stag, a runnable stag.

So a fateful hope lit up his eye,
    And he open'd his nostrils wide again,
And he toss'd his branching antlers high
    As he headed the hunt down the Charlock glen,
    As he raced down the echoing glen—
        For five miles more, the stag, the stag,
        For twenty miles, and five and five,
        Not to be caught now, dead or alive,
        The stag, the runnable stag.

Three hundred gentlemen, able to ride,
    Three hundred horses as gallant and free,
Beheld him escape on the evening tide,
    Far out till he sank in the Severn Sea,
    Till he sank in the depths of the sea—
        The stag, the buoyant stag, the stag
        That slept at last in a jewell'd bed
        Under the sheltering ocean spread,
        The stag, the runnable stag.

THOMPSON.

FRANCIS THOMPSON (1859–1907) is one of our truest religious lyrists, and his mystical apprehension of Christ inspired in *The Hound of Heaven,* the finest poem of its kind in our language. His longer poems riot too much with luxuriant verbiage, but among his shorter lyrics are many happy expressions of his love of flowers and children.

THE KINGDOM OF GOD.

O world invisible, we view thee,
O world intangible, we touch thee,
O world unknowable, we know thee,
Inapprehensible, we clutch thee.

Does the fish soar to find the ocean,
The eagle plunge to find the air—
That we ask of the stars in motion
If they have rumour of thee there ?

Not where the wheeling systems darken,
And our benumbed conceiving soars !—
The drift of pinions, would we hearken,
Beats at our own clay-shuttered doors.

The angels keep their ancient places;—
Turn but a stone, and start a wing !
'Tis ye, 'tis your estrangèd faces,
That miss the many-splendoured thing.

But (when so sad thou canst not sadder)
Cry;—and upon thy so sore loss
Shall shine the traffic of Jacob's ladder
Pitched between Heaven and Charing Cross.

Yea, in the night, my Soul, my daughter,
Cry—clinging Heaven by the hems;
And lo, Christ walking on the water
Not of Gennesareth, but Thames !

NOCTURN.

I walk, I only,
Not I only wake;
Nothing is, this sweet night,
But doth couch and wake
For its love's sake;
Everything, this sweet night,
Couches with its mate.
For whom but for the stealthy-visitant sun
Is the naked moon

Tremulous and elate ?
The heaven hath the earth
Its own and all apart;
The hushèd pool holdeth
A star to its heart.
You may think the rose sleepeth,
But though she folded is,
The wind doubts her sleeping;
Not all the rose sleeps,
But smiles in her sweet heart
For crafty bliss.
The wind lieth with the rose,
And when he stirs, she stirs in her repose:
The wind hath the rose,
And the rose her kiss.
Ah, mouth of me !
Is it then that this
Seemeth much to thee ?—
I wander only.
The rose hath her kiss.

TO A SNOWFLAKE.

What heart could have thought you ?—
Past our devisal
(O filigree petal !)
Fashioned so purely,
Fragilely, surely,
From what Paradisal
Imagineless metal,
Too costly for cost ?
Who hammered you, wrought you,
From argentine vapour ?—
" God was my shaper.
Passing surmisal,
He hammered, He wrought me,

From curled silver vapour,
To lust of His mind:—
Thou couldst not have thought me !
So purely, so palely,
Tinily, surely,
Mightily, frailly,
Insculped and embossed,
With His hammer of wind,
And His graver of frost."

DAISY.

Where the thistle lifts a purple crown
   Six foot out of the turf,
And the harebell shakes on the windy hill—
   O the breath of the distant surf !—

The hills look over on the South,
   And southward dreams the sea;
And with the sea-breeze hand in hand
   Came innocence and she.

Where 'mid the gorse the raspberry
   Red for the gatherer springs,
Two children did we stray and talk
   Wise, idle, childish things.

She listened with big-lipped surprise,
   Breast-deep mid flower and spine:
Her skin was like a grape whose veins
   Run snow instead of wine.

She knew not those sweet words she spake,
   Nor knew her own sweet way;
But there's never a bird, so sweet a song
   Thronged in whose throat that day.

Oh, there were flowers in Storrington
     On the turf and on the spray;
But the sweetest flower on Sussex hills
     Was the Daisy-flower that day !

Her beauty smoothed earth's furrowed face.
     She gave me tokens three:—
A look, a word of her winsome mouth,
     And a wild raspberry.

A berry red, a guileless look,
     A still word,—strings of sand !
And yet they made my wild, wild heart
     Fly down to her little hand.

For standing artless as the air,
     And candid as the skies,
She took the berries with her hand,
     And the love with her sweet eyes.

The fairest things have fleetest end,
     Their scent survives their close:
But the rose's scent is bitterness
     To him that loved the rose.

She looked a little wistfully,
     Then went her sunshine way:—
The sea's eye had a mist on it,
     And the leaves fell from the day.

She went her unremembering way,
     She went and left in me
The pang of all the partings gone,
     And partings yet to be.

She left me marvelling why my soul
    Was sad that she was glad;
At all the sadness in the sweet,
    The sweetness in the sad.

Still, still I seemed to see her, still
    Look up with soft replies,
And take the berries with her hand,
    And the love with her lovely eyes.

Nothing begins, and nothing ends,
    That is not paid with moan;
For we are born in other's pain,
    And perish in our own.

NEWBOLT.

SIR HENRY NEWBOLT (1862–1938) was poet, critic,
and novelist. He sang of the battlefield and the sea;
his poems, like those of Campbell, stir the blood, and
they are clearly the work of one in whom breathes
the best of our English spirit and tradition.

HE FELL AMONG THIEVES.

" Ye have robbed," said he, " ye have slaughtered and
    made an end,
  Take your ill-got plunder, and bury the dead:
What will ye more of your guest and sometime friend?"
    " Blood for our blood," they said.

He laugh'd: " If one may settle the score for five,
  I am ready; but let the reckoning stand till day:
I have loved the sunlight as dearly as any alive."
    " You shall die at dawn," said they.

He flung his empty revolver down the slope,
  He climbed alone to the Eastward edge of the trees;
All night long in a dream untroubled of hope
  He brooded, clasping his knees.

He did not hear the monotonous roar that fills
  The ravine where the Yassin river sullenly flows;
He did not see the starlight on the Laspur hills,
  Or the far Afghan snows.

He saw the April noon on his books aglow,
  The wistaria trailing in at the window wide;
He heard his father's voice from the terrace below
  Calling him down to ride.

He saw the gray little church across the park,
  The mounds that hide the loved and honoured dead;
The Norman arch, the chancel softly dark,
  The brasses black and red.

He saw the School Close, sunny and green,
  The runner beside him, the stand by the parapet wall,
The distant tape, and the crowd roaring between
  His own name over all.

He saw the dark wainscot and timbered roof,
  The long tables, and the faces merry and keen ;
The College Eight and their trainer dining aloof,
  The Dons on the daïs serene.

He watched the liner's stern ploughing the foam,
  He felt her trembling speed and the thrash of her
      screw;
He heard her passengers' voices talking of home,
  He saw the flag she flew.

And now it was dawn.   He rose strong on his feet,
    And strode to his ruined camp below the wood;
He drank the breath of the morning cool and sweet;
    His murderers round him stood.

Light on the Laspur hills was broadening fast,
    The blood-red snow-peaks chilled to a dazzling white:
He turned, and saw the golden circle at last,
    Cut by the Eastern height.

" O glorious Life, Who dwellest in earth and sun,
    I have lived, I praise and adore Thee."
                            A sword swept.
Over the pass the voices one by one
    Faded, and the hill slept.

VITAÏ LAMPADA.

There's a breathless hush in the Close to-night—
    Ten to make and the match to win—
A bumping pitch and a blinding light,
    An hour to play and the last man in.
And it's not for the sake of a ribboned coat,
    Or the selfish hope of a season's fame,
But his Captain's hand on his shoulder smote—
    " Play up ! play up ! and play the game ! "

The sand of the desert is sodden red,—
    Red with the wreck of a square that broke;—
The Gatling's jammed and the Colonel dead,
    And the regiment blind with dust and smoke.
The river of death has brimmed his banks,
    And England's far, and Honour a name,
But the voice of a schoolboy rallies the ranks:
    " Play up ! play up ! and play the game ! "

This is the word that year by year,
　　While in her place the School is set,
Every one of her sons must hear,
　　And none that hears it dare forget.
This they all with a joyful mind
　　Bear through life like a torch in flame,
And falling fling to the host behind—
　　" Play up ! play up ! and play the game ! "

DRAKE'S DRUM.

Drake he's in his hammock an' a thousand mile away,
　　(Capten, art tha sleepin' there below ?),
Slung atween the round shot in Nombre Dios Bay,
　　An' dreamin' arl the time o' Plymouth Hoe.
Yarnder lumes the Island, yarnder lie the ships,
　　Wi' sailor-lads a-dancin' heel-an'-toe,
An' the shore-lights flashin', and the night-tide dashin',
　　He sees et arl so plainly as he saw et long ago.

Drake he was a Devon man, an' rüled the Devon seas,
　　(Capten, art tha sleepin' there below ?),
Rovin' tho' his death fell, he went wi' heart at ease,
　　An' dreamin' arl the time o' Plymouth Hoe.
" Take my drum to England, hang et by the shore,
　　Strike et when your powder's runnin' low;
If the Dons sight Devon, I'll quit the port o' Heaven,
　　An' drum them up the Channel as we drummed them
　　　long ago."

Drake he's in his hammock till the great Armadas come,
　　(Capten, art tha sleepin' there below ?),
Slung atween the round shot, listenin' for the drum,
　　An' dreamin' arl the time o' Plymouth Hoe.
Call him on the deep sea, call him up the Sound,
　　Call him when ye sail to meet the foe;

Where the old trade's plyin' an' the old flag flyin'
　　They shall find him ware an' wakin', as they found him
　　　　long ago !

KIPLING.

RUDYARD KIPLING (1865–1936) has been called " the Laureate of the Empire." He brought into the literature of the eighteen-nineties a vigorous cheerful realism in strong contrast to the prevailing pessimism. His manly poetry, though often cruder than Newbolt's, has a robust patriotism and love of action in common with Newbolt's. In a quieter vein are his poems on Sussex and on flowers. Among his volumes of poetry are *Barrack-Room Ballads* (1892), and *The Seven Seas* (1896).

He was a novelist of India in *Kim,* and of school-life in *Stalky and Co.,* and a short-story writer as in *Wee Willie Winkie.* He wrote a history of the Irish Guards in the war of 1914–1918.

RECESSIONAL.

June 22, 1897.

God of our fathers, known of old,
　　Lord of our far-flung battle-line,
Beneath whose awful Hand we hold
　　Dominion over palm and pine—
Lord God of Hosts, be with us yet,
Lest we forget—lest we forget !

The tumult and the shouting dies;
　　The captains and the kings depart:
Still stands Thine ancient sacrifice,
　　An humble and a contrite heart.
Lord God of Hosts, be with us yet,
Lest we forget—lest we forget!

Far-called, our navies melt away;
   On dune and headland sinks the fire:
Lo, all our pomp of yesterday
   Is one with Nineveh and Tyre !
Judge of the Nations, spare us yet,
Lest we forget—lest we forget !

If, drunk with sight of power, we loose
   Wild tongues that have not Thee in awe,
Such boastings as the Gentiles use,
   Or lesser breeds without the Law—
Lord God of Hosts, be with us yet,
Lest we forget—lest we forget !

For heathen heart that puts her trust
   In reeking tube and iron shard,
All valiant dust that builds on dust,
   And guarding, calls not Thee to guard,
For frantic boast and foolish word—
Thy Mercy on Thy People, Lord !

SUSSEX.

God gave all men all earth to love,
   But since our hearts are small,
Ordained for each one spot should prove
   Beloved over all;
That as He watched Creation's birth,
   So we, in godlike mood,
May of our love create our earth
   And see that it is good.

So one shall Baltic pines content,
   As one some Surrey glade,
Or one the palm-grove's droned lament
   Before Levuka's trade.

Each to his choice, and I rejoice
  The lot has fallen to me
In a fair ground—in a fair ground—
  Yea, Sussex by the sea !

No tender-hearted garden crowns,
  No bosomed woods adorn
Our blunt, bow-headed, whale-backed Downs,
  But gnarled and writhen thorn—
Bare slopes where chasing shadows skim,
  And through the gaps revealed
Belt upon belt, the wooded, dim
  Blue goodness of the Weald.

Clean of officious fence or hedge,
  Half-wild and wholly tame,
The wise turf cloaks the white cliff edge
  As when the Romans came.
What sign of those that fought and died
  At shift of sword and sword ?
The barrow and the camp abide,
  The sunlight and the sward.

Here leaps ashore the full Sou' west
  All heavy-winged with brine,
Here lies above the folded crest
  The Channel's leaden line;
And here the sea-fogs lap and cling,
  And here, each warning each,
The sheep-bells and the ship-bells ring
  Along the hidden beach.

We have no waters to delight
  Our broad and brookless vales—
Only the dewpond on the height
  Unfed, that never fails,

Whereby no tattered herbage tells
    Which way the season flies—
Only our close-bit thyme that smells
    Like dawn in Paradise.

Here through the strong unhampered days
    The tinkling silence thrills;
Or little, lost, Down churches praise
    The Lord who made the hills:
But here the Old Gods guard their round,
    And, in her secret heart,
The heathen kingdom Wilfrid found
    Dreams, as she dwells, apart.

Though all the rest were all my share,
    With equal soul I'd see
Her nine-and-thirty sisters fair,
    Yet none more fair than she.
Choose ye your need from Thames to Tweed,
    And I will choose instead
Such lands as lie 'twixt Rake and Rye,
    Black Down and Beachy Head.

I will go out against the sun
    Where the rolled scarp retires,
And the Long Man of Wilmington
    Looks naked toward the shires;
And east till doubling Rother crawls
    To find the fickle tide,
By dry and sea-forgotten walls,
    Our ports of stranded pride.

I will go north about the shaws
    And the deep ghylls that breed
Huge oaks and old, the which we hold
    No more than " Sussex weed ";

Or south where windy Piddinghoe's
  Begilded dolphin veers,
And black beside wide-bankèd Ouse
  Lie down our Sussex steers.

So to the land our hearts we give
  Till the sure magic strike,
And Memory, Use, and Love make live
  Us and our fields alike—
That deeper than our speech and thought,
  Beyond our reason's sway,
Clay of the pit whence we were wrought
  Yearns to its fellow-clay.

God gives all men all earth to love,
  But since man's heart is small,
Ordains for each one spot shall prove
  Beloved over all.
Each to his choice, and I rejoice
  The lot has fallen to me
In a fair ground—in a fair ground—
  Yea, Sussex by the sea!

IF—.

If you can keep your head when all about you
  Are losing theirs and blaming it on you;
If you can trust yourself when all men doubt you,
  But make allowance for their doubting too;
If you can wait and not be tired by waiting,
  Or being lied about, don't deal in lies,
Or being hated don't give way to hating,
  And yet don't look too good, nor talk too wise;

If you can dream—and not make dreams your master;
  If you can think—and not make thoughts your aim,

If you can meet with Triumph and Disaster
  And treat those two impostors just the same;
If you can bear to hear the truth you've spoken
  Twisted by knaves to make a trap for fools,
Or watch the things you gave your life to, broken,
  And stoop and build 'em up with worn-out tools;

If you can make one heap of all your winnings
  And risk it on one turn of pitch-and-toss,
And lose, and start again at your beginnings
  And never breathe a word about your loss;
If you can force your heart and nerve and sinew
  To serve your turn long after they are gone,
And so hold on when there is nothing in you
  Except the Will which says to them: "Hold on!"

If you can talk with crowds and keep your virtue,
  Or walk with Kings—nor lose the common touch,
If neither foes nor loving friends can hurt you,
  If all men count with you, but none too much;
If you can fill the unforgiving minute
  With sixty seconds' worth of distance run,
Yours is the Earth and everything that's in it,
  And—which is more—you'll be a Man, my son!

YEATS.

WILLIAM BUTLER YEATS (1865–1939) stood at the
head of the Irish literary movement in drama and
poetry, and his work was largely inspired by Irish
traditions and fairy lore. His earlier productions,
such as the poetic plays *The Countess Cathleen*
(1892) and *Deirdre* (1907) and lyric volumes like *The
Wind among the Reads* (1899) were romantic. His
later work such as *A Full Moon in March* (1935) was
austere and awake to the tragic circumstances of the
day. He was the greatest poet of his time.

THE LAKE ISLE OF INNISFREE.

I will arise and go now, and go to Innisfree,
And a small cabin build there, of clay and wattles made:
Nine bean rows will I have there, a hive for the honey bee,
And live alone in the bee-loud glade.

And I shall have some peace there, for peace comes
    dropping slow,
Dropping from the veils of the morning to where the
    cricket sings;
There midnight's all a glimmer, and noon a purple glow,
And evening full of the linnet's wings.

I will arise and go now, for always night and day
I hear lake water lapping with low sounds by the shore;
While I stand on the roadway, or on the pavements grey,
I hear it in the deep heart's core.

WHEN YOU ARE OLD.

When you are old and grey and full of sleep,
    And nodding by the fire, take down this book,
    And slowly read; and dream of the soft look
Your eyes had once, and of their shadows deep;

How many loved your moments of glad grace,
    And loved your beauty with love false or true,
    But one man loved the pilgrim soul in you,
And loved the sorrows of your changing face;

And bending down beside the glowing bars
    Murmur, a little sadly, how love fled
    And paced upon the mountains overhead
And hid his face amid a crowd of stars.

THE SONG OF WANDERING AENGUS.

I went out to the hazel wood,
    Because a fire was in my head,
And cut and peeled a hazel wand,
    And hooked a berry to a thread;
And when white moths were on the wing,
    And moth-like stars were flickering out,
I dropped the berry in a stream
    And caught a little silver trout.

When I had laid it on the floor
    I went to blow the fire aflame,
But something rustled on the floor,
    And some one called me by my name:
It had become a glimmering girl
    With apple blossom in her hair
Who called me by my name and ran
    And faded through the brightening air.

Though I am old with wandering
    Through hollow lands and hilly lands,
I will find out where she has gone,
    And kiss her lips and take her hands;
And walk among long dappled grass,
    And pluck till time and times are done
The silver apples of the moon,
    The golden apples of the sun.

THE MAN WHO DREAMED OF FAERYLAND.

He stood among a crowd at Drumahair;
His heart hung all upon a silken dress,
And he had known at last some tenderness,
Before earth made of him her sleepy care;
But when a man poured fish into a pile,

It seemed they raised their little silver heads,
And sang how day a Druid twilight sheds
Upon a dim, green, well-belovèd isle,
Where people love beside star-laden seas;
How Time may never mar their faery vows
Under the woven roofs of quicken boughs:
The singing shook him out of his new ease.

He wandered by the sands of Lisadill;
His mind ran all on money, cares and fears,
And he had known at last some prudent years
Before they heaped his grave under the hill;
But while he passed before a plashy place,
A lug-worm with its grey and muddy mouth
Sang how somewhere to north or west or south
There dwelt a gay, exulting, gentle race;
And how beneath those three times blessèd skies
A Danaan fruitage makes a shower of moons,
And as it falls awakens leafy tunes:
And at that singing he was no more wise.

He mused beside the well of Scanavin,
He mused upon his mockers: without fail
His sudden vengeance were a country tale,
Now that deep earth has drunk his body in;
But one small knot-grass growing by the pool
Told where, ah, little, all-unneeded voice!
Old Silence bids a lonely folk rejoice,
And chaplet their calm brows with leafage cool;
And how, when fades the sea-strewn rose of day,
A gentle feeling wraps them like a fleece,
And all their trouble dies into its peace:
The tale drove his fine angry mood away.

He slept under the hill of Lugnagall;
And might have known at last unhaunted sleep

Under that cold and vapour-turbaned steep,
Now that old earth had taken man and all:
Were not the worms that spired about his bones
Proclaiming with a low and reedy cry,
That God had leaned His hands out of the sky,
To bless that isle with honey in His tones;
That none may feel the power of squall and wave,
And no one any leaf-crowned dancer miss
Until He burn up Nature with a kiss:
The man has found no comfort in the grave.

RUSSELL.

" A. E. " (GEORGE W. RUSSELL, 1867–1935) shared
with Yeats in the new Irish movement in poetry and
the theatre. As journalist he edited *The Irish
Statesman,* 1923–30.

BABYLON.

The blue dusk ran between the streets: my love was
    winged within my mind,
It left to-day and yesterday and thrice a thousand years
    behind.
To-day was past and dead for me, for from to-day my feet
    had run
Through thrice a thousand years to walk the ways of
    ancient Babylon.
On temple top and palace roof the burnished gold flung
    back the rays
Of a red sunset that was dead and lost beyond a million
    days.
The tower of heaven turns darker blue, a starry sparkle
    now begins;

The mystery and magnificence, the myriad beauty and the
    sins
Come back to me. I walk beneath the shadowy multitude
    of towers;
Within the gloom the fountain jets its pallid mist in lily
    flowers.
The waters lull me and the scent of many gardens and I
    hear
Familiar voices, and the voice I love is whispering in my
    ear.
Oh real as in dream all this; and then a hand on mine is
    laid;
The wave of phantom time withdraws; and that young
    Babylonian maid,
One drop of beauty left behind from all the flowing of
    that tide,
Is looking with the self-same eyes, and here in Ireland by
    my side.
Oh light our life in Babylon, but Babylon has taken wings,
While we are in the calm and proud procession of eternal
    things.

BINYON.

LAURENCE BINYON (1869-1943), a high official at the
British Museum, was an authority on art as well as a
poet. On the whole he was a scholarly and careful
poet rather than a born singer, but his lyrics often
charm, and during the Great War of 1914-1918 he
wrote some noble war poetry. Lines from "For the
Fallen" are engraved as a war memorial on the front
of the British Museum. Among his early volumes are
London Visions (1895, 1898). *The Sirens* (1924) and
The Idols (1928) show his sustained lyric power.

THE LITTLE DANCERS.

Lonely, save for a few faint stars, the sky
Dreams; and lonely, below, the little street
Into its gloom retires, secluded and shy.
Scarcely the dumb roar enters this soft retreat;
And all is dark, save where come flooding rays
From a tavern window: there, to the brisk measure
Of an organ that down in an alley merrily plays,
Two children, all alone and no one by,
Holding their tattered frocks, through an airy maze
Of motion, lightly threaded with nimble feet,
Dance sedately: face to face they gaze,
Their eyes shining, grave with a perfect pleasure.

FOR THE FALLEN.

With proud thanksgiving, a mother for her children,
England mourns for her dead across the sea.
Flesh of her flesh they were, spirit of her spirit,
Fallen in the cause of the free.

Solemn the drums thrill: Death august and royal
Sings sorrow up into immortal spheres.
There is music in the midst of desolation
And a glory that shines upon our tears.

They went with songs to the battle, they were young,
Straight of limb, true of eye, steady and aglow.
They were staunch to the end against odds uncounted,
They fell with their faces to the foe.

They shall grow not old, as we that are left grow old:
Age shall not weary them, nor the years condemn.
At the going down of the sun and in the morning
We will remember them

They mingle not with their laughing comrades again;
They sit no more at familiar tables of home;
They have no lot in our labour of the day-time:
They sleep beyond England's foam.

But where our desires are and our hopes profound,
Felt as a well-spring that is hidden from sight,
To the innermost heart of their own land they are
    known
As the stars are known to the Night;

As the stars that shall be bright when we are dust,
Moving in marches upon the heavenly plain,
As the stars that are starry in the time of our darkness,
To the end, to the end, they remain.

From THE SIRENS.

Hearken to the eternal lovers rejoicing !
A sunrise in their hearts, a music in their veins,
Their bodies make sweet singing to one another;
They bathe in beams from one another's eyes.
They rejoice to belong to the Eternal Delight
Upon whose universe of buoyance they are launched,
That questions not of its way nor of its haven
But is both way and haven where it hies.

They marvel to be born in a new element,
To meet like streams as they go chiming to the sea,
To move like flames that touch and tremble; and
    marvelling
They look back on the voided shell they quit.
Dawn within dawn, light within light, unfolds for them
The secret of the world that flowing overflows
The sun and the moon and the farthest of the stars,
And it abounds in them, and they in it.

Beautiful are their fears as the shy-footed fawns
Safe only in wildness from the old hunter, Time,
To be assured in shadow of the heart's solitude,
Where joy finds joy that never Time records.
They have made virgin words of that soiled alphabet
Wherewith have been written histories of sorrow,
Labour and long defeat, and proud and vain conquest;
And all their lore is those sufficing words.

Magnificent they match the music of a name
Against abhorred Silence and terrors of the abyss,
The trust of a smile against all-ignoring Night,
And one low voice against Oblivion's greed.
Difference drew them to the enamoured wrestle,
Chosen, inevitable dear antagonists;
They cry one to the other: " Alone I was not I,"
" O lovely danger ! " and " O my angel need ! "

" Because thy sweetness is so troubling and so sharp,
Full of blood-thrilling strangeness, unexplored peril,
Never to be possessed, always to be desired,
Thou unknown world, I will dare all for thee."
" Though in a moment thou hast made me to forget
All that I was and had, triumphing I hold thee;
To thy darkness of strength I give and commit me;
Here is thy world, O sail upon my sea ! "

As the East that quickens and flushes to the height
Answering the ardour of the West, and as a rose
Quivers on the western cloud before the dayspring,
Divided as the East and West they are:
But upon ways invisible to mortal sense
Moves their bright union, where was created new
Love's wondrous world; from the darkness it emerges;
It is their Evening and their Morning Star.

Out of the hollows of unpenetrated Night
From afar calls to them, though they have known it not,
A voice that is theirs, yet is not theirs, a new voice
Never yet heard, yet older than all things;
Laughter of a child's voice, sweeter than any sound
On the earth or in the air, voice of eternal joy,
Victorious over the bowed wisdom of mortals,
A well beyond the world, that springs and sings.

BELLOC.

HILAIRE BELLOC (*b.* 1870) is novelist, essayist, and historian as well as poet. Perhaps the best of all his large output is his travel-book, *The Path to Rome* (1902). He is a Roman Catholic by faith, and has a strongly individual masculine intellect.

THE SOUTH COUNTRY.

When I am living in the Midlands
    That are sodden and unkind,
I light my lamp in the evening:
    My work is left behind;
And the great hills of the South Country
    Come back into my mind.

The great hills of the South Country
    They stand along the sea,
And it's there walking in the high woods
    That I could wish to be,
And the men that were boys when I was a boy
    Walking along with me.

The men that live in North England
  I saw them for a day:
Their hearts are set upon the waste fells,
  Their skies are fast and grey;
From their castle-walls a man may see
  The mountains far away.

The men that live in West England
  They see the Severn strong,
A-rolling on rough water brown
  Light aspen leaves along.
They have the secret of the Rocks,
  And the oldest kind of song.

But the men that live in the South Country
  Are the kindest and most wise,
They get their laughter from the loud surf,
  And the faith in their happy eyes
Comes surely from our Sister the Spring
  When over the sea she flies;
The violets suddenly bloom at her feet,
  She blesses us with surprise.

I never get between the pines
  But I smell the Sussex air;
Nor I never come on a belt of sand
  But my home is there.
And along the sky the line of the Downs
  So noble and so bare.

A lost thing could I never find,
  Nor a broken thing mend:
And I fear I shall be all alone
  When I get towards the end.
Who will be there to comfort me
  Or who will be my friend?

I will gather and carefully make my friends
  Of the men of the Sussex Weald,
They watch the stars from silent folds,
  They stiffly plough the field.
By them and the God of the South Country
  My poor soul shall be healed.

If I ever become a rich man,
  Or if ever I grow to be old,
I will build a house with deep thatch
  To shelter me from the cold,
And there shall the Sussex songs be sung
  And the story of Sussex told.

I will hold my house in the high wood
  Within a walk of the sea,
And the men that were boys when I was a boy
  Shall sit and drink with me.

LINES TO A DON.

Remote and ineffectual Don
That dared attack my Chesterton,
With that poor weapon, half-impelled,
Unlearnt, unsteady, hardly held,
Unworthy for a tilt with men—
Your quavering and corroded pen;
Don poor at Bed and worse at Table,
Don pinched, Don starved, Don miserable;
Don stuttering, Don with roving eyes,
Don nervous, Don of crudities;
Don clerical, Don ordinary,
Don self-absorbed and solitary;
Don here-and-there, Don epileptic;
Don puffed and empty, Don dyspeptic;
Don middle-class, Don sycophantic,

Don dull, Don brutish, Don pedantic;
Don hypocritical, Don bad,
Don furtive, Don three-quarters mad;
Don (since a man must make an end),
Don that shall never be my friend.

*   *   *   *   *

Don different from those regal Dons !
With hearts of gold and lungs of bronze,
Who shout and bang and roar and bawl
The Absolute across the hall,
Or sail in amply bellowing gown
Enormous through the Sacred Town,
Bearing from College to their homes
Deep cargoes of gigantic tomes;
Dons admirable !   Dons of Might !
Uprising on my inward sight
Compact of ancient tales, and port
And sleep—and learning of a sort.
Dons English, worthy of the land;
Dons rooted; Dons that understand.
Good Dons perpetual that remain
A landmark, walling in the plain—
The horizon of my memories—
Like large and comfortable trees.

*   *   *   *   *

Don very much apart from these,
Thou scapegoat Don, thou Don devoted,
Don to thine own damnation quoted,
Perplexed to find thy trivial name
Reared in my verse to lasting shame.
Don dreadful, rasping Don and wearing,
Repulsive Don—Don past all bearing.
Don of the cold and doubtful breath,
Don despicable, Don of death;
Don nasty, skimpy, silent, level;

Don evil; Don that serves the devil.
Don ugly—that makes fifty lines.
There is a Canon which confines
A Rhymed Octosyllabic Curse
If written in Iambic Verse
To fifty lines. I never cut;
I far prefer to end it—but
Believe me I shall soon return.
My fires are banked, but still they burn
To write some more about the Don
That dared attack my Chesterton.

MEW.

CHARLOTTE MEW (1870–1928) had a hard life; first
there was poverty, then ill-health, then the death of the
sister she loved; finally she killed herself.   The bitterness of her experience coloured much of her poetry,
of which there are only two volumes, *The Farmer's
Bride* (1916), and *The Rambling Sailor* (1929).

THE CHANGELING.

Toll no bell for me, dear Father, dear Mother,
    Waste no sighs;
There are my sisters, there is my little brother
    Who plays in the place called Paradise,
Your children all, your children for ever;
        But I, so wild,
Your disgrace, with the queer brown face, was never.
    Never, I know, but half your child !

In the garden at play, all day, last summer,
    Far and away I heard
The sweet " tweet-tweet " of a strange new-comer,
    The dearest, clearest call of a bird.

It lived down there in the deep green hollow,
    My own old home, and the fairies say
The word of a bird is a thing to follow,
    So I was away a night and a day.

One evening, too, by the nursery fire,
    We snuggled close and sat round so still,
When suddenly as the wind blew higher,
    Something scratched on the window-sill.
A pinched brown face peered in—I shivered;
    No one listened or seemed to see;
The arms of it waved and the wings of it quivered,
    Whoo—I knew it had come for me;
    Some are as bad as bad can be !
All night long they danced in the rain,
Round and round in a dripping chain,
Threw their caps at the window-pane,
    Tried to make me scream and shout
    And fling the bedclothes all about:
I meant to stay in bed that night,
And if only you had left a light
    They would never have got me out.

Sometimes I wouldn't speak, you see,
    Or answer when you spoke to me,
Because in the long, still dusks of Spring
You can hear the whole world whispering;
    The shy green grasses making love,
    The feathers grow on the dear, grey dove,
    The tiny heart of the redstart beat,
    The patter of the squirrel's feet,
The pebbles pushing in the silver streams,
The rushes talking in their dreams,
    The swish-swish of the bat's black wings,

The wild-wood bluebell's sweet ting-tings,
 Humming and hammering at your ear,
 Everything there is to hear
In the heart of hidden things,
 But not in the midst of the nursery riot,
 That's why I wanted to be quiet,
 Couldn't do my sums or sing,
 Or settle down to anything.
 And when, for that, I was sent upstairs
 I *did* kneel down to say my prayers;
But the King who sits on your high church steeple
Has nothing to do with us fairy people !

'Times I pleased you, dear Father, dear Mother,
 Learned all my lessons and liked to play,
And dearly I loved the little pale brother
 Whom some other bird must have called away.
Why did They bring me here to make me
 Not quite bad and not quite good,
Why, unless They're wicked, do They want, in spite,
  to take me
 Back to their wet, wild wood ?
Now, every night I shall see the windows shining,
 The gold lamp's glow, and the fire's red gleam,
While the best of us are twining twigs and the rest of
  us are whining
 In the hollow by the stream.
Black and chill are Their nights on the wold;
 And They live so long and They feel no pain:
I shall grow up, but never grow old,
I shall always, always be very cold,
 I shall never come back again !

DAVIES.

W. H. DAVIES (1871–1940) told of his early life in his *Autobiography of a Super-Tramp* (1907), a tale of the same class as Borrow's *Lavengro*, but one of more complete vagabondage. He was a pure lyrist, whose clear limpid song is as unforced as that of the birds of which he often wrote.

LEISURE.

What is this life if, full of care,
We have no time to stand and stare

No time to stand beneath the boughs
And stare as long as sheep or cows.

No time to see, when woods we pass,
Where squirrels hide their nuts in grass.

No time to see, in broad daylight,
Streams full of stars, like skies at night.

No time to turn at Beauty's glance,
And watch her feet, how they can dance.

No time to wait till her mouth can
Enrich that smile her eyes began.

A poor life this if, full of care,
We have no time to stand and stare.

OH, SWEET CONTENT.

Oh, sweet content, that turns the labourer's sweat
    To tears of joy, and shines the roughest face;
How often have I sought you high and low,
    And found you still in some lone quiet place.

Here, in my room, when full of happy dreams,
    With no life heard beyond that merry sound
Of moths that on my lighted ceiling kiss
    Their shadows as they dance and dance around.

Or in a garden, on a summer's night,
    When I have seen the dark and solemn air
Blink with the blind bat's wings, and heaven's bright face
    Twitch with the stars that shine in thousands there.

THE MOON.

Thy beauty haunts me, heart and soul,
    Oh thou fair Moon, so close and bright;
Thy beauty makes me like the child,
    That cries aloud to own thy light:
The little child that lifts each arm,
To press thee to her bosom warm.

Though there are birds that sing this night
    With thy white beams across their throats,
Let my deep silence speak for me
    More than for them their sweetest notes:
Who worships thee till music fails
Is greater than thy nightingales.

SWEET STAY-AT-HOME.

Sweet Stay-at-Home, sweet Well-content,
Thou knowest of no strange continent:
Thou hast not felt thy bosom keep
A gentle motion with the deep;
Thou hast not sailed in Indian seas,
Where scent comes forth in every breeze.

Thou hast not seen the rich grape grow
For miles, as far as eyes can go;
Thou hast not seen a summer's night
When maids could sew by a worm's light;
Nor the North Sea in spring send out
Bright hues that like birds flit about
In solid cages of white ice—
Sweet Stay-at-Home, sweet Love-one-place.
Thou hast not seen black fingers pick
White cotton when the bloom is thick,
Nor heard black throats in harmony;
Nor hast thou sat on stones that lie
Flat on the earth, that once did rise
To hide proud kings from common eyes.
Thou hast not seen plains full of bloom
Where green things had such little room
They pleased the eye like fairer flowers—
Sweet Stay-at-Home, all these long hours.
Sweet Well-content, sweet Love-one-place,
Sweet, simple maid, bless thy dear face;
For thou hast made more homely stuff
Nurture thy gentle self enough;
I love thee for a heart that's kind—
Not for the knowledge in thy mind.

RAPTURES.

Sing for the sun your lyric, lark,
    Of twice ten thousand notes;
Sing for the moon, you nightingales,
    Whose light shall kiss your throats;
Sing, sparrows, for the soft, warm rain,
    To wet your feathers through;
And, when a rainbow's in the sky,
    Sing you, cuckoo—" Cuckoo ! "

Sing for your five blue eggs, fond thrush,
  By many a leaf concealed;
You starlings, wrens, and blackbirds sing
  In every wood and field:
While I, who fail to give my love
  Long raptures twice as fine,
Will for her beauty breathe this one—
  A sigh, that's more divine.

HODGSON.

RALPH HODGSON (*b.* 1871), is particularly notable for
the short lyrics in which he expresses his deep sympathy with the feelings of animals. His best-known
poem is probably *The Bull*, a more sustained lyric
than most, in which he penetrates into the dreaming
mind of an old bull about to die in a tropical country.

THE BELLS OF HEAVEN.

'Twould ring the bells of Heaven
  The wildest peal for years,
If Parson lost his senses
  And people came to theirs,
And he and they together
  Knelt down with angry prayers
For tamed and shabby tigers,
  And dancing dogs and bears,
And wretched, blind pit-ponies,
  And little hunted hares.

TIME, YOU OLD GIPSY MAN.

Time, you old gipsy man,
    Will you not stay,
Put up your caravan
    Just for one day?

All things I'll give you,
    Will you be my guest,
Bells for your jennet
    Of silver the best,
Goldsmiths shall beat you
    A great golden ring,
Peacocks shall bow to you,
    Little boys sing,
Oh, and sweet girls will
    Festoon you with may,
Time, you old gipsy,
    Why hasten away?

Last week in Babylon,
    Last night in Rome,
Morning, and in the crush
    Under Paul's dome;
Under Paul's dial
    You tighten your rein—
Only a moment,
    And off once again;
Off to some city
    Now blind in the womb,
Off to another
    Ere that's in the tomb.

Time, you old gipsy man,
    Will you not stay,
Put up your caravan
    Just for one day?

DE LA MARE.

WALTER DE LA MARE (*b.* 1873) is a poet of little children, and of all little creatures, of birds or of mice, of flowers, and of fairyland and its bewitching mysteries. He has the daintiest touch and the purest trill of song; his imagination is a cunning little sprite ever dancing fantastically among the common things of the countryside. His prose differs from his poetry chiefly in form; in his short stories and his novels we are again drawn into an unsuspected world where strange things happen. *The Memoirs of a Midget* is a tale of uncanny beauty.

SILVER.

Slowly, silently, now the moon
Walks the night in her silver shoon;
This way, and that, she peers, and sees
Silver fruit upon silver trees;
One by one the casements catch
Her beams beneath the silvery thatch ;
Couched in his kennel, like a log,
With paws of silver sleeps the dog;
From their shadowy cote the white breasts peep
Of doves in a silver-feathered sleep;
A harvest mouse goes scampering by,
With silver claws, and silver eye;
And moveless fish in the water gleam,
By silver reeds in a silver stream.

THE CHILDREN OF STARE.

Winter is fallen early
On the house of Stare;
Birds in reverberating flocks
Haunt its ancestral box;
Bright are the plenteous berries
In clusters in the air.

Still is the fountain's music,
The dark pool icy still,
Whereon a small and sanguine sun
Floats in a mirror on,
Into a West of crimson,
From a South of daffodil.

'Tis strange to see young children
In such a wintry house;
Like rabbits' on the frozen snow
Their tell-tale footprints go;
Their laughter rings like timbrels
'Neath evening ominous:

Their small and heightened faces
Like wine-red winter buds;
Their frolic bodies gentle as
Flakes in the air that pass,
Frail as the twirling petal
From the briar of the woods.

Above them silence looms,
Still as an arctic sea;
Light fails ; night falls ; the wintry moon
Glitters; the crocus soon
Will ope grey and distracted
On earth's austerity:

Thick mystery, wild peril,
Law like an iron rod:—
Yet sport they on in Spring's attire,
Each with his tiny fire
Blown to a core of ardour
By the awful breath of God.

NOD.

Softly along the road of evening,
  In a twilight dim with rose,
Wrinkled with age, and drenched with dew,
  Old Nod, the shepherd, goes.

His drowsy flock streams on before him,
  Their fleeces charged with gold,
To where the sun's last beam leans low
  On Nod the shepherd's fold.

The hedge is quick and green with briar,
  From their sand the conies creep;
And all the birds that fly in heaven
  Flock singing home to sleep.

His lambs outnumber a noon's roses,
  Yet, when night's shadows fall,
His blind old sheep-dog, Slumber-soon,
  Misses not one of all.

His are the quiet steeps of dreamland,
  The waters of no-more-pain,
His ram's bell rings 'neath an arch of stars,
  " Rest, rest, and rest again."

THE SUNKEN GARDEN.

Speak not—whisper not;
Here bloweth thyme and bergamot;
Softly on the evening hour,
Secret herbs their spices shower,
Dark-spiked rosemary and myrrh,
Lean-stalked, purple lavender;
Hides within her bosom, too,
All her sorrows, bitter rue.

Breathe not—trespass not;
Of this green and darkling spot,
Latticed from the moon's beams,
Perchance a distant dreamer dreams;
Perchance upon its darkening air,
The unseen ghosts of children fare,
Faintly swinging, sway and sweep,
Like lovely sea-flowers in the deep;
While, unmoved, to watch and ward,
Amid its gloomed and daisied sward,
Stands with bowed and dewy head
That one little leaden Lad.

THE LINNET.

Upon this leafy bush
   With thorns and roses in it,
Flutters a thing of light,
   A twittering linnet,
And all the throbbing world
   Of dew and sun and air
By this small parcel of life
   Is made more fair;
As if each bramble-spray
   And mounded gold-wreathed furze,
Harebell and little thyme,
   Were only hers;
As if this beauty and grace
   Did to one bird belong,
And, at a flutter of wing,
   Might vanish in song.

CHESTERTON.

GILBERT KEITH CHESTERTON (1874–1936) was poet, novelist, essayist, journalist, and critic. In all his work beauty, seriousness, and fun mingle, for he had the vision of the poet, the social reformer, the sincere Christian, and the humorist. His genius had the unusual combination of robustness and whimsicality. Among his prose tales are the fantastic story *The Napoleon of Notting Hill,* and the Father Brown stories of mystery and detection; notable in his critical work is his volume on Browning in " The English Men of Letters " Series.

THE DONKEY.

When fishes flew and forests walked
  And figs grew upon thorn,
Some moment when the moon was blood
  Then surely I was born;

With monstrous head and sickening cry
  And ears like errant wings,
The devil's walking parody
  On all four-footed things.

The tattered outlaw of the earth,
  Of ancient crooked will;
Starve, scourge, deride me: I am dumb,
  I keep my secret still.

Fools ! For I also had my hour;
  One far fierce hour and sweet:
There was a shout about my ears,
  And palms before my feet.

THE SONG OF QUOODLE.

They haven't got no noses,
  The fallen sons of Eve;
Even the smell of roses

Is not what they supposes;
But more than mind discloses
And more than men believe.

They haven't got no noses,
They cannot even tell
When door and darkness closes
The park a Jew encloses,
Where even the Law of Moses
Will let you steal a smell.

The brilliant smell of water,
The brave smell of a stone,
The smell of dew and thunder,
The old bones buried under,
Are things in which they blunder
And err, if left alone.

The wind from winter forests,
The scent of scentless flowers.
The breath of brides' adorning,
The smell of snare and warning,
The smell of Sunday morning,
God gave to us for ours.

*　　*　　*　　*　　*

And Quoodle here discloses
All things that Quoodle can,
They haven't got no noses,
They haven't got no noses,
And goodness only knowses
The Noselessness of Man.

A CIDER SONG.

The wine they drink in Paradise
They make in Haute Lorraine;
God brought it burning from the sod
To be a sign and signal rod
That they that drink the blood of God
Shall never thirst again.

The wine they praise in Paradise
They make in Ponterey,
The purple wine of Paradise,
But we have better at the price;
It's wine they praise in Paradise,
It's cider that they pray.

The wine they want in Paradise
They find in Plodder's End,
The apple wine of Hereford,
Of Hafod Hill and Hereford,
Where woods went down to Hereford,
And there I had a friend.

The soft feet of the blessed go
In the soft western vales,
The road the silent saints accord,
The road from Heaven to Hereford,
Where the apple wood of Hereford
Goes all the way to Wales.

MASEFIELD.

JOHN MASEFIELD (*b.* 1878) is Poet Laureate in succession to Robert Bridges. He is thoroughly English, and a poet of wide experience and achievement. *Salt Water Ballads* and *Dauber* are poems of the sea; *Reynard the Fox* is an epic of the hunting-field, *Right Royal* of a race-horse; *The Everlasting Mercy* (1911) and *The Widow in the Bye Street* are powerful realistic narratives; *Lollingdon Downs* gives his philosophy of man and earth. In prose he is a sturdy romancer; among his best tales are *Sard Harker* and *Odtaa*. In drama he has written some poetic plays like *Philip the Great*, and a very powerful prose tragedy in *Nan*.

SEA-FEVER.

I must down to the seas again, to the lonely sea and the sky,
And all I ask is a tall ship and a star to steer her by,
And the wheel's kick and the wind's song and the white
    sail's shaking,
And a grey mist on the sea's face and a grey dawn breaking.

I must down to the seas again, for the call of the running tide
Is a wild call and a clear call that may not be denied;
And all I ask is a windy day with the white clouds flying,
And the flung spray and the blown spume, and the sea-
    gulls crying.

I must down to the seas again, to the vagrant gypsy life,
To the gull's way and the whale's way where the wind's
    like a whetted knife;
And all I ask is a merry yarn from a laughing fellow-rover,
And quiet sleep and a sweet dream when the long trick's
    over.

UP ON THE DOWNS.

Up on the downs the red-eyed kestrels hover,
    Eyeing the grass.
The field-mouse flits like a shadow into cover
    As their shadows pass.

Men are burning the gorse on the down's shoulder;
A drift of smoke
Glitters with fire and hangs, and the skies smoulder,
And the lungs choke.

Once the tribe did thus on the downs, on these downs
    burning
Men in the frame,
Crying to the gods of the downs till their brains were
    turning
And the gods came.

And to-day on the downs, in the wind, the hawks the
    grasses,
In blood and air,
Something passes me and cries as it passes,
On the chalk downland bare.

From THE DAFFODIL FIELDS.

Still as high June, the very water's noise
Seemed but a breathing of the earth; the flowers
Stood in the dim like souls without a voice.
The wood's conspiracy of occult powers
Drew all about them, and for hours on hours
No murmur shook the oaks, the stars did house
Their lights like lamps upon those never-moving
    boughs.

Under their feet the woodland sloped away
Down to the valley, where the farmhouse lights
Were sparks in the expanse the moon made gray.
June's very breast was bare this night of nights.
Moths blundered up against them, grays and whites
Moved on the darkness where the moths were out,
Nosing for stickysweet with trembling uncurled snout.

But all this beauty was but music played,
While the high pageant of their hearts prepared.
A spirit thrilled between them, man to maid,
Mind flowed in mind, the inner heart was bared,
They needed not to tell how much each cared;
All the soul's strength was at the other's soul.
Flesh was away awhile, a glory made them whole.

THY EVERLASTING MERCY, CHRIST.

Up the slow slope a team came bowing,
Old Callow at his autumn ploughing,
Old Callow stooped above the hales,
Ploughing the stubble into wales;
His grave eyes looking straight ahead,
Shearing a long straight furrow red;
His plough-foot high to give it earth
To bring new food for men to birth.

O wet red swathe of earth laid bare,
O truth, O strength, O gleaming share,
O patient eyes that watch the goal,
O ploughman of the sinner's soul.
O Jesus, drive the coulter deep
To plough my living man from sleep.

Slow up the hill the plough team plod,
Old Callow at the task of God,
Helped by man's wit, helped by the brute
Turning a stubborn clay to fruit,
His eyes for ever on some sign
To help him plough a perfect line.
At top of rise the plough team stopped,
The fore-horse bent his head and cropped.
Then the chains chack, the brasses jingle,
The lean reins gather through the cringle,

The figures move against the sky,
The clay wave breaks as they go by.
I kneeled there in the muddy fallow,
I knew that Christ was there with Callow,
That Christ was standing there with me,
That Christ had taught me what to be,
That I should plough, and as I ploughed
My Saviour Christ would sing aloud,
And as I drove the clods apart
Christ would be ploughing in my heart,
Through rest-harrow and bitter roots,
Through all my bad life's rotten fruits.

O Christ who holds the open gate,
O Christ who drives the furrow straight,
O Christ, the plough, O Christ, the laughter
Of holy white birds flying after,
Lo, all my heart's field red and torn,
And Thou wilt bring the young green corn,
The young green corn divinely springing,
The young green corn for ever singing;
And when the field is fresh and fair
Thy blessèd feet shall glitter there.
And we will walk the weeded field,
And tell the golden harvest's yield,
The corn that makes the holy bread
By which the soul of man is fed,
The holy bread, the food unpriced,
Thy everlasting mercy, Christ.

(The Everlasting Mercy.)

BEAUTY.

I have seen dawn and sunset on moors and windy hills
Coming in solemn beauty like slow old tunes of Spain:
I have seen the lady April bringing the daffodils,
Bringing the springing grass and the soft warm April rain.

I have heard the song of the blossoms and the old chant
   of the sea,
And seen strange lands from under the arched white
   sails of ships;
But the loveliest things of beauty God ever has showed
   to me,
Are her voice, and her hair, and eyes, and the dear red
   curve of her lips.

BARING.

HON. MAURICE BARING (1874-1945), after being in
the Diplomatic Service, became war correspondent in
Manchuria (1904), and special correspondent in Russia
(1905-8).   In the Great War he served in the Air
Force.   His *Collected Poems* appeared in 1925.   He
has written several books on Russia, including *An
Outline of Russian Literature* (1914).

IN MEMORIAM, A. H.

*(Auberon Herbert, Captain Lord Lucas, R.F.C.; killed
November 3, 1916.)*

> The wind had blown away the rain
> That all day long had soaked the level plain.
> Against the horizon's fiery wrack,
> The sheds loomed black.
> And higher, in their tumultuous concourse met,
> The streaming clouds, shot-riddled banners, wet
> With the flickering storm,
> Drifted and smouldered, warm
> With flashes sent
> From the lower firmament.

And they concealed—
They only here and there through rifts revealed
A hidden sanctuary of fire and light,
A city of chrysolite.

We looked and laughed and wondered, and I said:
That orange sea, those oriflammes outspread
Were like the fanciful imaginings
That the young painter flings
Upon the canvas bold,
Such as the sage and the old
Make mock at, saying it could never be;
And you assented also, laughingly.
I wondered what they meant,
That flaming firmament,
Those clouds so grey so gold, so wet so warm,
So much of glory and so much of storm,
The end of the world, or the end
Of the war—remoter still to me and you, my friend.

Alas ! it meant not this, it meant not that:
It meant that now the last time you and I
Should look at the golden sky,
And the dark fields large and flat,
And smell the evening weather,
And laugh and talk and wonder both together.

The last, last time.   We nevermore should meet
In France, or London street,
Or fields of home.   The desolated space
Of life shall nevermore
Be what it was before.
No one shall take your place.
No other face

Can fill that empty frame.
There is no answer when we call your name.
We cannot hear your step upon the stair.
We turn to speak and find a vacant chair.
Something is broken which we cannot mend.
God has done more than take away a friend
In taking you; for all that we have left
Is bruised and irremediably bereft.
There is none like you.   Yet not that alone
Do we bemoan;
But this; that you were greater than the rest,
And better than the best.

O liberal heart fast-rooted to the soil,
O lover of ancient freedom and proud toil,
Friend of the gipsies and all wandering song,
The forest's nursling and the favoured child
Of woodlands wild—
O brother to the birds and all things free,
Captain of liberty !
Deep in your heart the restless seed was sown;
The vagrant spirit fretted in your feet;
We wondered could you tarry long,
And brook for long the cramping street,
Or would you one day sail for shores unknown,
And shake from you the dust of towns, and spurn
The crowded market-place—and not return ?
You found a sterner guide;
You heard the guns.   Then, to their distant fire,
Your dreams were laid aside;
And on that day, you cast your heart's desire
Upon a burning pyre;
You gave your service to the exalted need,
Until at last from bondage freed,
At liberty to serve as you loved best,
You chose the noblest way.   God did the rest.

So when the spring of the world shall shrive our
     stain,
After the winter of war,
When the poor world awakes to peace once more,
After such night of ravage and of rain,
You shall not come again.
You shall not come to taste the old Spring weather,
To gallop through the soft untrampled heather,
To bathe and bake your body on the grass.
We shall be there, alas !
But not with you.   When Spring shall wake the earth,
And quicken the scarred fields to the new birth,
Our grief shall grow.   For what can Spring renew
More fiercely for us than the need of you ?

That night I dreamt they sent for me and said
That you were missing, " missing, missing—dead ":
I cried when in the morning I awoke,
And all the world seemed shrouded in a cloak;
But when I saw the sun,
And knew another day had just begun,
I brushed the dream away, and quite forgot
The nightmare's ugly blot.
So was the dream forgot.   The dream came true.
Before the night I knew
That you had flown away into the air
Forever.   Then I cheated my despair.
I said
That you were safe—or wounded—but not dead.
Alas ! I knew
Which was the false and true.

And after days of watching, days of lead,
There came the certain news that you were dead.
You had died fighting, fighting against odds,
Such as in war the gods

Æthereal dared when all the world was young;
Such fighting as blind Homer never sung,
Nor Hector nor Achilles never knew;
High in the empty blue.

High, high, above the clouds, against the setting sun,
The fight was fought, and your great task was done.

Of all your brave adventures this the last
The bravest was and best;
Meet ending to a long embattled past, .
This swift, triumphant, fatal quest,
Crowned with the wreath that never perisheth,
And diadem of honourable death;
Swift Death aflame with offering supreme
And mighty sacrifice,
More than all mortal dream;
A soaring death, and near to Heaven's gate;
Beneath the very walls of Paradise.
Surely with soul elate,
You heard the destined bullet as you flew,
And surely your prophetic spirit knew
That you had well deserved that shining fate.

Here is no waste,
No burning Might-have-been,
No bitter after-taste,
None to censure, none to screen,
Nothing awry, nor anything misspent;
Only content, content beyond content,
Which hath not any room for betterment.

God, Who had made you valiant, strong and swift,
And maimed you with a bullet long ago,
And cleft your riotous ardour with a rift,
And checked your youth's tumultuous overflow,

Gave back your youth to you,
And packed in moments rare and few
Achievements manifold
And happiness untold,
And bade you spring to Death as to a bride,
In manhood's ripeness, power and pride,
And on your sandals the strong wings of youth.
He let you leave a name
To shine on the entablatures of truth,
Forever:
To sound forever in answering halls of fame.

For you soared onwards to that world which rags
Of clouds, like tattered flags,
Concealed; you reached the walls of chrysolite,
The mansions white;
And losing all, you gained the civic crown
Of that eternal town,
Wherein you passed a rightful citizen
Of the bright commonwealth ablaze beyond our ken.

Surely you found companions meet for you
In that high place;
You met there face to face
Those you had never known, but whom you knew:
Knights of the Table Round,
And all the very brave, the very true,
With chivalry crowned;
The captains rare,
Courteous and brave beyond our human air;
Those who had loved and suffered overmuch,
Now free from the world's touch.
And with them were the friends of yesterday,
Who went before and pointed you the way;
And in that place of freshness, light and rest,

Where Lancelot and Tristram vigil keep
Over their King's long sleep,
Surely they made a place for you,
Their long-expected guest,
Among the chosen few,
And welcomed you, their brother and their friend,
To that companionship which hath no end.

And in the portals of the sacred hall
You hear the trumpet's call,
At dawn upon the silvery battlement,
Re-echo through the deep
And bid the sons of God to rise from sleep,
And with a shout to hail
The sunrise on the city of the Grail:
The music that proud Lucifer in Hell
Missed more than all the joys that he forwent.
You hear the solemn bell
At vespers, when the oriflammes are furled;
And then you know that somewhere in the world,
That shines far-off beneath you like a gem,
They think of you, and when you think of them
You know that they will wipe away their tears,
And cast aside their fears;
That they will have it so,
And in no otherwise;
That it is well with them because they know,
With faithful eyes,
Fixed forward and turned upwards to the skies,
That it is well with you,
Among the chosen few,
Among the very brave, the very true.

THOMAS.

EDWARD THOMAS (1878–1917), poet and essayist, was killed in the war of 1914–1918. His writings reveal his sensitive love and observation of nature. As a naturalist he was partly inspired by the work of Richard Jefferies, on whom he wrote a book.

ADLESTROP.

Yes. I remember Adlestrop—
The name, because one afternoon
Of heat the express-train drew up there
Unwontedly. It was late June.

The steam hissed. Someone cleared his throat.
No one left and no one came
On the bare platform. What I saw
Was Adlestrop—only the name,

And willows, willow-herb, and grass,
And meadowsweet and haycocks dry,
No whit less still and lonely fair
Than the high cloudlets in the sky.

And for that minute a blackbird sang
Close by, and round him, mistier,
Farther and farther, all the birds
Of Oxfordshire and Gloucestershire.

OUT IN THE DARK.

Out in the dark over the snow
The fallow fawns invisible go
With the fallow doe;
And the winds blow
Fast as the stars are slow.

Stealthily the dark haunts round
And, when a lamp goes, without sound
At a swifter bound
Than the swiftest hound,
Arrives, and all else is drowned;

And I and star and wind and deer
Are in the dark together—near,
Yet far,—and fear
Drums on my ear
In that sage company drear.

How weak and little is the light,
All the universe of sight,
Love and delight,
Before the might,
If you love it not, of night.

LIGHTS OUT.

I have come to the borders of sleep,
The unfathomable deep
Forest where all must lose
Their way, however straight,
Or winding, soon or late;
They cannot choose.

Many a road and track
That, since the dawn's first crack,
Up to the forest brink,
Deceived the travellers,
Suddenly now blurs,
And in they sink.

Here love ends,
Despair, ambition ends,
All pleasure and all trouble,

Although most sweet or bitter,
Here ends in sleep that is sweeter
Than tasks most noble.

There is not any book
Or face of dearest look
That I would not turn from now
To go into the unknown
I must enter and leave alone
I know not how.

The tall forest towers;
Its cloudy foliage lowers
Ahead, shelf above shelf;
Its silence I hear and obey
That I may lose my way
And myself.

MONRO.

HAROLD MONRO (1879–1932) founded *The Poetry Review* (1911), and also the Poetry Bookshop. He was a contributor to *Georgian Poetry*.

MILK FOR THE CAT.

When the tea is brought at five o'clock,
And all the neat curtains are drawn with care,
The little black cat with bright green eyes
Is suddenly purring there.

At first she pretends, having nothing to do,
She has come in merely to blink by the grate ;
But, though tea may be late or the milk may be sour,
She is never late.

And presently her agate eyes
Take a soft large milky haze,
And her independent casual glance
Becomes a stiff hard gaze.

Then she stamps her claws or lifts her ears,
Or twists her tail and begins to stir,
Till suddenly all her lithe body becomes
One breathing trembling purr.

The children eat and wriggle and laugh;
The two old ladies stroke their silk:
But the cat is grown small and thin with desire,
Transformed to a creeping lust for milk.

The white saucer like some full moon descends
At last from the clouds of the table above;
She sighs and dreams and thrills and glows,
Transfigured with love.

She nestles over the shining rim,
Buries her chin in the creamy sea;
Her tail hangs loose; each drowsy paw
Is doubled under each bending knee.

A long dim ecstasy holds her life;
Her world is an infinite shapeless white,
Till her tongue has curled the last holy drop,
Then she sinks back into the night,

Draws and dips her body to heap
Her sleepy nerves in the great arm-chair,
Lies defeated and buried deep
Three or four hours unconscious there.

COLUM.

PADRAIC COLUM (*b.* 1881) is an Irish poet and dramatist. His work in both kinds shows a mingling of fantasy and realism.

A DROVER.

To Meath of the pastures,
From wet hills by the sea,
Through Leitrim and Longford,
Go my cattle and me.

I hear in the darkness
Their slipping and breathing—
I name them the bye-ways
They're to pass without heeding;

Then the wet, winding roads,
Brown bogs with black water;
And my thoughts on white ships
And the King o' Spain's daughter.

O! farmer, strong farmer!
You can spend at the fair;
But your face you must turn
To your crops and your care.

And soldiers—red soldiers!
You've seen many lands;
But you walk two by two,
And by captain's commands.

O! the smell of the beasts,
The wet wind in the morn;
And the proud and hard earth
Never broken for corn;

And the crowds at the fair,
The herds loosened and blind,
Loud words and dark faces
And the wild blood behind.

(O ! strong men, with your best
I would strive breast to breast,
I could quiet your herds
With my words, with my words.)

I will bring you, my kine,
Where there's grass to the knee;
But you'll think of scant croppings
Harsh with salt of the sea.

DRINKWATER.

JOHN DRINKWATER (1882–1937) was poet, dramatist, and writer on literature. Like many Georgian poets he found much of his poetic inspiration in the beauty of the country. As a dramatist his greatest success was in plays built round prominent historical figures— *Abraham Lincoln* (1918), *Mary Stewart* (1921). He wrote a biography of Byron.

OLTON POOLS.

Now June walks on the waters,
And the cuckoo's last enchantment
Passes from Olton pools.

Now dawn comes to my window
Breathing midsummer roses,
And scythes are wet with dew.

Is it not strange for ever
That, bowered in this wonder,
Man keeps a jealous heart ? . . .

That June and the June waters
And birds and dawn-lit roses,
Are gospels in the wind,

Fading upon the deserts,
Poor pilgrim revelations ? . . .
Hist . . . over Olton pools !

THE MIDLANDS.

Black in the summer night my Cotswold hill
    Aslant my window sleeps, beneath a sky
Deep as the bedded violets that fill
    March woods with dusky passion.   As I lie
Abed between cool walls I watch the host,
    Of the slow stars lit over Gloucester plain,
And drowsily the habit of these most
    Beloved of English lands moves in my brain,
While silence holds dominion of the dark,
Save when the foxes from the spinneys bark.

I see the valleys in their morning mist
    Wreathed under limpid hills in moving light,
Happy with many a yeoman melodist;
    I see the little roads of twinkling white
Busy with fieldward teams and market gear
    Of rosy men, cloth-gaitered, who can tell
The many-minded changes of the year,
    Who know why crops and kine fare ill or well;
I see the sun persuade the mist away,
Till town and stead are shining to the day.

I see the wagons move along the rows
    Of ripe and summer-breathing clover-flower;
I see the lissom husbandman who knows
    Deep in his heart the beauty of his power,
As, lithely pitched, the full-heaped fork bids on
    The harvest home.   I hear the rickyard fill
With gossip as in generations gone,
    While wagon follows wagon from the hill.
I think how, when our seasons all are sealed,
Shall come the unchanging harvest from the field.

I see the barns and comely manors planned
    By men who somehow moved in comely thought,
Who, with a simple shippon to their hand,
    As men upon some godlike business wrought;
I see the little cottages that keep
    Their beauty still where since Plantagenet
Have come the shepherds happily to sleep,
    Finding the loaves and cups of cider set;
I see the twisted shepherds, brown and old,
Driving at dusk their glimmering sheep to fold.

And now the valleys that upon the sun
    Broke from their opal veils are veiled again,
And the last light upon the wolds is done,
    And silence falls on flocks and fields and men;
And black upon the night I watch my hill,
    And the stars shine, and there an owly wing
Brushes the night, and all again is still,
    And, from this land of worship that I sing,
I turn to sleep, content that from my sires
I draw the blood of England's midmost shires.

FLECKER.

JAMES ELROY FLECKER (1884–1915) is perhaps best known for his oriental play *Hassan,* rich in poetry and magnificent as a spectacle. Neither this nor *Don Juan,* a promising but imperfect play, was staged before his death. As a poet he is on the whole marked by a restrained richness of phrasing and imagination.

THE OLD SHIPS.

I have seen old ships sail like swans asleep
Beyond the village which men still call Tyre,
With leaden age o'ercargoed, dipping deep
For Famagusta and the hidden sun
That rings black Cyprus with a lake of fire;
And all those ships were certainly so old—
Who knows how oft with squat and noisy gun,
Questing brown slaves or Syrian oranges,
The pirate Genoese
Hell-raked them till they rolled
Blood, water, fruit and corpses up the hold.
But now through friendly seas they softly run,
Painted the mid-sea blue or the shore-sea green,
Still patterned with the vine and grapes in gold.

But I have seen
Pointing her shapely shadows from the dawn
And image tumbled on a rose-swept bay,
A drowsy ship of some yet older day;
And, wonder's breath indrawn,
Thought I—who knows—who knows—but in that same
(Fished up beyond Aeaea, patched up new
—Stern painted brighter blue—)
That talkative, bald-headed seaman came
(Twelve patient comrades sweating at the oar)

From Troy's doom-crimson shore,
And with great lies about his wooden horse
Set the crew laughing, and forgot his course.

It was so old a ship—who knows—who knows ?
—And yet so beautiful, I watched in vain
To see the mast burst open with a rose,
And the whole deck put on its leaves again.

THE DYING PATRIOT.

Day breaks on England, down the Kentish hills,
Singing in the silence of the meadow-footing rills,
Day of my dreams, O day !
   I saw them march from Dover, long ago,
    With a silver cross before them, singing low,
Monks of Rome from their home where the blue seas break in foam,
    Augustine with his feet of snow.

Noon strikes on England, noon on Oxford town,
—Beauty she was statue cold—there's blood upon her gown:
Noon of my dreams, O noon !
   Proud and godly kings had built her, long ago,
    With her towers and tombs and statues all arow,
With her fair and floral air and the love that lingers there,
    And the streets where the great men go.

Evening on the olden, the golden sea of Wales,
When the first star shivers and the last wave pales:
O Evening dreams !
   There's a house that Britons walked in, long ago,
    Where now the springs of ocean fall and flow,
And the dead robed in red and sea-lilies overhead
    Sway when the long winds blow.

Sleep not, my country: though night is here, afar
Your children of the morning are clamorous for war:
Fire in the night, O dreams !

    Though she send you as she sent you long ago,
      South to desert, East to ocean, West to snow,
West of these out to seas colder than the Hebrides I
      must go
Where the fleet of stars is anchored and the young Star-
      captains glow.

WOLFE.

HUMBERT WOLFE (1885–1940) struck a new individual note in poetry, combining satire with lyric
beauty. His chief poems were *Requiem* (1927) and
The Uncelestial City (1930), but he seemed never quite
to find his true scope as a poet. Just before his death
he followed the progress of the war with biting
epigrammatic verses against the enemy.

A THRUSH IN THE TRENCHES.

Suddenly he sang across the trenches,
    Vivid in the fleeting hush
As a star-shell through the smashed black branches,
    A more than English thrush.

Suddenly he sang, and those who listened
    Nor moved nor wondered, but
Heard, all bewitched, the sweet unhastened
    Crystal Magnificat.

One crouched, a muddied rifle clasping,
 And one a filled grenade,
But little cared they, while he went lisping
 The one clear tune he had.

Paused horror, hate and Hell a moment,
 (You could almost hear the sigh)
And still he sang to them, and so went
 (Suddenly) singing by.

(Requiem).

A BOTTICELLI FACE.

  . . . . I have seen the face,
And I could think only of tenderness,
Such as a girl might have been when she is smiling,
Infinitely young, infinitely beguiling,
And like a boy's lips wild with the romance
Of boyhood's effortless omnipotence,
Or when upon the evening one white petal
Of the last bird's song stirs the air a little,
And all the petalled beauties that ever were
In song and eve enchant the listener,
And there's nothing in the world but tenderness—
All that and more than that were in the face.

(News of the Devil).

SASSOON.

SIEGFREID SASSOON (*b.* 1886) served in France and
Palestine in the war of 1914–1918. His realistic
war poems, though in general below those of Wilfred
Owen, possessed both pathos and satire. He has
continued to write poetry, but his most lasting work
is likely to be his autobiographical prose such as
Memoirs of a Fox-hunting Man (1928) and *The Weald
of Youth* (1942).

EVERYONE SANG.

Everyone suddenly burst out singing;
And I was filled with such delight
As prisoned birds must find in freedom,
Winging wildly across the white
Orchards and dark green fields; on; on; and out
    of sight.

Everyone's voice was suddenly lifted,
And beauty came like the setting sun.
My heart was shaken with tears, and horror
Drifted away . . . O but Everyone
Was a bird; and the song was wordless; the
    singing will never be done.

THE DUG-OUT.

Why do you lie with your legs ungainly huddled,
And one arm bent across your sullen cold
Exhausted face ?   It hurts my heart to watch you,
Deep-shadow'd from the candle's guttering gold;
And you wonder why I shake you by the shoulder;
Drowsy, you mumble and sigh and turn your head....
You are too young to fall asleep for ever;
And when you sleep you remind me of the dead.

BROOKE.

RUPERT BROOKE (1887–1915) was one of the most
promising of our young poets to die in the war of
1914–1918.   He expressed the mood of youth—the
idealism, the gaiety, the cynicism, the keen sense of
beauty, and the love of life and unsated interest in all
life has to offer. *Poems* appeared in 1911, *1914 and
Other Poems* in 1915.

THE SOLDIER.

If I should die, think only this of me:
   That there's some corner of a foreign field
That is for ever England.   There shall be
   In that rich earth a richer dust concealed;
A dust whom England bore, shaped, made aware,
   Gave, once, her flowers to love, her ways to roam,
A body of England's, breathing English air,
   Washed by the rivers, blest by suns of home.

And think, this heart, all evil shed away,
   A pulse in the eternal mind, no less
      Gives somewhere back the thoughts by England
         given;
Her sights and sounds; dreams happy as her day;
   And laughter, learnt of friends; and gentleness,
      In hearts at peace, under an English heaven.

THE OLD VICARAGE, GRANTCHESTER.

Café des Westens, Berlin, May 1912.

Just now the lilac is in bloom,
All before my little room;
And in my flower-beds, I think,
Smile the carnation and the pink;
And down the borders, well I know,
The poppy and the pansy blow. . . .
Oh! there the chestnuts, summer through,
Beside the river make for you
A tunnel of green gloom, and sleep
Deeply above; and green and deep
The stream mysterious glides beneath,
Green as a dream and deep as death.—
Oh, damn! I know it! and I know
How the May fields all golden show,
And when the day is young and sweet,

Gild gloriously the bare feet
That run to bathe. . . .

Du lieber Gott !

Here am I, sweating, sick, and hot,
And there the shadowed waters fresh
Lean up to embrace the naked flesh.
Temperamentvoll German Jews
Drink beer around; and *there* the dews
Are soft beneath a morn of gold.
Here tulips bloom as they are told;
Unkempt about those hedges blows
An English unofficial rose;
And there the unregulated sun
Slopes down to rest when day is done,
And wakes a vague unpunctual star,
A slippered Hesper; and there are
Meads towards Haslingfield and Coton
Where *das Betreten's* not *verboten.*

Εἴθε γενοίμην . . . would I were
In Grantchester, in Grantchester !—
Some, it may be, can get in touch
With Nature there, or Earth, or such.
And clever modern men have seen
A Faun a-peeping through the green,
And felt the Classics were not dead,
To glimpse a Naiad's reedy head,
Or hear the Goat-foot piping low. . . .
But these are things I do not know.
I only know that you may lie
Day long and watch the Cambridge sky,
And, flower-lulled in sleepy grass,
Hear the cool lapse of hours pass,
Until the centuries blend and blur
In Grantchester, in Grantchester. .

Still in the dawnlit waters cool
His ghostly Lordship swims his pool,
And tries the strokes, essays the tricks,
Long learnt on Hellespont, or Styx;
Dan Chaucer hears his river still
Chatter beneath a phantom mill;
Tennyson notes, with studious eye,
How Cambridge waters hurry by. . . .
And in that garden, black and white,
Creep whispers through the grass all night;
And spectral dance, before the dawn,
A hundred Vicars down the lawn;
Curates, long dust, will come and go
On lissom, clerical, printless toe;
And oft between the boughs is seen
The sly shade of a Rural Dean. . . .
Till, at a shiver in the skies,
Vanishing with Satanic cries,
The prim ecclesiastic rout
Leaves but a startled sleeper-out,
Grey heavens, the first bird's drowsy calls,
The falling house that never falls.

God ! I will pack, and take a train,
And get me to England once again !
For England's the one land, I know,
Where men with Splendid Hearts may go;
And Cambridgeshire, of all England,
The shire for Men who Understand;
And of *that* district I prefer
The lovely hamlet Grantchester.
For Cambridge people rarely smile,
Being urban, squat, and packed with guile;
And Royston men in the far South
Are black and fierce and strange of mouth;
At Over they fling oaths at one,

And worse than oaths at Trumpington,
And Ditton girls are mean and dirty,
And there's none in Harston under thirty,
And folks in Shelford and those parts,
Have twisted lips and twisted hearts,
And Barton men make cockney rhymes,
And Coton's full of nameless crimes,
And things are done you'd not believe
At Madingley on Christmas Eve.
Strong men have run for miles and miles
When one from Cherry Hinton smiles;
Strong men have blanched and shot their wives,
Rather than send them to St. Ives;
Strong men have cried like babes, by dam,
To hear what happened at Babraham.
But Grantchester ! ah, Grantchester !
There's peace and holy quiet there,
Great clouds along pacific skies,
And men and women with straight eyes,
Lithe children lovelier than a dream,
A bosky wood, a slumbrous stream,
And little kindly winds that creep
Round twilight corners, half asleep.
In Grantchester their skins are white,
They bathe by day, they bathe by night;
The women there do all they ought;
The men observe the Rules of Thought.
They love the Good; they worship Truth;
They laugh uproariously in youth;
(And when they get to feeling old,
They up and shoot themselves, I'm told). . . .

Ah God ! to see the branches stir
Across the moon at Grantchester !
To smell the thrilling-sweet and rotten,
Unforgettable, unforgotten

River-smell, and hear the breeze
Sobbing in the little trees.
Say, do the elm-clumps greatly stand,
Still guardians of that holy land?
The chestnuts shade, in reverend dream,
The yet unacademic stream?
Is dawn a secret shy and cold
Anadyomene, silver-gold?
And sunset still a golden sea
From Haslingfield to Madingley?
And after, ere the night is born,
Do hares come out about the corn?
Oh, is the water sweet and cool,
Gentle and brown, above the pool?
And laughs the immortal river still
Under the mill, under the mill?
Say, is there Beauty yet to find?
And Certainty? and Quiet kind?
Deep meadows yet, for to forget
The lies, and truths, and pain? . . . Oh! yet
Stands the Church clock at ten to three?
And is there honey still for tea?

TURNER.

W. J. TURNER (1889-1947) as a lyric poet followed
no school. His last volume of poems was *Fossils
of a Future Time?* (1946). He was also a music critic,
and wrote studies of Beethoven and Mozart.

ROMANCE.

When I was but thirteen or so
    I went into a golden land,
Chimborazo, Cotopaxi
    Took me by the hand.

My father died, my brother too,
    They passed like fleeting dreams,
I stood where Popocatapetl
    In the sunlight gleams.

I dimly heard the master's voice
    And boys far-off at play,
Chimborazo, Cotopaxi
    Had stolen me away.

I walked in a great golden dream
    To and fro from school—
Shining Popocatapetl
    The dusty streets did rule.

I walked home with a gold dark boy
    And never a word I'd say,
Chimborazo, Cotopaxi
    Had taken my speech away:

I gazed entranced upon his face
    Fairer than any flower—
O shining Popocatapetl
    It was thy magic hour:

The houses, people, traffic seemed
    Thin fading dreams by day,
Chimborazo, Cotopaxi
    They had stolen my soul away !

NICHOLS.

ROBERT NICHOLS (1893–1944) was one of the Georgian poets. He fought in France, and *Ardours and Endurances* (1917) contained both war poetry and Keatsian beauty. Modern influences hardly affected his poetry.

THE TOWER.

It was deep night, and over Jerusalem's low roofs
The moon floated, drifting through high vaporous woofs.
The moonlight crept and glistened silent, solemn, sweet,
Over dome and column, up empty, endless street;
In the closed, scented gardens the rose loosed from the
    stem
Her white showery petals; none regarded them;
The starry thicket breathed odours to the sentinel palm;
Silence possessed the city like a soul possessed by calm.

Not a spark in the warren under the giant night,
Save where in a turret's lantern beamed a grave, still
    light;
There in the topmost chamber a gold-eyed lamp was lit—
Marvellous lamp in darkness, informing, redeeming it !
For, set in that tiny chamber, Jesus, the blessed and
    doomed,
Spoke to the lone apostles as light to men entombed;
And spreading His hands in blessing, as one soon to be
    dead,
He put soft enchantment into spare wine and bread.

The hearts of the disciples were broken and full of tears,
Because their Lord, the spearless, was hedged about with
    spears;
And in His face the sickness of departure had spread a
    gloom,

At leaving His young friends friendless.
> They could not forget the tomb.
He smiled subduedly, telling, in tones soft as voice of
the dove,
The endlessness of sorrow, the eternal solace of love;
And lifting the earthly tokens, wine and sorrowful bread,
He bade them sup and remember One who lived and
was dead;
And they could not restrain their weeping.
> But one rose up to depart,
Having weakness and hate of weakness raging within his
heart,
And bowed to the robed assembly whose eyes gleamed
wet in the light.
Judas arose and departed: night went out to the night.

Then Jesus lifted His voice like a fountain in an ocean
of tears,
And comforted His disciples and calmed and allayed
their fears.
But Judas wound down the turret, creeping from floor
to floor,
And would fly; but one leaning, weeping, barred him
beside the door.
And he knew her by her ruddy garment and two yet-
watching men:
Mary of Seven Evils, Mary Magdalen.
And he was frighted at her. She sighed: " I dreamed
him dead.
We sell the body for silver. . ."
> Then Judas cried out and fled
Forth into the night ! . . . The moon had begun to
set:
A drear, deft wind went sifting, setting the dust afret;
Into the heart of the city Judas ran on and prayed
To stern Jehovah lest his deed make him afraid.

But in the tiny lantern, hanging as if on air,
The disciples sat unspeaking. Amaze and peace were
    there.
For *His* voice, more lovely than song of all earthly birds,
In accents humble and happy spoke slow, consoling
    words.

Thus Jesus discoursed, and was silent, sitting upright,
    and soon
Past the casement behind Him slanted the sinking moon;
And, rising for Olivet, all stared, between love and dread,
Seeing the torrid moon a ruddy halo behind his head.

GRAVES.

ROBERT GRAVES (*b.* 1895) has developed a long way
from his early poetry, and *Collected Poems* (1938)
made a severe selection from his volumes up to 1926.
His poetic life has been a tense struggle after truth,
but he has remained a true lyric poet. *I, Claudius*
(1934) is among his notable novels, and *Goodbye to
All That* (1929) was a striking autobiography.

A BOY IN CHURCH.

" Gabble-gabble, . . . brethren, . . . gabble-
    gabble ! "
  My window frames forest and heather.
I hardly hear the tuneful babble,
  Not knowing nor much caring whether
The text is praise or exhortation,
Prayer or thanksgiving, or damnation.

Outside it blows wetter and wetter,
  The tossing trees never stay still.
I shift my elbows to catch better

The full round sweep of heathered hill.
The tortured copse bends to and fro
In silence like a shadow-show.

The parson's voice runs like a river
  Over smooth rocks.   I like this church:
The pews are staid, they never shiver,
  They never bend or sway or lurch.
" Prayer," says the kind voice, " is a chain
That draws down Grace from Heaven again."

I add the hymns up, over and over,
  Until there's not the least mistake.
Seven-seventy-one. (Look ! there's a plover !
  It's gone !) Who's that Saint by the lake ?
The red light from his mantle passes
Across the broad memorial brasses.

It's pleasant here for dreams and thinking,
  Lolling and letting reason nod,
With ugly serious people linking
  Sad prayers to a forgiving God. . . .
But a dumb blast sets the trees swaying
With furious zeal like madmen praying.

IN THE WILDERNESS.

Christ of his gentleness
Thirsting and hungering
Walked in the wilderness;
Soft words of grace He spoke
Unto lost desert-folk
That listened wondering.
He heard the bitterns call
From ruined palace-wall,
Answered them brotherly.

He held communion
With the she-pelican
Of lonely piety.
Basilisk, cockatrice,
Flocked to His homilies,
With mail of dread device,
With monstrous barbèd stings,
With eager dragon-eyes;
Great bats on leathern wings
And poor blind broken things,
Foul in their miseries.
And ever with Him went,
Of all His wanderings
Comrade, with ragged coat,
Gaunt ribs—poor innocent—
Bleeding foot, burning throat,
The guileless old scape-goat;
For forty nights and days
Followed in Jesus' ways,
Sure guard behind Him kept,
Tears like a lover wept.

BLUNDEN.

EDMUND BLUNDEN (*b.* 1896) won the Hawthornden
Prize in 1922 for *The Shepherd and Other Poems of
Peace and War,* and his considerable work is collected
in *Poems* 1914-30 and *Poems* 1930-40. His sensitive
observation of nature remains, but his poetry has also
been very sensitive to the unrest of the times.

THE LONG TRUCE.

Rooks in black constellation slowly wheeling
Over this pale sweet sky, and church-bells pealing
Our homely pilgrims to the fount of healing;

The cypresses that swartly gather nigh,
The grey conventicle that claims the sky
Where the white rugged road climbs patient by;

The day and hour, the obedience of good people
To the commandment singing from the steeple,
All speak a calm sea where there's scarce a ripple.

I bless my chance that finds me this deep leisure,
The voice of Sabbath with its lulling measure,
I bless this England for such serious pleasure.

And gravely as I go I reach that grove
Where once the Cavalier and Roundhead strove,
And think, this peace rewards their rival love:

I see them now at truce eternal lying,
With no hoarse trumpet summoning, none replying—
Only in sweet content for England vying.

MIDNIGHT.

The last-lighted windows have darkened,
    The last courting pair have gone home,
And moon and wind and the little shriek-owl
    All over the country roam.

The chimneys and roofs of the village
    Like a mystical figure are drawn
On a cloud's white veil that sleeps and shines
    From the church to the sign of the Swan.

Between blue and silver the by-road
    Runs, hides and again gleams free;
The moon seems loitering, like the wind
    That kisses the hawthorn tree.

Far glistens that tree in the meadow,
    But the spirit of love hither borne
In glimmerings and sighings, O can such a joy
    Be the wind in the moonlit thorn ?

SITWELL.

EDITH SITWELL (*b.* 1887) began as a revolutionary in
verse with *Wheels,* an annual anthology (1916-21),
remarkable for its new technique.   Russian ballet, jazz
and French poets like Baudelaire and Rimbaud have
strongly influenced her, and *A Poet's Notebook* (1943)
shows her preoccupation with the music of verse.
Collected Poems (1930) must now be read in the light
of her greatest poetry in *A Song of the Cold* (1945).

THE LITTLE GHOST WHO DIED FOR LOVE.*

" Fear not, O maidens, shivering
As bunches of the dew-drenched leaves
In the calm moonlight . . . it is the cold sends
        quivering
My voice, a little nightingale that grieves.

Now Time beats not, and dead Love is forgotten . . .
The spirit too is dead and dank and rotten,

---

* Deborah Churchill, born in 1678, was hanged in
1708 for shielding her lover in a duel.   His opponent
was killed, her lover fled to Holland, and she was
hanged in his stead, according to the law of the time.
The chronicle said : "Though she died at peace with
God, this malefactor could never understand the justice of her sentence, to the last moment of her life."

And I forget the moment when I ran
Between my lover and the sworded man—
Blinded with terror lest I lose his heart.
The sworded man dropped, and I saw depart

Love and my lover and my life . . . he fled
And I was strung and hung upon the tree.
It is so cold now that my heart is dead
And drops through time . . . night is too dark to see

Him still. . . . But it is spring; upon the fruit-
    boughs of your lips,
Young maids, the dew like India's splendour drips.
Pass by among the strawberry beds, and pluck the
    berries
Cooled by the silver moon; pluck boughs of cherries
That seem the lovely lucent coral bough
(From streams of starry milk those branches grow)
That Cassiopeia feeds with her faint light,
Like Ethiopia ever jewelled bright.

Those lovely cherries do enclose
Deep in their sweet hearts the silver snows,

And the small budding flowers upon the trees
Are filled with sweetness like the bags of bees.

Forget my fate . . . but I, a moonlight ghost,
Creep down the strawberry paths and seek the lost

World, the apothecary at the Fair.
I, Deborah, in my long cloak of brown
Like the small nightingale that dances down
The cherried boughs, creep to the doctor's bare
Booth . . . cold as ivy in the air,
And, where I stand, the brown and ragged light
Holds something still beyond, hid from my sight.

Once, plumaged like the sea, his swanskin head
Had wintry white quills . . . 'Hearken to the
    Dead . . .
I was a nightingale, but now I croak
Like some dark harpy hidden in night's cloak,
Upon the walls; among the Dead, am quick.
Oh, give me medicine, for the world is sick;
Not medicines planet-spotted like fritillaries
For country sins and old stupidities,
Nor potions you may give a country maid
When she is lovesick . . . love in earth is laid,
Grown dead and rotten ' . . .   So I sank me down,
Poor Deborah in my long cloak of brown.
Though cockcrow marches crying of false dawns
Shall bury my dark voice, yet still it mourns
Among the ruins,—for it is not I
But this old world, is sick and soon must die ! "

GLOSSARY.

ABEIGH (STAND): *keep aloof.*

ABERDOUR: *Aberdeen.*

ABUNE: *above.*

ACADEMES: *academies.*

ACHILLES: the bravest of the Greeks who fought in the war against Troy. He is the chief hero of the *Iliad.* According to the legend he was vulnerable only in the heel.

ACQUENT: *acquainted.*

ACQUIST: *acquirement.*

AFFRAY: *frighten.*

AGINCOURT: a village in Northern France, where, in a desperate battle on October 25th, 1415, the English under Henry V. defeated the French army.

AGLEY (GANG): *(go) wrong.*

AGNES, ST.: a Christian martyr said to have been killed in 304; patron saint of young girls. On St. Agnes' Eve (20th January) it used to be common for girls to try to discover their future husbands by performing various rites.

AIRTS: *directions.*

AJAX: one of the Greek heroes who fought at Troy.

ALCESTIS: wife of Admetus, king of Pherae in Thessaly, who according to a Greek legend gave her life to redeem her husband from death, but was rescued from the other world by Hercules, "Jove's great son."

ALCHEMY: power of transmuting a substance into gold.

ALGARSIFE: eldest son of the Tartar king Cambuscan in Chaucer's unfinished *Squire's Tale.* By a magic horse of brass (see CAMBUSCAN) he was to win a lady named Theodera.

ALLAY: *cool.*

427

AMALTHEA: a Cretan nymph who fed Zeus (Jupiter) with the milk of a goat. Zeus broke off one of the goat's horns and endowed it with the property of becoming filled with any food or drink the possessor wished.

AMARANTHUS: a flower that remains long without withering; literally the *unfading flower*.

AMPHION: a son of Jupiter, of whom it was fabled that by the sound of his lyre given him by Mercury he built the walls of Thebes.

ANADYOMENE: a painting showing Venus rising from the sea.

ANODYNES: *pain-relieving medicines*.

ANUBIS: an Egyptian god of darkness.

APOLLO: son of Zeus, and an important deity of the ancient Greeks, who was worshipped as the god of prophecy, poetry, and music.

ARBUTHNOT: Dr. John Arbuthnot (1667–1735) was a prominent physician, and a friend of Pope and Swift.

ARCADY: Arcadia in ancient Greece, a mountainous district inhabited by shepherds, where Pan, the god of shepherds, dwelt.

ARGUS: a king in Greek mythology, set by Juno to guard Io whom Jupiter had transformed into a cow. He had a hundred eyes. Hermes (Mercury) charmed Argus to sleep by his lyre and then cut off his head. Juno put his hundred eyes into the tail of the peacock, her sacred bird.

ARTHUR: a British chieftain who rallied the Celtic tribes against the Saxons in the sixth century. He became magnified into a great mythological figure around whom and his Knights of the Round Table many legends grew.

ASHTAROTH: a Hebrew name for the Syrian goddess Astarte, equivalent to the Greek Venus.

ASKLENT: *aslant*.

ASPHODEL: a plant which, in Greek mythology, covered the meadows of Hades, the abode of the dead.

ASSOIL: *absolve, pardon*.

ATOMIES: tiny creatures.

ATTEMPERED: *suited.*

ATTIC BOY: Cephalus, son of Deioneus king of Sicily; he was very fond of hunting.

AUGUSTINE: Saint Augustine (d. 613?), first Archbishop of Canterbury; he was sent from Rome to England by the Pope in 596 to convert the English.

AURORA: goddess of dawn.

AVILION: the site of this place mentioned in the Arthurian legends is located variously. Some of the romances located it near Glastonbury, others made it a mythical isle of Paradise.

AVIS'D (WELL): *with careful attention.*

BAÄLIM: Phoenician gods.

BACCHANAL: devotee of Bacchus.

BACCHUS: god of wine; the ivy was sacred to him.

BAIAE'S BAY: a watering-place in Campania in Italy.

BAITH: *both.*

BALTIC, BATTLE OF: in 1800 Russia, Prussia, Sweden, and Denmark, acting under the influence of Napoleon, formed a coalition which maintained an armed neutrality hostile to British interests. In April 1801 a British fleet appeared off Copenhagen, silenced the Danish batteries, and captured most of the Danish ships. The victory was mainly due to the brilliant tactics of Nelson, though he was only second in command.

BARKEN'D: *tanned.*

BASSARID: a votary of Bacchus.

BARTON: farm-yard.

BAULDRICK: *a belt.*

BAYONA: a town on the west coast of Galicia, in Spain, near Cape Finisterre.

BELLERUS: a name coined by Milton from Bellerium, the Roman name for Land's End. Bellerus is imagined as giving a name to the promontory. " By the fable of Bellerus old " = Land's end.

BESPRENT: *besprinkled.*

BESTRUTTED: *swollen.*

BICKERING: *angry chattering.*

BIELD: *shelter.*

BIG: *build.*

BILBOS: swords from Bilboa in Spain, a place noted for the excellent swords made there.

BIN: *are.*

BIRK: *birch.*

BLABBING: *revealing secrets.*

BLEER'T: *bleared.*

BLIN': *blind.*

BOLUS: *big pill.*

BONIVARD: François de Bonivard (1496–1570), a native of Geneva, famous for his six years' imprisonment in the Castle of Chillon.

BOSKY: *bushy, consisting of brushwood.*

BOTTICELLI: Sandro Botticelli (1444–1510), the famous Florentine painter.

BOURNE: *limit of territory.*

BRAES: *hillsides.*

BRAID LETTER: letter written on a broad sheet.

BRATTLE: *hurry, scamper.*

BRAW: *handsome.*

BREDE: *anything plaited, embroidery.*

BROCKET: a stag in its second year.

BROW, BAY AND TRAY: the antler proper, and the second and third branches of a stag's horn.

BUCKINGHAM: George Villiers, second Duke of Buckingham (1628–87); he was one of Charles II.'s ministers, but later opposed the King's policy, as in supporting the Exclusion Bill, 1680–1, for his share in which action Dryden satirised him in *Absalom and Achitophel.*

BUGLE-BRACELET: a bracelet of black beads.

BURD: *maiden.*

BUSKIN'D: the buskin was a kind of half-boot with thick soles worn by actors in Greek tragedy to add to their height.

BYRE: *cow-shed.*

CALEDONIE: *Scotland.*

CAMBALL: there are two men called Cambalo in Chaucer's unfinished *Squire's Tale;* one, the younger son of the Tartar king Cambuskan, was to help his sister Canace to regain for a falcon, who was possibly an enchanted princess, her lost lover. Canace had been enabled to speak with the falcon by a magic ring she had been given. The second Cambalo was to fight Canace's two brothers in the lists.

CAMBUSKAN: a Tartar king in the *Squire's Tale* who received as presents from the king of Araby and Ind a magic horse of brass and a magic sword; from the same king came Canace's ring.

CAMILLA: queen of the Volsci, who was said to run so swiftly that she could run over a field of corn without bending the corn; in Vergil's *Aeneid* she helps Turnus against Aeneas.

CANACE: see CAMBALL.

CANTY: *gay, lively.*

CAREENED: *heeled over.*

CARLINE: *old woman.*

CASSIOPEIA: wife of Cepheus, king of Ethiopia, and mother of Andromeda; she was turned into the well-known constellation.

CATES: *dishes, delicacies.*

CECILIA: St. Cecilia, the patroness of music. She is regarded as the inventor of the organ, the "mingled world of sound." Her martyrdom is said to have taken place in 230 A.D.

CEDARN: *formed of cedar trees.*

CERBERUS: a dog with three heads, which in Greek mythology was supposed to guard the entrance of Hades.

CHANNERIN': *fretting.*

CHAPMAN: George Chapman (1559?-1634), poet and dramatist; best remembered for his verse translations of the *Iliad* (1611) and the *Odyssey* (1614).

CHATTERTON: Thomas Chatterton (1752-70) wrote some remarkable poetry which he tried to pass off as the work of a fifteenth-century priest named Rowley. In proud despair he committed suicide. See p. 14.

CHAUCER: Geoffrey Chaucer (1340 ?–1400); see pp. 4–5.

CHILLON: a castle at the eastern end of Lake Geneva. See BONIVARD.

CIMMERIAN DESERT: the Cimmerians were a mythical people who dwelt in darkness.

CITHERN: a kind of guitar used in the sixteenth and seventeenth centuries.

CITHOLE: a stringed musical instrument of the late Middle Ages.

CLAVER'SE: John Graham of Claverhouse, Viscount Dundee (1649 ?–89); he was outlawed in 1689 for his support of James II., raised a Scottish army in James's support, and won the battle of Killie-crankie, but he was killed in the battle.

CLOSE-HEADS: *entries to blind allies (closes).*

COCK: *cock-boat, dinghy.*

CONVENTION, THE LORDS OF: the Scottish Parliament.

COOST: *tossed.*

CORONACH: *Highland dirge.*

CORONAL: *crown of flowers.*

CORREGGIO : Antonio Allegri, generally known as Correggio (1494–1534), a great Italian painter.

CORREI: a hollow in a hillside; now spelt *corrie.*

CORTEZ: Hernando Cortes (1485–1547), a Spanish soldier, conqueror of Mexico; Keats is wrong in attributing this first vision of the Pacific Ocean to him. See DARIEN.

CORYDON: a common name for a shepherd in pastoral poetry.

COTYTTO: a Thracian goddess of magic and wanton revelry.

COUTHIE: *affable, familiar.*

CRANREUCH: *hoar-frost.*

CRESSY: scene of Edward III.'s victory over the French in 1346.

CRINGLE: *metal ring.*

CRISPIN, ST.: patron saint of shoemakers; St. Crispin's day is October 25th.

CROMWELL: Oliver Cromwell (1599–1658), from 1644 lieutenant-general of the Parliament's army against Charles I., and from 1653 to 1658 Lord Protector of England.

CROUSE: *merry.*

CRUISE, EARTHEN: *earthenware jar.*

CUMBER: *trouble.*

CYNOSURE: *centre of attraction ;* in the constellation Little Bear, known to the Greeks as Cynosure (dog's tail), is the Pole Star.

CYNTHIA: the Moon (as a goddess).

CYTHERĒA: Venus, so called from the island of Cythera in the Aegean Sea, where she was worshipped.

DAIMEN ICKER: *an ear of corn now and then.*

DAN: *Master ;* it is a corruption of the Latin *dominus.*

DANAAN: when Danae, daughter of Acrisius king of Argos and of Eurydice, was shut in a tower of brass, Jupiter obtained access to her by turning himself into a golden shower.

DAPHNE: Daphne, fleeing from the love of Apollo, called upon the gods to help her, and was then turned into a laurel.

DARIEN: a district round Panama on the isthmus between North and South America. In 1513 Vasco Nuñez de Balboa "upon a peak in Darien" saw the Pacific Ocean. Keats wrongly gives this vision to Cortez.

DAS BETRETEN: *treading on (the grass).*

DAW: *dawn.*

DECORE: *adorn.*

DESCRIES: *reveals.*

DIANA: daughter of Jupiter and Latona, goddess of the chase, and the moon.

DIAPASON: *complete harmony* (Milton); *great burst of harmony* (Crashaw); *the whole range of notes in the scale* (Dryden).

DIDO: queen of Carthage; when Aeneas, in his travels after the fall of Troy, was driven on her coasts, she fell in love with him, and when he left again she killed herself.

DIGHT: *arranged, decked, adorned.*

DIS' WAGGON: Dis was another name for Pluto, king of the underworld; when he saw Proserpine gathering flowers on the plains of Enna in Sicily, he caught her up in his chariot.

DISWITTED: *deprived of her wits, crazy.*

DIVIDING: *making division,* a term in music denoting the dividing of each of a succession of long notes into several short ones.

DOLPHIN: a sea-creature not unlike a porpoise.

DOUCE: *sober, sedate.*

DOXY: *sweetheart.*

DREE: *suffer, endure.*

DRYADS: wood-nymphs or inferior divinities in Greek mythology, believed to live in trees.

DRYOPE: a nymph of Arcadia, mother of Pan by Mercury.

DULCIMER: an ancient musical instrument held by some to be the ancestor of the piano.

DULE: *grief.*

DU LIEBER GOTT: *Dear God!*

DUNDEE: see CLAVER'SE.

DUNNIEWASSALS: Highland clansmen of superior rank.

DURELESS: *not lasting.*

EBON: *black.*

EFTSOONS: *soon after, forthwith.*

ELDERN: *old.*

ELISA: *Queen Elizabeth.*

ELYSIAN: from or belonging to Elysium, in Greek mythology the place set apart for the abode of the blessed after dead.

EMBAY: *bathe.*

EMIT: *ant.*

ENSAFFRONING: *colouring with saffron (yellow).*

EPODE: *third division in an Ode.*

EREMITE: *devotee,* original sense *hermit.*

ERST: *first, formerly.*

ESSAY: *attempt.*

ETHIOP QUEEN: Cassiopea; Neptune sent a sea-monster to ravage Ethiopia because Cassiopea boasted that she was more beautiful than the Nereides, the sea-nymphs.

EUPHROSYNE: with her sisters Aglaia and Thalia, one of the three Graces, personifications in Greek mythology of grace, gentleness, and beauty, who attended upon Venus.

EURYDICE: the wife of Orpheus. When she died Orpheus went to Hades and so pleased Pluto by his playing on the lyre that Pluto promised to restore Eurydice to life if Orpheus did not turn to look behind him until he reached the earth again; Orpheus, however, turned too soon, and his wife vanished for ever.

EYN: *eyes.*

FASHES: *troubles.*

FAUNS: woodland deities worshipped by the Romans and by them identified with the Greek satyrs. They were represented with short horns, pointed ears, tails, and goats' feet.

FAUSE: *false.*

FAYS: *fairies.*

FEALTY: *loyalty.*

FEATEOUSLY: *gracefully.*

FLASKET: *little flask.*

FLEECH'D: *begged.*

FLORA: the goddess of flowers.

FLYTING: *scolding, angry dispute.*

FOGGAGE: *moss.*

FOWLS: *birds* (in Spenser).

FU': *full.*

GANG: *go.*

GANYMED: a beautiful youth, the cup-bearer of Jupiter.

GART: *caused.*

GATLING: a kind of machine-gun.

GAWDS: *glittering trifles, toys.*

GAZA: a town in Judea where Samson, pulling down the pillars, killed, with himself, many of the Philistines; see Judges, ch. xvi.

GENNESARETH: see St. Matthew, ch. xiv.

GHOSTLY LORDSHIP: the poet Lord Byron who spent a good deal of his time at Cambridge swimming in the Cam.

GIN: *if.*

GLANVIL: Joseph Glanvil (1636–80), a clergyman, in whose *Vanity of Dogmatizing* (1661) Arnold read the story of the Scholar Gipsy.

GLISTER: *glitter.*

GOAT-FOOT: *satyr.*

GOWD, GOWDEN: *gold, golden.*

GRAIL: the Holy Dish at Christ's Last Supper, in which Joseph of Arimathea, according to legend, collected blood from Christ's pierced side, and which Joseph later brought to England. Malory's *Morte Darthur* tells how it suddenly vanished from King Arthur's hall and how Sir Gawain vowed to seek it, and set off with many other knights in that noble quest.

GRAITH'D: *adorned, equipped.*

GRASSMARKET: a street in Edinburgh.

GRAT HIS EEN: *wept.*

GRISAMBER: ambergris; it was formerly used a good deal in cookery.

GRYTE: *great.*

GUARDED MOUNT: St. Michael's Mount near Penzance.

GUERDON: *reward.*

GULES: the name given in heraldic language to the colour crimson.

GULLIES: *knives.*

HALD: *dwelling.*

HALES: *handles of plough.*

HAMADRYADS: nymphs who lived in trees.

HAMPDEN: John Hampden (1594–1643) opposed Charles I.'s exaction of ship-money, and was one of the King's chief opponents in the quarrel between him and Parliament which led to the Civil War; he was killed in a skirmish with Prince Rupert's troops.

HAMMON: an Egyptian god whose temple was in the deserts of Lybia.

HANDSEL: *gift.*

HAPPY ISLES: fabulous islands in the Western Ocean believed by the ancients to be the abode of the blessed. By some they have been identified with the Canary Isles.

HARBOURER: a man whose duty, on the morning of a meet of a stag-hunt, is to find the covert in which a runnable stag is lying.

HARROWED: *raided ;* according to old belief, when Christ harrowed hell he took away from Satan the souls of the just, such as Abraham, who had been in the keeping of Satan from their deaths until the coming of Christ.

HEAL: *healthy.*

HEBE: the cupbearer of the gods, in which office Ganymed succeeded her.

HECAT': Hecate, the classical goddess of witches, identified with Diana and the Moon.

HECTOR: son of King Priam and Hecuba, he was the bravest of the Trojans and their leader in the siege of Troy by the Greeks.

HELLESPONT: the modern Dardanelles, the strait between Europe and Asia; in classical legend Leander swam it to see his love Hero.

HERCULES: a heroic character in classical myth, famous for his strength; he was son of Zeus (Jupiter). As a baby Hercules strangled two serpents; in his manhood, in penance for slaying some of his children, he was made to undergo twelve "labours" (see HESPERIDES), and many other notable deeds were ascribed to him. By the Romans he was worshipped as the god of physical strength. The pillars of Hercules are the heights on each side of the straits of Gibraltar, so-called because Hercules was said to have rent them asunder.

HERMES: the messenger of the gods, and the patron of travellers; Hermes was his name among the Greeks, Mercury among the Romans. See ARGUS. THRICE-GREAT HERMES in *Il Penseroso* was Hermes Trismegistus, a fabulous Egyptian king famous for his knowledge.

HESPER: Hesperus, the Evening Star.

HESPERIDES: the three daughters of Hesperus; they guarded, together with a dragon, the golden apples which it was one of the labours of Hercules to obtain. They lived on some islands in the west, called after them the Hesperides.

HIE: *hasten.*

HIPPOCRENE: a fountain sacred to the Muses near Mount Helicon, a mountain in Greece, also sacred to them.

HIST: *summoned in silence.*

HISTIE: *barren.*

HIZZIE: *young girl.*

HOMER: the great blind epic poet of Ancient Greece; he is supposed to have lived about 1000 B.C., and to have written the *Iliad* and the *Odyssey.*

HUMOROUS STAGE: stage on which man's " humours " or particular traits of character, are shown.

HYADES: a group of seven stars in the head of the constellation Taurus.

HYLAS: a beautiful youth who is represented in Greek mythology as drawing water for Hercules.

HYMEN: the god of the marriage ceremony; so HYMENEAL means *belonging to the marriage ceremony.*

IBERIANS: the Spaniards of Greek and Roman times.

IDA: a mountain range of Asia Minor; the city of Troy was situated at the base of this range.

ILKA: *each one.*

INDIAN STEEP: the Himalaya Mountains.

INGLE BENCH: *seat by the fire-side.*

ISIS: an Egyptian goddess, wife of Osiris.

ISLINGTON: a village in Norfolk.

ITYLUS: son of Aedon, and of Zethus brother of Amphion; Aedon, who out of jealousy wished to kill her sister Niobe's eldest son, slew Itylus by mistake.

JACOB'S LADDER: to Jacob (we are told in Genesis, ch. xxvii.), came from God a vision of a ladder "set up on the earth, and the top of it reached to heaven: and behold the angels of God ascending and descending on it."

JAW: *wave*.

JENNET: small Spanish horse.

JONSON'S LEARNED SOCK: Ben Jonson's learned comedies. See SOCK, and p. 87.

JOVE: Jupiter, who dethroned his father Saturn and the older gods, and became supreme in their place. Falling in love with Leda he turned himself into a swan, and so deceived her into letting him approach her. Greatest of his children was his son Hercules.

JUBAL: "the father of all such as handle the harp and organ," Genesis, ch. iv. 21.

JUNO: wife of Jove, and queen of heaven.

KEMS: *combs*.

KERCHIEFT: *clad with a kerchief*, i.e. *a woman's head-dress*.

KEST: *cast*.

KITLING: *like a kitten's*.

KUBLA KHAN: Grand Khan of the Mongols and Emperor of China. He was a powerful Prince and extended his sway over most of Asia, and even as far as Hungary in Europe.

LAITH: *loath*.

LAMB: the Lamb of God, Christ.

LANCELOT: the noblest of King Arthur's Knights, yet he made love disloyally to Queen Guinevere; he took part in the quest of the Holy Grail.

LANE, THY: *alone.*

LASHER: *weir.*

LAUCH: *laugh.*

LAUD: *praise.*

LAVE: *rest.*

LEDA: wife of Tyndarus, king of Sparta. Jove, seeing her bathing, fell in love with her (see JOVE).

LEES: *dregs.*

LETHEWARDS: into oblivion. In classical mythology Lethe was one of the rivers of Hades; the dead, before crossing it, had to drink of its waters, and so gained complete oblivion of their earthly lives.

LETTING: *hindering.*

'LIGHT: *alight, descend.*

LIMNING: *painting.*

LINDENS: *lime-trees.*

LINN: *waterfall.*

LOGRES: *Britain.*

LOTUS-EATERS: a people who ate the fruit of the lotus, which made one forget one's home. Tennyson's poem describes the visit to their land of Ulysses and his ships, and the Chorus expresses their feelings there.

LOWPIN': *leaping.*

LUBRIC: *smooth.*

LUCAN: a Roman poet (39–65 A.D.). Having been concerned in a plot against the Emperor Nero, Lucan was ordered to kill himself. He had his veins opened in his bath, and while dying recited an appropriate passage from one of his poems.

LUCIFER: the name (it means *light-bearing*) of Satan while he was still an archangel before he was expelled from heaven; also the name of the morning-star, the planet Venus when it appears in the sky before sunrise.

LYAEUS: a name of Bacchus.

LYCEAN MT.: a mountain in Arcadia in Greece, sacred to Pan in whose honour festivals were held there.

LYDIAN MEASURES: one of the three moods or measures in music recognised by the Greeks. It was soft and enervating. The others were Doric and Phrygian.

LYONES: Cornwall.

MAENADS: priestesses of Bacchus.

MANDRAKE: a narcotic plant, round which many superstitions have gathered. Its root was supposed to resemble a human form.

MARROWS: *companions.*

MAUN: *must.*

MAW: *stomach.*

MAZER: *drinking-bowl.*

MEDEA: a daughter of a king of Colchis, a district in Asia east of the Black sea. She was famous for her skill in magic and for her barbarous cruelty. Her chariot was drawn by dragons.

MEIKLE: *great.*

MEMNON'S MOTHER: Aurora, goddess of the dawn; she was the wife of Tithonus, and mother of Memnon, king of Ethiopia.

MEMPHIAN: of the city of Memphis in Egypt.

MERLIN: the great sage and magician of the Arthurian legends.

MEXIQUE BAY: Gulf of Mexico.

MIRK: *dark.*

MOLOCH: a god of the Phoenicians to whom human sacrifices were made because of his cruelty.

MOLY: a miraculous plant said by Homer to have been given to Odysseus by Hermes as a protection against the sorceries of Circe.

MONS MEG: an ancient piece of artillery of great size for the age in which it was constructed. It is still in Edinburgh Castle.

MONTROSE: James Graham, Marquis of Montrose (1612–50), leader of the Scottish Royalists in the Civil War (1642–5); he was hung in Edinburgh in 1650 after an unsuccessful attempt to win Scotland for Charles II.

MORPHEUS: the god of sleep.

MORRICE: a costume dance.

MOTE: *may, must.*

MUSAEUS: an ancient Greek poet, said by some to be son of Orpheus.

MUSES: the Nine Muses who presided over the various branches of the arts of music, poetry, astronomy, and dancing.

NA: *no, not.*

NAIADES: in Greek mythology nymphs of lakes and fountains.

NAMANCOS: a town in Galicia, Spain, near Cape Finisterre.

NEEBOUR: *neighbour.*

NELSON AND THE NORTH: see BALTIC, BATTLE OF.

NEREID: *sea-nymph.*

NINEVEH: a former city on the river Tigris, once the famous capital of the Assyrian empire.

ORIFLAMMES: *streaks in the sky like richly-coloured banners;* the oriflamme was a banner of the early kings of France.

ORMUS: a town on an island near the entrance of the Persian Gulf, once famous as a mart for jewels and pearls.

ORPHEUS: a poet and musician who, according to Greek mythology, moved inanimate objects by his music. See EURYDICE.

ORUS: son of Isis; sun-god of the ancient Egyptians.

OSIRIS: the ancient Egyptian god of Day and Resurrection.

PAEAN: *song of thanksgiving.*

PALE (p. 124): *limits.*

PAN: god of forests, pastures, and flocks.

PARDS: panthers, animals sacred to Bacchus.

PATINES: *circular pieces of metal.*

PATTLE: *ploughstaff.*

PEERS: *equals, contemporaries.*

PELLEAS and PELLENORE: Knights of King Arthur's "Table Round."

PELOPS' LINE: Pelops was king of Pisa in that part of southern Greece which was later, after Pelops, called Pelopennesus. A curse laid upon him and his descendants gave rise to a series of tragedies dealt with by Greek dramatists, notably by Sophocles; Milton is referring to the dramas of Sophocles.

PENEUS: a river of Thessaly in Greece, rising from Mount Pindus, and so called after Peneus, a son of Oceanus.

PENT: *confined.*

PEOR: a Phoenician god.

PHILOMEL: *the nightingale.*

PHOEBUS: the name given to Apollo as the sun-god.

PHOENIX: a fabulous Arabian bird of which only one was said to exist; it lived for 500 years, and then was consumed by fire, to rise again from its own ashes.

PIEMONTESE: the troops of Charles Emmanuel II., Duke of Savoy and Prince of Piedmont, who persecuted the Vaudois or Waldenses (a religious sect who dwelt chiefly in the valleys of the Cottonian Alps) because of their religion.

PINDUS: a mountain in Thessaly, sacred to the Muses and Apollo.

PLAT: *plot of ground.*

PLATO: Plato (427–347 B.C.), the great Greek philosopher, whose most famous book is the *Republic*, the first representation of an ideal commonwealth.

PLUTO: the god of the lower world, Hades; also known as Dis.

POITIERS: scene of the Black Prince's victory over the French in 1356.

POW: *head.*

PROMETHEAN FIRE: Prometheus in Greek mythology, when fire was taken away from mankind by Jupiter, restored the gift of fire to them again.

PROSERPINA: daughter of the goddess Ceres, and queen of the underworld; see DIS.

PROSPICE: *look forward.*

PROTEUS: a sea-god in Greek mythology.

PUGGING: *thievish.*

PUMICE ISLE: island containing pumice, a kind of volcanic lava.

PUSS: *a hare.*

QUOODLE: a dog in Chesterton's novel *The Flying Inn.*

RACK: *drifting-clouds.*

REBECKS: *fiddles.*

RIN: *run.*

RIOU: Captain Riou, who commanded the " Amazon " Frigate in the Battle of the Baltic, and was killed in the action.

ROW: *roll.*

RUTH: in the Old Testament book of *Ruth*, Ruth accompanied Naomi her mother-in-law, whose husband and sons were all dead, from Moab to Bethlehem, and there she worked as a gleaner in the fields of Boaz, who later married her.

SAG: *sagging.*

SAIR: *sore.*

SATURN: chief of the gods until Jupiter overthrew him.

SATYRS: forest deities in Greek mythology, half human and half animal in appearance, and generally represented as following the god Dionysus (Bacchus). See FAUNS.

SAWS: *sayings.*

SCAITH: *harm.*

SEAREST: *most withered.*

SENNACHERIB: king of Assyria; see 2 Chronicles, ch. xxxii. 21.

SENSIBLE: *sensitive.*

SEQUACIOUS: *accustomed to follow.*

SERAPHIM: one of the nine orders of angels.

SHAW: *a wooded dell.*

SHEEN: *bright, shining.*

SHEND: *blame, put to shame.*

SHEUGH: *trench.*

SHIPPON: *cowshed.*

SIC: *such.*

SICILIAN MUSE: the Muse of Pastoral poetry. Theocritus, the first writer of pastorals, was born at Syracuse in Sicily.

SIDNEY: Sir Philip Sidney; see p. 48. When dying on the battlefield he refused a cup of water so that another might have it.

SKEIGH: *proud.*

SLEE: *sly.*

SMOOR'D: *smothered.*

SNELL: *bitter.*

SOCK: light shoe used by actors in classical comedy; so = comedy.

SOPHOCLES: the Greek tragic dramatist (495–406 B.C.).

STARR'D: *ill-fated.*

STAW: *stole.*

STEER: *disturb.*

STIBBLE: *stubble.*

'STILL: *distill.*

STOURE: *dust.*

STROW: *strew.*

STYGIAN: *belonging to the underworld.*

STYX: the river Styx, supposed by the ancients to encircle the infernal regions.

SWART: *dark.* By the " swart star " Milton means Sirius, the Dog Star, which brings heat and makes the flowers dark.

SYDNAEAN SHOWERS: the allusion is to SIDNEY above and the charm of his conversation.

SYKE: *ditch.*

SYLVAN: *belonging to a wood.*

SYRINX: a nymph who, at her own request, was turned into a reed to escape the undesired love of Pan.

SYRTES: shifting sand-banks off the Mediterranean coast of Africa.

TABOR: *small drum.*

TARGET: *a light shield.*

TASSIE: *cup.*

TEEN: *sorrow.*

TELEMACHUS: a son of Ulysses and Penelope.

TEMPE: a valley or mountain gorge in Thessaly between the mountains Olympus and Ossa; it was a favourite resort of Apollo.

TEMPERAMENTVOLL: *high-spirited.*

TEMPLAR, KNIGHTS: members of a powerful religious and secular order founded about 1118 mainly to protect Christ's Sepulchre at Jerusalem and guard pilgrims to the Holy Land.

TENT: *take care of.*

THAMMUZ: a Phoenician god, identified with the Syrian Adonis.

THEBES: an ancient Greek city in Boeotia around whose earliest history many Greek legends arose; from the sixth century to the fourth century B.C. Thebes was constantly at war with Athens and Sparta with varying success, but in 335 B.C. Alexander the Great destroyed the city, sparing only the house of the poet Pindar. The story of Thebes was very popular in England and France in the Middle Ages.

THESSALY: a country in North-East Greece.

THESTYLIS: a country woman; no particular woman is meant.

THOLE: *endure.*

THRAVE: *two dozen sheaves of corn.*

THYRSIS: conventional name for a shepherd.

TIMBREL: a musical instrument like a tambourine.

TIMOTHEUS: a musician of Boeotia in Greece and a favourite of Alexander the Great.

TIRE (ATTIC): *dress (Athenian).*

TINED: *bearing horns.*

TITHE-PIG: a pig received by a parson in payment of tithes.

TITHON'S BED: Tithonus, son of Laomedon, king of Troy; see AURORA.

TRAMMEL: *ensnare*.

TRISTRAM: one of King Arthur's Knights; the story of his tragic love for Iseult, wife of Mark, king of Cornwall, is one of the great stories of the Arthurian cycle.

TRIPLE TYRANT: the Pope, so-called by Milton because of his triple Tiara.

TRITON: a sea-god, son of Poseidon (Neptune); he had a spiral shell, by blowing which he could calm the sea.

TROY: or Ilium, was a city in Phrygia in Asia Minor. The famous siege of Troy, the subject of the *Iliad*, was undertaken by the Greeks to recover Helen, wife of Menelaus, king of Sparta, who had been carried off by Paris, son of Priam, king of Troy; it lasted ten years. The Greeks finally gained an entrance into the city by the device of a wooden horse, sent as a gift, which was full of Greek soldiers.

TRYST (SET): (*made*) *appointment*.

TURTLES: *turtle-doves*.

TUSCAN'S EARLY ART: the painting and sculpture of Tuscany in the thirteenth and following centuries; Florence was one of the chief cities famous for its artists.

TYPHON: brother of Osiris, the Egyptian god; the lower part of his body was represented as a crocodile's tail.

TYRE: a trading city of Phoenicia; the Tyrians founded, among other trading cities, Carthage.

TYRIAN HUE: purple; so-called from a dye made in ancient Tyre from certain molluscs.

ULYSSES: King of Ithaca, one of the Greek heroes who fought at Troy. He was famous for his wisdom in council. *Ulysses* is the Latinised form of *Odysseus*, the name of the hero of the *Odyssey*.

UNCO': *very*.

UNFLEAD: *unskinned*, i.e. with its crust unbroken.

UNSPHERE: call from his place among the dead (as if he were a star in heaven).

UNWIN, MARY: Mary Unwin (1724–96) was the close friend of the poet Cowper, who first went to live as a boarder in her house in 1765.

UTHER: one of the petty kings of Britain in the days of the Saxon invasions; reputed father of King Arthur.

VAWARD: *vanguard.*

VENUS: goddess of Love and Beauty. She had a magic girdle (*zone*) which could give beauty and arouse love. Her chariot was often represented as drawn by doves. Cupid was her son.

VERBOTEN: *prohibited, forbidden.*

VERMEIL: *vermilion.*

VESTA: goddess of the hearth; in her sanctuary was a fire tended by Vestal Virgins whose duty it was never to let it go out.

WAD: *would.*

WAIN: *waggon.*

WA'S: *walls.*

WATER-WRAITH: *phantom on the water.*

WATTLED COTES: sheep-cotes made of osiers woven together in hurdles.

WEAL: *prosperity.*

WEET: *wet.*

WEST PORT: a gate of Edinburgh.

WHAUPS: *curlews.*

WHILES: *sometimes.*

WHIST: *silenced.*

WIGHT: *man, creature.*

WILFRID: Wilfrid (634?–709), Archbishop of York; in his wanderings he twice visited pagan Sussex.

WIST: *knew.*

WRACKS: *wrecks.*

YCLEPT: *called.*

ZEPHYR, ZEPHYRUS: the west wind.

ZIMRI: Dryden's allegorical name for BUCKINGHAM.

ZONE: *girdle.*

WITHDRAWN